JN077473

Baseball in Occupied Japan

JAPANESE SOCIETY SERIES
General Editor: Yoshio Sugimoto

Baseball in Occupied Japan

US Postwar Cultural Policy

By

TAKESHI TANIKAWA

Kyoto University Press

TRANS
PACIFIC
PRESS

This English edition published in 2021 jointly by:

Kyoto University Press
69 Yoshida Konoe-cho
Sakyo-ku, Kyoto 606-8315, Japan
Telephone: +81-75-761-6182
Fax: +81-75-761-6190
Email: sales@kyoto-up.or.jp
Web: http://www.kyoto-up.or.jp

Trans Pacific Press Co., Ltd
2nd Floor, Hamamatsu-cho Daiya Building
2-2-15 Hamamatsu-cho, Minato-ku, Tokyo
105-0013, Japan
Telephone: +81-50-5371-9475
Email: info@transpacificpress.com
Web: http://www.transpacificpress.com

© Takeshi Tanikawa 2021.
Edited by Miriam Riley, Armidale, Australia.
Designed and set by Ryo Kuroda, New York, USA.
Printed by Asia Printing Office Corporation, Nagano, Japan.

Distributors

USA and Canada
Independent Publishers Group (IPG)
814 N. Franklin Street
Chicago, IL 60610, USA
Telephone inquiries: +1-312-337-0747
Order placement: 800-888-4741 (domestic only)
Fax: +1-312-337-5985
Email: frontdesk@ipgbook.com
Web: http://www.ipgbook.com

Europe, Oceania, Middle East and Africa
EUROSPAN
Gray's Inn House,
127 Clerkenwell Road
London, EC1R 5DB
United Kingdom
Telephone: +44-(0)20-7240-0856
Email: info@eurospan.co.uk
Web: https://www.eurospangroup.com/

Japan
For purchase orders in Japan, please contact any
distributor in Japan.

China
China Publishers Services Ltd
718, 7/F., Fortune Commercial Building,
362 Sha Tsui Road, Tsuen Wan, N.T.
Hong Kong
Telephone: +852-2491-1436
Email: edwin@cps-hk.com

Korea, Taiwan
MHM Limited
1-1-13-4F, Kanda-Jinbocho,
Chiyoda-ku, Tokyo 101-0051 JAPAN
Telephone: +81-(0)3-3518-9449
Email: sales@mhmlimited.co.jp

Southeast Asia
Alkem Company Pte Ltd
1, Sunview Road #01-27, Eco-Tech@Sunview
Singapore 627615
Telephone: +65 6265 6666
Email: enquiry@alkem.com.sg

The publication of this book was supported by a Grant-in-Aid for Publication of Scientific Research Results
(Grant Number 20HP5246), provided by the Japan Society for the Promotion of Science.

ISBN 978-1-920901-98-1 (hardback)
ISBN 978-1-925608-01-4 (paperback)
ISBN 978-1-925608-02-1 (eBook)

For my daughter, Mayuri,
who gave me the joy of being a father

Contents

Figures

Tables

Photographs

Author's Biography

Takeshi Tanikawa is Visiting Professor of Film History in the Graduate School of Political Science, Waseda University, and has been a freelance cinema journalist and film critic for nearly three decades.

After working for Nippon Herald Film Co. as publicity staff and marketing director for eight years, he plied between journalism and academia, publishing more than thirty books (in Japanese), and obtaining an MA in cultural science from Saitama University, where his thesis won the prestigious 1st Kyoto Film Culture Award.

Under a Fulbright Scholarship, he worked on his dissertation at the East Asian Institute, Columbia University, earning him a Ph.D. in sociology from Hitotsubashi University, which was later published (in Japanese) by Kyoto University Press as *American Films and the Occupation Policy* (2002).

Following two-and-a-half years as an associate professor of cultural studies at the College of Humanities, Ibaraki University, Dr. Tanikawa was invited by Waseda University to assume his current position. His recent publications (in Japanese) include *All About Post-World War II Chushingura Films* (2013) and *Kouraiya Three Brothers and Films* (2018).

Acknowledgements

The idea for this book came to me in 1999 while I was living in New York City, thanks to the Fulbright Journalist Program, as a visiting research scholar at Columbia University. I was enjoying my life there and frequently visited Shea Stadium to root for the New York Mets, the team which was founded and officially had their first home game at old Polo Ground on April 13, 1962, exactly one week after I was born in Tokyo. Although I was concentrating on my Ph.D. dissertation, which was focused on the formulation and implementation of U.S. film policy toward occupied Japan, it occurred to me that baseball, like motion picture, may have been a most effective tool used by the U.S. military occupation to democratize the Japanese people.

Since then, I have been searching for an opportunity to conduct research on U.S. sports policy in occupied Japan. Although over the next eight or nine years I was constantly busy organizing or joining other research projects, I managed to find time to devote to this topic, and had written the prototype of this manuscript by the end of 2009. In April 2009, when I had decided to focus on baseball (sports) within the wider frame of U.S. international cultural diplomacy policy, Dr. Yuka Tsuchiya of Ehime University, a distinguished scholar and long-time friend, invited me to join her new research project on cultural diplomacy. This approach brought fruitful results and its perspective enriched my manuscript which I revised over the following six years.

Some parts of early versions of Chapters One and Two appeared in Volumes I, II and IV of *Senryouki-Zasshi-Shiryou-Taikei: Taishu-Bunka-Hen* (The occupation period periodical materials compendium: Popular culture series) (2008–2009). Also, an early version of Chapter Three was published in *Studies of Korean & Chinese Humanities* (No. 18, 2006), and Chapter Six appeared in *Intelligence* (No. 3, 2003). All of the above publications were written in Japanese. The remaining chapters were composed solely for this book, but small parts of Chapters Four and Five appeared in Japanese in Yuka Tsuchiya and Shunya Yoshimi (eds), *Occupying Eyes, Occupying Voices: CIE/USIS Films and VOA Radio in Asia during the Cold War* (2012).

I wish to express my appreciation to Dr. Yuka Tsuchiya, who now works for Kyoto University, and Dr. Shunya Yoshimi of the University of Tokyo among many other members of the cultural diplomacy research project who always offered me generous advice. I owe a sincere debt of gratitude to the archivists at the National Archives and Records Administration both at College Park (Maryland) and in New York City, and to Eiko Sakaguchi, Amy Wasserstrom and many staff at the Gordon W. Prange Collection, University of Maryland. I also wish to thank Yoichi Nagata, who kindly gave me much advice on the manuscript of this book from the viewpoint of an expert on baseball history.

Finally, I would like to thank Dr. Martin C. Babicz, who patiently helped me to proofread and polish my original manuscript which had many problems as English is my second language. Akiko Mori and Amy Kiyota also assisted me in the early stage of translating the original Japanese manuscript into English. Gary Mitchem and Miriam Riley helped to polish the manuscript as copyeditors. Even though I received tremendous suggestions from them, some unsophisticated phrases may remain, for which I am entirely responsible. Tetsuya Suzuki generously agreed to publish the manuscript despite the severe environment surrounding the publishing industry in Japan. Prof. Michael Krenn kindly agreed to write the Preface, and Junichi Munetoshi gave the book wonderful attire with his cover design.

Aside from direct quotations from original materials written in English, I translated all quotations from various sources with the help of Akiko and Amy, most notably from the Gordon W. Prange Collection. Also, I translated some quotations apparently written in English originally but which I was only able to obtain as a Japanese translation. Please see the relevant notes for details.

Preface

From being an afterthought in the field of U.S. diplomatic history, or a colorful diversion from the 'real' issues of international relations, cultural diplomacy has taken its place among the key elements now under consideration by historians of America's foreign affairs. In the past thirty years or so, the study of how and why the United States utilized culture as a foreign policy tool to influence friends, contradict and attack enemies, and construct an image of America that, whether accurate or inaccurate, would serve as an important component of the diplomatic machinery used to achieve U.S. goals.

Cultural diplomacy is one aspect of what Joseph S. Nye Jr. referred to as 'soft power'. While this has turned out to be a remarkably elastic term, in its most basic form it denotes the use of diplomatic tools designed to 'attract' and 'persuade', rather than force or coerce (through the so-called 'hard power' tools of military action or economic and political pressure). In its cultural form, soft power involves the application of any number of different approaches that have as their main goal the construction of an attractive and influential national image. This, in turn, can be utilized by a nation such as the United States to convince other nations to follow its lead and to willingly adhere to its foreign policy goals or, conversely, to refute the efforts of America's enemies to portray the United States in unflattering ways.

The study of U.S. diplomatic history, which had heretofore focused almost exclusively on America's application of 'hard power' to achieve its ends, took note of Nye's research and began to examine more carefully the ways in which culture had also been part of the nation's Cold War arsenal. The result was a tremendous outpouring of important books and articles examining nearly every aspect of American culture and its application to U.S. foreign policy. At least initially, much of the focus was on the more traditional forms of culture—ballet, symphony orchestras, fine painting and sculpture, theatrical productions, opera—and many other American cultural productions were extensively studied in terms of how and why they were utilized as diplomatic weapons by the United States. Very quickly, however, scholars began to look at more modern and popular examples of American culture, such as modern dance, experimental theater, abstract expressionism and pop art, jazz, rock and roll, Hollywood films and television. Sport also attracted the attention of scholars, and soon there were studies about the international competitions for medals and national influence at the Olympics, while other researchers examined the use of sports figures (such as tennis star Althea Gibson and boxers such as Archie Moore and Jersey Joe Walcott) and teams (for example, the Harlem Globetrotters) as unofficial cultural diplomats in U.S. government publications and tours sponsored by the Department of State and the United States Information Agency.

It is hardly surprising that baseball featured in a number of book and articles on U.S. cultural diplomacy. It was, after all, the truly 'American' sport. Thomas W. Zeiler's important study, *Ambassadors in Pinstripes: The Spalding World Baseball Tour and the Birth of the American Empire* (2006), examined the world tour undertaken by two teams of professional American baseball players in the late-nineteenth century. Although this was purely a private undertaking, organized and financed by the sporting goods king Albert Spalding, Zeiler made it clear that the tour was designed to do more than encourage foreign buyers to purchase Spalding's baseball equipment. As an early example of sport as cultural diplomacy, it was also supposed to speak to American manliness and masculinity, teamwork and competitive spirit. Taking a more comprehensive view of baseball's role in American foreign policy, Robert Elias's, *The Empire Strikes Out: How Baseball Sold U.S. Foreign Policy and Promoted the American Way Abroad* (2010), argued that the sport was — or, at least, should have been — more than a none-too-subtle attempt to spread the word about America's ideology and strength by serving as a shining example of globalization in action as other nations adopted baseball as part of their sporting activities.

As significant as all of the work on U.S. cultural diplomacy has been, however, the field has also been plagued by questions and criticisms that, more or less, remain only partially addressed. First and foremost has been the criticism that the studies of U.S. cultural diplomacy focus almost entirely on America as the purveyor of cultural artifacts and productions, with the foreign nations and audiences as relatively passive recipients who have the limited choices of liking, or not liking, what they see, hear or experience. In short, the relationship has been a decidedly one-way street. Second, some scholars have argued that the very concept of cultural diplomacy has been expanded to include so many different aspects of international relations that it tends to lose all meaning. In particular, the position is forwarded that non-governmental examples of such 'diplomacy' are nothing more than the normal — and somewhat trivial — cultural exchanges between peoples and nations that take place on a daily basis. For example, in an early — and, as I now understand, unsophisticated — review of the Zeiler book on baseball, I flippantly asked whether this was diplomacy at all. Finally, an endless source of debate surrounds the question of the impact of cultural diplomacy. Yes, it may be entertaining: people might like it; they might even seek to copy it in one form or another. But the issue remains as to what kind of influence cultural diplomacy has on the intended audience and how this influence translates to concrete and measurable results in the field of foreign policy. Finally, there is the matter of the participants in America's cultural diplomacy — the actors, singers, musicians, artists and athletes. What, exactly, is their role? Are they merely 'performers', sent on stage by the U.S. government to say the right things and act like 'good Americans'? Or, do they willingly participate, either because of their sense of patriotism and duty or their dedication to using art as a way to reach a global audience?

At first glance, one might consider Takeshi Tanikawa's contribution to the field as simply another interesting piece of the puzzle. By focusing on the role of baseball in the U.S. occupation of Japan after World War II, the book appears to repeat the same story of a dominating United States (more dominating, in fact, because of its military occupation of Japan), pushing one of its cultural assets onto a Japanese people who view the effort with a mix of curiosity and suspicion. Tanikawa's book does more than add another 'case study' to the growing field of research on U.S. cultural diplomacy in the post-World War II era. It positively moves that field forward by directly addressing the questions raised above.

Tanikawa clearly argues that U.S. officials were certainly interested in using baseball as a cultural tool during their efforts to rebuild and reshape postwar Japan. While banning traditional Japanese sports such as *budo* or kendo, the American occupiers felt that baseball would not only provide the Japanese with a less militaristic style of competition but would also be an effective advertisement for the American values of fair play, sportsmanship and teamwork. Indeed, in an interesting aside, the author notes that General Douglas MacArthur, the commander of the U.S. occupation forces, was an avid baseball fan. There is far more to the story, however: 'the revival of baseball in the post-World War II era should be remembered as a collaborative work'. It might surprise some readers to discover that barely three months after the atomic bombs were dropped on Japan professional baseball was already starting up. The Japanese were not merely recipients of this American cultural product. Baseball was already popular in Japan prior to the war and had, in many ways, become a lucrative business. As Tanikawa cogently argues, baseball was not forced upon a passive and defeated Japanese people. Japanese businessmen were just as active in promoting the resurgence of the sport, and actively worked with the Americans to ensure its revival. Collaboration, not dominance, was the key to baseball's success.

In terms of the precise impact of baseball as cultural diplomacy in Japan, even the author admits that it is often difficult to precisely quantify its effectiveness. However, Tanikawa manages to make a convincing argument that baseball should not be viewed as a stand-alone element in America's goals in Japan. Instead, baseball was merely one aspect of the '3-S Policy' in which the U.S. government sought to use the 'screen' (movies designed to inculcate the values of democracy, American power and capitalism), 'sex' (the subtle encouragement of erotic outlets to distract the Japanese people from their stress and disappointment after the war) and 'sports' (baseball, of course, but also the introduction of American-style boxing). In short, Tanikawa argues that cultural diplomacy was more than one art exhibit, or concert, or ballgame. It was a coherent package of cultural tools to achieve the desired ends, and Japan's remarkable political, economic and social resurrection from the ashes of World War II does suggest that it was also an effective package.

Finally, an extremely interesting and significant section of this book looks at the role played by Jackie Robinson, who became the first African American to play in Major League Baseball in 1947. Robinson became a staple of U.S. cultural diplomacy in the years after World War II, featured in stories in State Department publications and on Voice of America radio broadcasts. Not only did he serve to promote the growth of baseball in Japan, but he was also useful in addressing America's embarrassing race problem by showing that African Americans could, in fact, succeed in breaking the color line. And unlike other African Americans, such as W.E.B. Du Bois, Paul Robeson and the expatriate Josephine Baker, who later became personae non gratae because of their attacks on America's sorry record in civil rights, Robinson remained a willing participant who sought to use his worldwide popularity to sustain his role as a spokesperson for the American way of life. Robinson would later tour Japan with the rest of the Brooklyn Dodgers.

In these ways, and many others too numerous to mention here, Tanikawa's study serves to not simply push the boundaries of the study of U.S. cultural diplomacy into different locales, time periods, or use of cultural tools. This book uses the exploration of the use of American baseball in Japan after World War II to seriously and significantly address some of the most important questions and criticisms that continue to limit the field. In doing so, he revises our understanding of the purposes, implementation and results of America's cultural diplomacy in the early years of the Cold War.

Michael L. Krenn
Appalachian State University

Introduction

In the wake of World War II, Japan, a defeated nation, was occupied by the U.S.-led Allied Powers. The Allied Powers included not only the major participants—the U.S., the U.K. and Australia—but also the Soviet Union, a last-minute addition after years of neutrality. The real enforcement of the occupation was, however, executed by U.S. forces alone, despite the fact that the British Commonwealth Occupation Force, which included the Australian military, helped in the disarmament.

General Douglas MacArthur was appointed as Supreme Commander for the Allied Powers (SCAP), while also holding the post of Supreme Commander for the U.S. Army Forces Pacific (AFPAC). Through this position, Gen. MacArthur assumed reign over Japan from Emperor Hirohito, who had been portrayed as a god-like figure and the supreme ruler of the Empire of Japan as Arahitogami.[1] Although Gen. MacArthur's organization was called GHQ (General Headquarters) by the Japanese people, the term was more complicated as it referred to two separate entities—GHQ/SCAP and GHQ/AFPAC.

Although it is difficult to clarify whether the military tension between the Soviet Union and the U.S. emerged during World War II or in the post-war era, it is clear that GHQ started to implement policy according to U.S. national interests, and the U.S. began to regard the Soviet Union as a speculative adversary. This suggests that public and cultural diplomacy policies from both the East and West were developing in Japan as an occupied nation in the Far East, which was completely different from the division of Germany into East and West.

The U.S. government might have been eager to strengthen certain images worldwide that conveyed that the U.S. as a democratic nation had the capacity to create a more prosperous society than a socialist nation such as the Soviet Union. Thus, the U.S. administration established a democratic nation in occupied Japan. This thriving democracy was what the U.S. wanted not only the Japanese people, but also people all over the world, to know through mass media and various other kinds of tools.

I conducted research on films used as propaganda resources to pursue the occupation goals and analyzed them in my Ph.D. dissertation. Through this process, I gradually came to realize that sports, like films, were also utilized as an extremely important tool during the occupation. In this book, I have two key aims: first, to examine how the U.S. government carried out

---

1 Arahitogami: A god who appears to this world as the figure of a human being.

its cultural diplomacy policy during the occupation of Japan within the arena of 'sports' by looking at the way in which this policy was cultivated through films; and second, to explore how sport was utilized as effective cultural diplomacy during the occupation.

Under U.S. supervision, the Japanese film industry was controlled via strict regulations governing what movies ought and ought not to be shown. Samurai films, for example, were perceived as feudalistic. Particularly, films that depicted vengeance, such as from the Chushingura genre, were banned. Instead, the production of films that featured modern values was encouraged, including those that included romantic kissing scenes, and a carefully selected abundance of U.S. films were distributed to inculcate Western or U.S. social values and modern customs.

In the case of Japanese sports, *budo* (Japanese martial arts) were recognized as associated with feudalism, and especially kendo (Japanese fencing) was viewed as celebrating the Shinto religion and was strictly prohibited. On the other hand, playing and watching baseball games, which was considered American-like, was encouraged as an effective teamwork- and sportsmanship-building tool. Therefore, GHQ regarded the opportunity for Japanese people to be reintroduced to the essence of U.S. baseball as important.

Why was baseball emphasized over other sports? I suspect that a number of reasons exist, but there is no single correct and definitive answer. It seems that the most significant factor was that *yakyu* — the Japanese word for 'baseball', or Japan's own version of 'baseball' — had been very popular among the average Japanese people and had developed certain features distinct from its U.S. counterpart before the occupation. In addition, the fact that Gen. MacArthur himself was a huge fan of baseball cannot be ignored.

Gen. MacArthur enjoyed playing baseball while attending military academy. Later, he served as the chief captain of the U.S. Army baseball team according to a pamphlet on the Army-Navy baseball game of 1920 (see Fig. 0.1).

After departing Japan in April 1951 to move to New York, Gen. MacArthur frequently attended Brooklyn Dodgers games while the team's home-field was Ebbets Field. When Gen. MacArthur was invited by Walter O'Malley, the new owner of the Dodgers who had recently acquired the team from Branch Rickey, to cooperate in promoting the team to other veteran soldiers, he commented, 'somebody said, if you want to see a real game of baseball, go over to Ebbets Field, so here I am'.[2] This quote shows his love and understanding of sports in his own words and also functioned to advertise baseball.

Commonly known as the '3-S Policy', a provision of three elements — Screen (movies), Sports and Sex — was established by GHQ rule and disseminated among the Japanese people so as to reduce the sense of unease during the occupation. For the focus of this study, it is more useful to investigate what was achieved in Japan as a result of the occupation and what specific measures were taken in the occupation policies rather than examining why the policies favored sports, especially baseball. It is also important to note that baseball was not solely promoted by GHQ/SCAP but was also closely linked to the hidden agenda of Japan's professional baseball society to revive its own baseball industry.

In reality, the revival of Japanese baseball in the post-World War II era should be remembered as a collaborative effort between Japanese baseball leaders and Gen. MacArthur's right-hand man. Ryuji Suzuki, Sotaro Suzuki and Matsutaro Shoriki, the heads of Japan's professional baseball leagues, and Maj. Gen. William F. Marquat, one of the Bataan Boys known as Gen. MacArthur's right-hand man during his tenure in the Philippines, worked together to promote 'the use of baseball' in U.S.-occupied Japan.

Figure 0.1 'Army-Navy Game 1920' pamphlet, Annapolis, Maryland, May 29, 1920
Source: Takeshi Tanikawa Collection.

---

2 Carl Prince, *Brooklyn's Dodgers: The Bums, the Borough and the Best of Baseball, 1947–1957* (Oxford University Press, 1996), p. 30.

As I will discuss in Chapter One, the first Japanese professional baseball game between East and West was held on November 23, 1945, only 100 days after the end of the war, followed by a professional baseball pennant race. The Tokyo Big Six Baseball League games took place in the spring of 1946, and the revival of the inter-city baseball tournament followed in the summer of that year. In addition, in the spring of 1947, the Junior High School Baseball Tournament (now, the High School Baseball Tournament) was revived, signifying that Japan's baseball was definitely on the way to recovery.

The memoirs and biographies of Japanese professional baseball affiliates reveal that the planned goal of Maj. Gen. Marquat for the Japanese professional baseball industry was two-fold: to introduce the system of the two major American leagues and to establish a commissionership that was expected to bring strong leadership to the sport. Furthermore, the San Francisco Seals' visit to Japan to promote the recovery of the Japan-U.S. baseball relationship provided a great opportunity to convince Japanese society that the objectives of the U.S. occupation of Japan were being carried out through the medium of 'baseball'. In other words, the Seals' visit was meant to be an enticing event to exhibit the recovery of the Japan-U.S. relationship and to show how a Far East country was being reconstructed and becoming a democratic nation, no longer posing a threat to the rest of the world. Simply, the visit was designed to establish diplomatic relations with the United States. I will explore the true meaning of the Seals' visit in Chapter Seven.

Despite the 1949 agreement that resulted from negotiations between Japanese professional baseball affiliates and Maj. Gen. Marquat to appoint Matsutaro Shoriki as commissioner prior to the Seals' visit, Shoriki was rejected by Courtney Whitney, the head of the Government Section, and Charles A. Willoughby, the head of the G-2. The commissionership was finally reintroduced in 1951. On the other hand, the launching of the two major leagues system went smoothly while Japan was in a state of excitement over the Seals' visit. On November 26, 1949, only twenty days after the Seals left Japan, Japan's baseball league announced its dismissal. On the same day, four existing teams—the Nankai Hawks, Hankyu Braves, Daiei Stars and Tokyu Flyers—along with three new teams—the Mainichi Orions, Kintetsu Pearls and Nishitetsu Lions—organized the Taiheiyo Baseball Association (later, the Pacific League). On December 15, the Central League was established with the Yomiuri Giants, Shochiku Robins, Hanshin Tigers and Chunichi Dragons as well as newcomers the Maruha Team (Taiyo-Gyogyo, later called the Taiyo Whales), Hiroshima Carp and Nishi-Nippon

Shinbun (Nishi-Nippon Pirates). Ultimately, the two major leagues system was successfully and comprehensively established.

In the meantime, strict regulations governing the film industry had been legislated by GHQ/SCAP—no sword-fighting films (*chanbara*) or *jidaigeki* (costume play) which, like Chushingura, include themes of revenge. Regulations were simultaneously imposed in the sports environment— particularly *budo*, such as kendo, judo, *kyudo* and sumo, was forced to reform under a completely different approach to that taken in the baseball industry. The only way for *budo* to survive was to highlight its 'sports' aspect as physical exercise over its previous emphasis on fostering one's mind or spirit.

As I discuss in Chapters Two and Three, there was an attempt to transform sports such as judo and sumo as *Ozumo* (professional sport) into 'spectator sports' by internationalization or commercialization. Kendo, which was perceived by GHQ/SCAP as a sport directly associated with the *bushido* spirit (way of the warrior)—samurai sports—suffered the most. The Dainippon Butoku Kai, the headquarters of the Kendo Association, was forced to close; its assets were forfeited and its goods confiscated. Furthermore, practicing kendo as physical education at schools was prohibited, and schools' kendo equipment was seized. Judo, on the other hand, prevailed and became JUDO, a popular combative international sport featuring colorful uniforms, while kendo maintained its traditional style and garb.

At the same time, occupation era boxing called '*kento*' (it was more commonly called '*kento*' than 'boxing' in post-World War II Japan), as a fighting sport like *judo*, became popular. The *kento* industry regarded the restriction of *budo* by GHQ as a great opportunity to popularize their sport among the Japanese people. A Cinderella story, boxer Yoshio Shirai became the first Japanese world champion. Shirai trained under the scientific method promoted by Dr. Alvin Robert Cahn, who, while working for the natural resources agency at GHQ/SCAP, developed a rigorous physical management, nutrition guidance and coaching theory. It was symbolic that a Japanese boxer could become a world champion during the occupation because of the practical and scientific methods of the American style of training. This was completely at odds with the traditional methods that were based on a non-scientific approach to training founded on mental focus.

The way in which GHQ/SCAP implemented policies that promoted sports as one of the resources to democratize Japan was not limited to 'providing' sports to the Japanese people (to encourage sports as leisure and to promote 'baseball' to spectators) or 'not providing' *budo* (by prohibiting *budo* at school, and transforming *budo* as combative sports into sports based on practical and scientific methods).

Baseball was encouraged not only as a sport to play or watch, but also to be viewed on film, especially for those unable to watch a professional baseball game in their local area. Enjoying baseball via film was quite popular among the Japanese people, which is evidenced by various data.

The United Newsreel sponsored by the Central Motion Picture Exchange (CMPE), which was established as a government subsidiary of the Civil Information and Education Section (CIE) of GHQ/SCAP and promoted democracy through selected Hollywood feature films, frequently showed news on the training methods of the American professional baseball leagues. Furthermore, the Shochiku-franchised movie theaters screened news on the Spring High School Baseball tournament (the new high school system began in 1948), and the Daiei-operated (foreign) movie theaters showed a short informational film entitled *Let's Play Baseball*, sponsored by the CIE.[3]

The fact that sports, particularly baseball, was promoted through the United Newsreel and short informational films sponsored by either the CMPE or CIE, which was part of the promotion of the democratization of Japan, proves that GHQ-operated 'sports promotion' was being accomplished. This was assisted by the proclamation of the importance of sports to the Japanese people by the staff of the education department of the CIE through a new magazine published by a Japanese publisher.

Chapter Four explores how many of the CIE's films were concerned with sports, and the extent to which these films influenced the ordinary Japanese throughout the country.

Under the occupation, the Office of International Information and Culture Affairs (OIC) of the U.S. State Department that was promoting global-scale public policies in the Far East had a direct channel in the form of the CIE and CMPE to control occupied Japan. The OIC actively utilized Jack Roosevelt 'Jackie' Robinson in order to develop positive images about America. The OIC took advantage of the fact that Robinson, as an African American athlete, was on the verge of becoming a Major League Baseball player despite his race, a symbol of the unification of American society. This suggested that the U.S. had a superior society devoid of inequality, and through Robinson's experiences, demonstrated that racism was a thing of the past.

---

3 At the time, Shochiku and Daiei were major Japanese film studios, and both later came to acquire professional baseball teams.

I will explore more details about Jackie Robinson in Chapter Five and Six, including a Voice of America (VOA) special radio program and the 'The Robinson Story' provided by the OIC and published in a Japanese baseball magazine.

It is difficult to obtain quantitative evidence on how the public policies under the U.S. occupation were carried out, and how effective they were. Rather, the extent to which Japan made progress may be taken to represent the effectiveness of these policies. As a stepping-stone, Japan took advantage of the Korean War and achieved highly successful economic growth; eventually, Japan became the nation with the second highest GNP, next to the U.S. (the People's Republic of China assumed this position in 2009). It is fair to say that this was the U.S.'s desired outcome.

In terms of sports, it is possible that Japan's success exceeded the U.S.'s expectations. Today, Japan is respected because it has provided distinguished ballplayers via the Japanese professional baseball leagues to the American major leagues, and these players play well in the U.S. Also, in the World Baseball Classic (WBC) which was established as a world-class international tournament, Japan achieved victory in the first and second games held in 2006 and 2009. In the third games held in 2013, Japan lost its championship and was relegated to third place. Notwithstanding the defeat, generally speaking, Japan has certainly proved its strength in baseball.

Considering these achievements, it is meaningful to first examine Japan during the occupation and evaluate whether or not the roots of the current situation emerged during this period.

The Revival of '*Yakyu*' and the Japan-U.S. Relationship

▌ Democratization through sports

For Americans, baseball is the 'National Pastime', and is regarded as the de facto sport of the nation. Although the U.S. occupation of Japan following World War II helped ingrain baseball into Japanese culture, the sport, called *yakyu* in Japanese, had been particularly popular in Japan long before the start of the war.

Baseball was first introduced in Japan in the early 1870s at the beginning of the Meiji era, and it quickly grew in popularity. Soon college baseball leagues and junior high school (now high school) tournaments were founded. In 1920, Atsushi Kono, a star player for the Waseda University baseball team that toured the U.S. in 1905, played a key role in establishing the Nippon Athletic Association, Japan's first professional baseball team. The team, also known as the Shibaura Association, played their games at a ballpark in Shibaura, Tokyo. The team's goal was to operate as a business with the income generated from admission fees, but the devastation caused by the Great Kanto Earthquake of 1923 forced it to dissolve in 1924.

Ichizo Kobayashi, the president of Hankyu Railway in Kansai and later the founder of the Hankyu Braves, reestablished the Shibaura Association later that year. The scarcity of opponents, however, permanently forced it out of business in 1929. Both men were later enshrined in the Japanese Baseball Hall of Fame for their pioneering efforts, Kono in 1960 and Kobayashi in 1968.

Throughout the 1920s and 1930s, more than sixty-five goodwill tours were embarked upon by baseball teams of all levels—university, semi-professional, Negro leagues, Nikkei League and Major League—on both sides of the Pacific.

Year	Team	Travel	Level
1920	Honolulu Asahi	to Japan	Nikkei League
1920	Seattle Mikados	to Japan	Nikkei League
1920	Herb Hunter's All-Stars	to Japan	Professional
1920	UC Berkeley	to Japan	University
1920	University of Chicago	to Japan	University
1920	Waseda	to the U.S.	University
1921	Hawaii All-Stars	to Japan	Nikkei League
1921	Hawaii Hilo	to Japan	Nikkei League
1921	Hawaii Nippon	to Japan	Nikkei League
1921	Seattle Asahi	to Japan	Nikkei League
1921	Vancouver Asahi	to Japan	Nikkei League
1921	Canadian Stars	to Japan	Semi-professional
1921	Sherman Indian School	to Japan	High School
1921	Suquamish Indians (Wash.)	to Japan	Semi-professional
1921	University of California	to Japan	University
1921	University of Washington	to Japan	University
1921	Waseda	to the U.S.	University
1922	Herb Hunter's All-Stars	to Japan	Professional
1922	University of Indiana	to Japan	University
1923	Seattle Asahi—Mikados	to Japan	Nikkei League
1924	Fresno Athletic Club	to Japan	Nikkei League
1924	Meiji	to the U.S.	University
1925	Philadelphia Bobbies	to Japan	Female semi-professional
1925	San Jose Asahi	to Japan	Nikkei League
1925	Damai (Osaka Mainichi)	to the U.S.	Professional
1925	University of Chicago	to Japan	University
1926	Honolulu Asahi	to Japan	Nikkei League
1926	Stanford University	to Japan	University
1926	University of California	to Japan	University
1926	University of Washington	to Japan	University
1927	Wakayamma High	to the U.S.	High School
1927	Philadelphia Royal Giants	to Japan	Negro League
1927	Aratani Guadalupe Packers	to Japan	Nikkei League
1927	Fresno Athletic Club	to Japan	Nikkei League
1927	University of California	to Japan	University
1927	Waseda	to the U.S.	University
1928	Stockton Yamato	to Japan	Nikkei League
1928	Instructional Tour with Ty Cobb	to Japan	Professional
1928	University of Illinois	to Japan	University
1928	University of Southern California	to Japan	University
1928	Keio	to the U.S.	University
1929	University of Michigan	to Japan	University
1929	University of California	to Japan	University
1929	Meiji	to the U.S.	University
1930	University of Chicago	to Japan	University
1931	Shogyo—Hiroshima High School	to the U.S.	High School
1931	Kono Alameda All-Stars	to Japan	Nikkei League
1931	LA Nippon	to Japan	Nikkei League
1931	Herb Hunter and Fred Lieb All-Stars	to Japan	Professional
1931	Hosei	to the U.S.	University
1931–32	Philadelphia Royal Giants	to Japan	Negro League
1932	Instructional: Hunter, O'Doul, Lyons, Berg	to Japan	Professional
1932	Athens Athletic Club (CA)	to Japan	Semi-professional
1932	University of Michigan	to Japan	University
1932	University of Hawaii	to Japan	University
1932	Rikkyo University	to the U.S.	University
1933	Seattle Taiyos (Suns)	to Japan	Nikkei League
1933	Waseda	to the U.S.	University
1933–34	Philadelphia Royal Giants	to Japan	Negro League
1934	Babe Ruth and Lou Gehrig All-Stars	to Japan	Professional

Table 1.1 U.S.-Japan baseball tours, 1920–1934

Through the goodwill efforts of teams at all levels, baseball continued to grow in popularity in the 1930s. In an attempt to expand its circulation to become a national newspaper, the *Yomiuri Shimbun* staged a number of events to attract readership. One of the most famous events organized by the newspaper was a baseball game in 1931 called the 'Japan-U.S. Great Baseball Game'. The game included professional players from the U.S. and star players of the Tokyo Big Six Baseball League from Japan—first baseman Henry Louis 'Lou' Gehrig of the New York Yankees was among the ballplayers on the U.S. side.[1]

Three years later, the *Yomiuri Shimbun* invited another group of American professional baseball players to visit Japan. In the early 1930s, there was no baseball player more famous than George Herman 'Babe' Ruth, and Matsutaro Shoriki, the president of the *Yomiuri* Newspaper Group, was determined that Ruth would join the team of American athletes that would visit Japan in 1934.

To that end, Shoriki asked Sotaro Suzuki, a reporter who covered American baseball for the *Yomiuri*, to persuade Ruth to make the trip. Suzuki enlisted the help of Frank 'Lefty' O'Doul, an outfielder with the New York Giants who had been a member of the group of American players who visited Japan in 1931. O'Doul had played for the Yankees with Ruth in the early 1920s. With O'Doul's help, Suzuki convinced Ruth to take part in the tour. Sotaro Suzuki later depicted in his book how this came about. Suzuki claims that he visited Ruth at a barber salon near Ruth's apartment on West 88th Street, New York City, in the morning of October 1, 1934. Before Ruth's haircut was finished, O'Doul had also arrived to help Suzuki in his attempt to convince Ruth to come to Japan. Ruth did not hide his reluctance, but when Suzuki showed him the poster for the American players' 1934 tour of Japan which was already printed and which featured Ruth's portrait and explained how deeply Japanese baseball fans wanted Ruth to come, Ruth broke into laughter and finally agreed to make the trip.[2] Later, under the occupation, the name 'Lefty O'Doul' once again became widely recognized.

---

1 Prior to the 'Japan-U.S. Great Baseball Game', several U.S. teams traveled to Japan and played games against Japanese teams. In 1908, the 'Reach All Americans' team, which included six Major League Baseball (MLB) players, played games against Waseda University team, etc. Then, in 1913, the New York Giants and the Chicago White Sox set out on a worldwide tour including Japan, and Herb Hunter's All-Stars, which consisted of Minor and Major League players came to Japan in 1920. In 1922, selected MLB players returned to Japan and played six games against Tokyo Big Six Baseball League teams.

2 Sotaro Suzuki, *Nihon Pro-Yakyu Gaishi* (Another history of Japanese professional baseball) (Baseball Magazine-Sha, 1976), pp. 161–163.

The 1934 tour of Japan by American players was an unqualified success. Professional baseball in Japan had always kept its gaze on the game's homeland—America. Not only were Japanese fans excited to see American stars play baseball, but their own players also gave them reason to be proud. During the tour, at the Kusanagi Kyuujou baseball stadium in Shizuoka Prefecture, Japanese pitcher Eiji Sawamura performed magnificently and fans responded with an extended applause, signifying Japanese success in baseball. The spectators were not only impressed by the skill of the American players, but also by the fact that Japanese baseball players could hold their own against a team from the 'baseball homeland' that included famous players such as Babe Ruth, Lou Gehrig and Jimmie Foxx. The pride felt by the Japanese audience in watching Sawamura's great performance and their admiration for the 'baseball homeland' were two sides of the same coin.

With the success of the 1934 tour, the Greater Japan Tokyo Baseball Club (Dainippon Tokyo Yakyu Kurabu) was established at the end of the year. Two years later, Japan's first professional league, the Japanese Baseball League (Nihon Shokugyou Yakyu Renmei), was set up. O'Doul's influence on Japanese baseball continued beyond the 1934 tour. In 1935, he helped arrange for the Greater Japan Tokyo Baseball Club to undertake a 110-game tour of the U.S. Because the team's name was so long, O'Doul suggested that the club adopt the nickname the Tokyo Giants, after O'Doul's team in New York.

Despite the success of Japanese baseball in the 1930s, *yakyu* could not have progressed without establishing a relationship with the U.S. Relations between the two countries broke down completely following the Pearl Harbor Attack in December 1941. Baseball is one of the symbols of American culture, and although it was a sport that came from the 'enemy', it was not banned in Japan during World War II. For instance, during the Manchuria Great Match in the summer of 1940, all nine Japanese baseball teams were sent to Manchuria including celebrity players such as Tetsuharu Kawakami, the first baseman of the Tokyo Giants. Instead of looking at baseball as a symbol of American culture, Japan stressed its unique relationship to the sport. Baseball in Japan was originally adapted as *yakyu*, a localized form of the game, and it was emphasized as being congruent with *budo*, Japanese martial arts. As Sadao Araki, the head of the education ministry, noted: 'Bats, balls and gloves must be handled with loving care, such as a samurai would expend on his sword'.[3]

Because of the war with the U.S., the use of English phrases was prohibited in Japan. As a result, Japanese terms came to replace those from the 'enemy's language'. For example, 'strike one' became '*yoshi, ippon*'. During the war, uniforms, which originally bore Arabic numerals, were revised to be written in kanji (Chinese characters). Even though Japan was hit hard by the war, baseball lingered there until the autumn of 1944. As the war approached an end, however, the dissolution of the professional baseball teams was finally determined on November 10, 1944. Ten days later, the close of baseball was marked by a farewell ceremony. Japan surrendered to the Allies nine months later.

Exactly 100 days after Japan's announcement of surrender on August 15, 1945, baseball returned to Japan. On November 22, 1945, with the support of the American occupational authority—General Headquarters, Supreme Commander for the Allied Powers (GHQ/SCAP)—an East versus West game was played in Japan.

Japan experienced such a quick and seamless transition from war to occupation that the American-led occupation was considered a success. In fact, until the recent Iraq War changed perceptions of U.S. occupation policy, the American occupation of Japan was often cited as a model to be followed. While chants of '*Kichiku-Bei-Ei*' ('The Devil to the U.S. and U.K.') were common in Japan right up until the end of the war, the Japanese people seemed to welcome the U.S. from the very day the Allied occupation began and the Imperial leaders, including Hideki Tojo, fell from power and were executed as war criminals. Unlike the occupation of Iraq, the American occupation of Japan benefited from the long-term diplomatic relationship that had existed between the U.S. and Japan prior to the war. The occupation period in Japan was the time to rebuild the friendly relationship that had once existed between the two nations.

One of the symbols of the friendship between the U.S. and Japan in the pre-war period was the numerous goodwill tours between the two countries, especially the Major League tours in 1931 and 1934. The Japanese people

---

3 Comment made by Sadao Araki in 'Japanese Political Diary' sent to the U.K. just after the Japanese government relinquished the Tokyo Olympics of 1940. This document is introduced in Yasuhiro Sakaue, *Nippon Yakyu-no-Keifugaku* (Seikyusha Library 15, 2001), pp. 171–172. (Original source: Japanese Political Diary, September 8, 1938 (FO371/22189/22248), National Archives of the U.K.).

were baseball enthusiasts and were thrilled with Babe Ruth's and Lou Gehrig's visit. Due to this passion for the sport, the leaders of Japan's baseball industry — including Matsutaro Shoriki, Sotaro Suzuki, Takizo Matsumoto and Ryuji Suzuki, a Japanese baseball executive who would later serve as the president of the Central League — approached GHQ/SCAP at the start of the occupation to seek permission to reconstruct Japan's baseball industry. The leaders of GHQ/SCAP agreed, believing they could utilize Japanese enthusiasm for baseball to help create a less antagonistic occupation.

Baseball became an effective tool in the GHQ/SCAP policy of 'democratization through sports'. Both Japanese citizens and occupying troops recognized that they could work to rebuild the U.S.-Japan friendship through *yakyu*. U.S. authorities believed that, by popularizing American sports, especially baseball, the U.S. could inculcate its social values and Americanize post-war Japan. The Japanese, on the other hand, emphasized the importance of recognizing the difference between American baseball with its rational approach and the Japanese version of the game with its focus on 'spiritual acquisition' as the first step in its cultural revival.

Proof that the U.S. occupation plan to establish democracy in Japanese society was effectively serving both American and Japanese goals can be found in articles published during the occupation. Japanese intellectuals and GHQ/SCAP staff writers took the same tone in their writing, and their articles were often published side by side in the same periodical.

One of the proponents of Japanese baseball during the occupation was Itaru Nii, an intellectual and former journalist for the *Osaka-Mainichi* newspaper and the *Tokyo-Asahi* newspaper. Nii would eventually become a professor at the Bunka Gakkuin, known for his liberal international views, and he later served as the mayor of Tokyo's Suginami Ward. Nii wrote an article for the inaugural issue of *Sports*, a periodical published by Taiiku Nihon Sha, Tokyo. In it he stated:

> Young Japanese baseball players, for example, may cry when they are defeated. This tends to be viewed as a positive reaction in Japan. In my opinion, it is old-fashioned Japanese-style sentiment where passion and patience were overly emphasized. It is, however, impossible to win a baseball game without hard training and excellent skills. It is a delusion and unscientific of the Japanese to think they can win a game only with passion.

The Japanese fought against America with the same mentality. Hideki Tojo [general of the Imperial Japanese Army] acted like a male cheerleader at a baseball game energetically waving a folding fan with the Rising Sun. Eventually, the Japanese were defeated, so the mentality did not work.

As evidenced by the cheerleaders analogy, the mindset of 'Japanese passion' made the defeated athletes cry, showing similarities to the illogical beliefs that led Japan to the tragic consequences of the war.

This is because we did not understand the meaning of sports. It is not aimless effort or simply being passionate, but scientific analogies and excellent skills that will lead the athletes or soldiers to victory.

Sports with scientific principles—this reinvigorates the minds of the athletes. Hereafter, the mentality of Japan's sports must depart from the negative mindset of the past.[4]

Maj. John W. Norviel, the physical educator of the Civil Information and Education Section (CIE) of GHQ/SCAP, contributed an article in the same first issue of *Sports*.[5] In it, Norviel wrote:

Sports will provide Japan with a great opportunity to promote democracy. In addition, it will make a great contribution to democratizing sports organizations and their development of athletic leagues and competitions. If the major obstacles are removed, the future of Japan's sports development is certainly promising.[6]

'The major obstacles' noted in the above passage refers to the lack of equipment available for the implementation of the democratization policies through sports. Norviel's article noted the details of the actual equipment problem, which will be discussed in greater depth in Chapter Three. Even in

---

4 Nii Itaru, 'Supōtsu to Minshushugi' (Sports and democracy), *Sports*, June 1946 (inaugural issue), pp. 6–7.

5 According to 'Sengo Kyouiku Kaikaku Shiryou 2' (Post-war education reform documents 2), which is regarded as the basic source on the organizational transition of the CIE, he served in the area of physical education throughout the occupation period. See Hideo Sato, ed., *Sengo Kyouiku Kaikaku Shiryou 2: Rengoukaku Saiko-Shireikan Soushireibu Minkan Jouhou Kyouiku Kyoku no Jinji to Kikou* (The staff rosters and organization charts of the C.I. & E. Section, GHQ/SCAP: Compiled from GHQ/SCAP telephone directories) (National Institute for Educational Research of Japan, 1984).

6 Maj. John W. Norviel, 'Nihon Supōtsu no Tameni' (For the progress of Japan's sports), *Sports*, June 1946, p. 9.

the context of sport, *budo* implicitly encouraged militarism. Although *budo* was banned from the school curriculum, *budo* equipment was ironically converted into baseball equipment.

GHQ/SCAP occupation policy was a double-edged sword as the administration distributed equipment for kendo, the Japanese martial art of swordsmanship, to be used as baseball equipment. Thus, kendo equipment was first confiscated on the basis of *budo*'s connection to feudalism, and then redistributed in the name of democracy. Contradictions within the occupation policy were not limited to sports. GHQ/SCAP also banned *chanbara* films (literally, 'sword fighting movies'), while promoting those that featured kissing scenes, like *Hatachi no Seishun* (Shochiku, 1946).[7]

An article written by an anonymous GHQ/SCAP staffer of the Maebashi military government headquarters entitled 'Effects of democracy's adaptation to sports' argued that sports, especially baseball games, were greatly influencing Japan to move toward democracy. The article stated, 'Suppose that one starts to play baseball, he would simultaneously engrave in his mind the notion of "teamwork"—to cooperate with other team members and to assume his own responsibilities in order to accomplish his own role in the team. This is the spirit of democracy'.[8]

The fact that the words of a Japanese intellectual and a GHQ/SCAP staffer resonated with each other in the same periodical indicate that the 'democratization of Japan through sports' was not carried out solely via GHQ/SCAP policy, but as a collaboration between GHQ/SCAP and the Japanese people.

While suffering from a lack of equipment, the recovery project helped Japan's baseball industry gradually grow. The effort of Sotaro Suzuki, who dealt with all the negotiations on the MLB tours to Japan in the pre-war period, was substantial. Maj. Gen. William F. Marquat, the head of the Economic and Scientific Section (ESS), was responsible for the GHQ/SCAP initiative on the baseball recovery project. Marquat put Tsuneo 'Cappy' Harada, one of his subordinates, in charge of restarting Japanese sports, and it was Harada who negotiated with the Japanese side. It seems clear, however, that the person who drew the grand design of the baseball recovery project was Marquat, while Harada was just someone who worked under Marquat's supervision. Marquat

---

7 Kyoko Hirano, *Mr. Smith goes to Tokyo: Japanese Cinema under the American Occupation, 1945–1952* (Smithsonian Institution Press, 1992), pp. 154–165.

8 'Undou-Kyougi no Minshushugi ni Oyobosu Eikyo' (Effects of democracy's adaptation to sports), *All Sports*, October 15, 1946, p. 5.

repaired the U.S.-Japan baseball relationship via the San Francisco Seals, which at the time was managed by none other than Lefty O'Doul. Marquat also completed the task of establishing a commissionership and a two major leagues system in Japan as proposed by Matsutaro Shoriki, whom Marquat agreed to nominate as the first commissioner. As noted in the Introduction, however, Shoriki was forced to resign immediately due to strong opposition from Courtney Whitney, the head of the Government Section (GS).[9] The role that Marquat fulfilled and the meaning of the San Francisco Seals' visit to Japan in 1949 will be discussed in detail in Chapter Seven.

Marquat prioritized bringing the comforts of home to American troops stationed in Japan. Consequently, he permitted the establishment of a Coca-Cola factory in Yokohama to refresh occupying soldiers with an American soft drink. Japanese institutions were given American names, including Tokyo Takarazuka Theatre, which was renamed the Ernie Pyle Theatre, and the Jingu Kyujou baseball stadium became the Stateside Park. In addition to the Stateside Park, the Korakuen Kyujou baseball stadium and the Hanshin Koshien Kyujou baseball stadium came under GHQ/SCAP supervision over the short term.[10]

GHQ/SCAP used such facilities for their own recreational activities, such as the 1949 4th of July Sports Program, which consisted of an all-star baseball game between the Occupation League All-Stars and Tokyo League All-Stars at Stateside Park, and softball games at Doolittle Field (Hibiya Park) (see Fig. 1.1). It was difficult for Japanese individuals or organizations to get permission to use such facilities.

In her book, *Transpacific Field of Dreams: How Baseball Linked the United States and Japan in Peace and War* (2012), Sayuri Guthrie-Shimizu introduces the fact that, in 1935, Matsutaro Shoriki, the president of the *Yomiuri* Newspaper Group, was assaulted by a crazed ultranationalist who believed the morally depraved Americans were desecrating the sacred

---

9 Masaru Hatano, *Nichibei Yakyu Shi: Major wo Oikaketa 70 Nen* (History of U.S.-Japan baseball: 70 years chasing the Major League) (PHP, 2001), pp. 197–199; Theodore Cohen, *Nihon-Senryou-Kakumei: GHQ karano Shougen* (The third turn: MacArthur, the Americans and the rebirth of Japan) (TBS Britannica, 1983), p. 150.

10 *Korakuen no 25 Nen* (25 years of Korakuen) (Korakuen Stadium, 1963), pp. 156–160; Kyushi Yamato, *Shinsetsu Nihon Yakyuu-shi: Showa hen sonogo* (True history of Japanese baseball: Showa Era vol. 5) (Baseball Magazine-Sha, 1979), pp. 27, 115–116.

ballpark adjacent to the Jingu Shrine.[11] It is not certain that GHQ/SCAP requisitioned the Jingu Kyujou baseball stadium as facilities to comfort U.S. military personnel and the civilians who worked for them, but it seems a persuasive theory that the ultranationalists regarded the Jingu Kyujou baseball stadium as something related to the Japanese wartime Shinto belief that Jingu was a sacred place. In any case, GHQ/SCAP continued to use the Jingu Kyujou baseball stadium under the name Stateside Park until March 31, 1952, when they took down the 'Stateside Park' sign and replaced it with one reading 'Jingu Stadium'.[12]

Figure 1.1 '4th of July Sports Program' pamphlet, 1949
Source: Takeshi Tanikawa Collection.

---

11 Sayuri Guthrie-Shimizu, *Transpacific Field of Dreams: How Baseball Linked the United States and Japan in Peace and War* (University of North Carolina Press, 2012), p. 202.

12 Ibid., p. 235.

The East-West Baseball Match

The resumption of baseball games perhaps offered a symbol of the return of an era of peace. With the support of GHQ/SCAP, baseball returned to Japan exactly 100 days after the end of World War II. As the first step of the baseball revival, the East-West game took place on November 23, 1945. The game featured well-known professional players of the wartime era as well as new players like Hiroshi Oshita from the Tokyo Big Six Baseball League. Although the Jingu Stadium had not allowed professional baseball teams to use its facilities in the past, GHQ/SCAP permitted the game to be played in the venue, a gesture that left a strong impression on the Japanese people about the new era of Japanese professional baseball.

Kenzo Hirose, the official recordkeeper of professional baseball games in Japan later inducted into Japan's Baseball Hall of Fame, was a walking sports dictionary who detailed the East-West game in the January 1946 issue of the periodical *Yakyu-kai*.

It was unrealistic to have high expectations of the East-West game, which was held as scheduled, because it was organized quickly without a preparatory period. The athletes were ordered to enthusiastically participate in a couple of practices with a ball for only a few days. What could one expect under these circumstances? The event was, however, more significant for the fact that Jingu Stadium was being permitted to be used by *professional baseball teams* for the first time under the supervision of GHQ/SCAP, which had never been allowed previously.

> It was a warm, sunny day in early spring; there was no wind, making it a perfect day for a baseball game, just like the day of the So-Kei (Waseda vs. Keio) game. It had rained on the 22nd and the game scheduled for that day was cancelled. On the 23rd, however, there was a clear sky and nice, warm temperature, like you could almost fall asleep under the sunlight. Regarding the game itself, I have nothing to write in detail. The batters of the East and West teams hit balls easily due to the lack of practice of the pitcher, the outfielders had not yet retrieved their usual speed, great eyesight, etc., so they could not impress the audience. It turned out to be a messy end to the game: the East team won with 13-9.[13]

---

13 Kenzo Hirose, 'Saiken Nihon Yakyu: Tosai-Taikou-Yakyu Kansenki' (Rebuilding Japanese baseball: Watching the East-West game), *Yakyu-kai*, Vol. 36, No. 1, January 1946, Hakubun-Kan, pp. 4–5.

A number of major players who actively played in the pre-war and post-war eras were missing from the lineup in the 1945 East-West game, including Tetsuharu Kawakami, known as the 'God of Batting'. His absence drew national attention. He refused to return to the Giants, in what was known as the 'Kawakami Hold-Out issue', unless the team agreed to pay him a re-signing fee of 30,000 yen. If the Giants refused his demand, he threatened to return to farming at his home in Kumamoto Prefecture. Kawakami's demands were reasonable because a baseball player's physical condition is his primary resource. From the league's perspective, the case of Kawakami was symbolic, and it inaugurated a new era in which professional athletes began to claim the rights to their services. Kawakami, also known as 'Red Bat', and Hiroshi Oshita, known as 'Blue Bat', a slugger for the Senators[14] who later became the home run king of the Pacific League after the Japanese professional baseball league split into two leagues after the 1949 season, pioneered Japan's professional baseball in the post-war era. Both players were extremely popular among Japan's younger fans.

Another player who was missing from the East-West game lineup was Russian-born Victor Starffin, a star player and ace pitcher, who along with Eiji Sawamura, led the Giants in the pre-war era. Starffin retired from baseball during the war, ostensibly for health reasons. Many suspect that the real reason behind Starffin's retirement was because he was forced to change his name to 'Hiroshi Suda' due to the wartime prohibition on English names. Starffin resumed his baseball career after the war. In 1946, a new club called the Pacific offered Starffin a contract. The Giants, claiming 'priority negotiation right', responded by suing the Nihon Yakyu Renmei (Japanese Baseball League), resulting in what is known as 'the Starffin issue'.[15]

The controversies surrounding Japanese baseball during the turbulent post-war period indicate that frequent misunderstandings occurred between teams and players regarding the impact of the war on inter-relational contracts from the pre-war era.

---

14 Another team, the Tokyo Senators, existed in Japan in the pre-war era, but there is no connection between that team and the Senators, a team born after the war.

15 Pacific became the Taiyo Robbins in 1947, and later the Shochiku Robbins in 1950. After the merger with the Taiyo Whales, it changed its name to the Yokohama Bay Stars. In 2011, it became the Yokohama DeNA Bay Stars. The name of the Japanese Baseball League changed from Nihon Shokugyou Yakyu Renmei to Nihon Yakyu Renmei in 1939. Nihon Yakyu Renmei (Japanese Baseball Association) operated the Japanese Baseball League, which was called 'Nihon Dai League' for a short period of time after World War II, and then changed to 'Pro Yokyu League'.

The Emperor and baseball

Overshadowed by college baseball, especially the celebrated So-Kei-Sen matches between Waseda and Keio, professional baseball suffered from a negative image in the pre-war years. Following the war, GHQ/SCAP's partnership with league officials and a rising interest in the star players catapulted professional baseball into the nation's consciousness. The professional teams enjoyed unprecedented popularity in the post-war period. It didn't hurt that many of the game's enthusiasts were famous, world-class figures. Among the celebrities that passionately followed the game were Hachiro Sato, a well-known poet, children's author and lyricist who would later become a famous television personality; Shuuoushi Mizuhara, a poet and essayist; and Ango Sakaguchi, a new-wave writer. Although they sometimes offered severe criticism for the purpose of encouraging the players or teams, they basically wrote of their love of professional baseball passionately to support the Nihon Yakyu Renmei to increase its popularity.

Sakaguchi's 1948 essay, 'Japan's professional baseball won't be professional', argued that while the professional sumo-wrestling world was profound, Japan's pro baseball players lacked professionalism. He compared Japanese players to American players and argued that the first and second hitters in Japanese lineups did not perform on the base with the consistency of their American counterparts.[16]

Sports essays by the likes of Ango Sakaguchi never drew the attention of researchers in the field of literature, and Sakaguchi's essay is not included in the complete works of Sakaguchi in either the Chikuma Shobo or Toujusha versions.

Professional baseball also benefited from the fact that Emperor Hirohito Showa was a baseball fan. Although baseball seemed a poor representation of traditional Japan, because Emperor Showa was a fan, the sport gained a new level of prestige. Baseball also helped give the Emperor his new identity as a meaningful and modern figure in the post-war era. After World War II, two faces of the Showa Emperor were emphasized intentionally. One was the image of the Emperor as scientist, and the other was the image of the Emperor as sports lover. Apparently, baseball helped in the transformation of the Emperor from a symbolic deity (Arahitogami) to an amiable unifier of citizens.

---

16 Ango Sakaguchi, 'Nihon-Yakyu-wa-Puro-ni-Arazu' (Japan's professional baseball won't be professional), *Baseball Magazine*, Vol. 3, No. 8, August 1948, Koubun-Sha, pp. 16–17.

On June 25, 1959, the Emperor became the first Japanese monarch to attend a professional baseball game when he attended a game between the Yomiuri Giants and Hanshin Tigers. The event achieved legendary status not only because the Emperor was present but because of Shigeo Nagashima's dramatic game-winning home run, giving the Giants a 5-4 victory over the Tigers. The Emperor's love of sumo-wrestling was already established, as he often appeared at tournaments at Kokugikan, the national sumo arena.

Considering his status and position, the Emperor could not publicly acknowledge his favorite team or even convey to the public that he was only interested in professional baseball. Japan officially learned of the Emperor's interest in baseball on August 3, 1947, when he attended the 18th Inter-City Match Amateur Baseball Tournament game at Korakuen Stadium. Three years later, the Emperor attended a So-Kei game of the Tokyo Big Six Baseball League. In October 1947, a special edition of *Yakyu Shonen* contained an article by Yutaka Fukuyu, a journalist from the *Mainichi Shimbun*, called 'Sports lovers: The Emperor Hirohito and Sir Mikasanomiya' (see Fig. 1.2).[17]

兩陛下後樂園球場へ

Figure 1.2 Showa Emperor and Empress appearing at Korakuen Stadium
Source: Takeshi Tanikawa Collection, photograph taken by Yutaka Fukuyu, 'Ryouheika Korakuen Kyujou e' (Emperor and Empress go to Korakuen Stadium), Yakyu Shonen *(special edition), October 1947.*

---

17 Yutaka Fukuyu, 'Supōtsu wo Aisareru Tennōheika to Mikasanomiya' (Sports lovers: The Emperor Hirohito and Sir Mikasanomiya), *Yakyu Shonen*, October 1947, Shoubun-kan, pp. 2–3.

The article included a photograph of both men. As the periodical was directed at young readers who were not yet influenced by the Emperor's prestigious image in the pre-war era and during the war, it is possible that the article may have been published on behalf of the Imperial Household Agency.

Baseball was returning to Japan at a rapid rate. With the season opening on April 27, 1946, Japanese professional baseball, which at that time consisted of only one league, resumed its long-anticipated pennant race. That spring, the Tokyo Big Six Baseball League was revived. The Inter-City Match Amateur Baseball Tournament and the Middle-School Baseball Summer Tournament followed in the summer of the same year. In the next year, on March 30, 1947, the Selected Middle-School Baseball Tournament resumed.[18] Two years after the end of the war, baseball leagues and tournaments on all levels — professional, university, industrial and scholastic — were back and thriving more than ever.

Baseball returned with the strong backing of GHQ/SCAP. Speaking at the opening ceremony of the Selected Middle-School Baseball Tournament, Maj. Gen. Marquat, the head of the Economic and Scientific Section, pointed out that 'Japan's baseball enthusiasm is unprecedented. It was the right decision that this game paid attention to sports at the school physical education level, and preached to promote it'.[19]

Jean MacArthur, the wife of Gen. Douglas MacArthur, the American general who administered the occupation from 1945 to 1951, attended a charity game at Jingu Stadium on August 24, 1949. The game, which was organized by the U.S. Armed Forces newspaper *Stars and Stripes* to benefit victims of the 1949 Hokuriku Earthquake, was the first professional game staged at Jingu Stadium since baseball returned to Japan with the East-West game of November 1945. Although three pennant races had been held since the 1945 East-West game, all of them were played at Korakuen Stadium when held in Tokyo. With the support of GHQ/SCAP, the charity game was held at Jingu Stadium. Using baseball to support victims of natural disaster was likely part of GHQ/SCAP's plan to democratize Japan through baseball. Further evidence of GHQ/SCAP using baseball to promote democracy can be seen in the congratulatory message Gen. MacArthur sent to the participants of the Sou-Kei-Sen match in June 1949:

---

18 Kyushi Yamato, *Shinsetsu Nihon Yakyuu-shi: Showa hen sonogo* (True history of Japanese baseball: Showa Era vol. 5) (Baseball Magazine-Sha, 1979), pp. 92, 109, 112–113, 115–116.

19 Masaru Hatano, p. 196.

It is almost impossible to discover a resource, besides the University Sports Competition, that can help build man's great personality. In such a narrow sense, it is 'baseball' that both Japanese and U.S. citizens would be deeply interested in. Baseball helps nourish one's endurance and a great sense of teamwork. Moreover, it also helps promote a sense of emulation that is necessary for our society to expand socio-economic liberty. I was a member of the baseball team at West Point around the time when the legendary match of the So-Kei University game was held for the first time back in 1903. I have been a great baseball enthusiast and supporter since then. I believe that members of both teams, which still exist, are the same as me. When I see Japanese people's enthusiasm for baseball from their childhood, I simultaneously observe that baseball helps build a great and practical moral sense that would resolve important issues to rebuild the nation. As a former baseball athlete and baseball lover, I would address my extolment to you, the players from Waseda and Keio Universities. I wish that happiness be with the stronger team.[20]

MacArthur's message implies the existence of GHQ/SCAP's policy to 'democratize Japan through sports'. Or, perhaps, such a policy should be defined as 'Americanizing post-war Japan by popularizing baseball to inculcate its social values'. Reviving baseball in Japan meant restoring Japan as a nation. It also signified that the goal of the U.S. occupation of Japan was to reconstruct the U.S.-Japan relationship. Finally, the revival of baseball was designed to restore the friendship that existed between the U.S. and Japan in the pre-war period.

---

20 'Ma-Gensui Sou-Kei-Sen ni Shukuji' (Gen. MacArthur sent a congratulatory message to the Sou-Kei-Sen), *Baseball Magazine*, Vol. 4, No. 10, August 1949, Koubun-Sha, p. 48. (Translation from the Japanese.)

Sports Industry Reform Under the U.S. Occupation

▌ Reforming *budo*

GHQ/SCAP implemented a policy that used baseball to promote democratization. At the same time, it adopted strict regulations restricting *budo*, Japan's traditional martial arts, because they were perceived as encouraging the wartime nationalism and militarism. Kendo, judo and *kyudo* (Japanese archery) were permitted to continue under one condition: they had to be dissociated from a past strongly linked to the Japanese aristocracy and promoted simply as sports. Traditionally, the practitioners of these martial arts were the *bushi*/samurai, members of a military elite who served the nobility and adhered to a severe code of honor.

In contrast, sumo was viewed as a 'professional sport' because, unlike other forms of *budo* which relied on individual training methods, sumo included professional tournaments at its highest level. The difference between amateur and professional sports can best be distinguished by whether or not the main objective of the business is to attract spectators. It was GHQ/SCAP policy to transform Japan's existing sports from participatory to spectator sports, increasing the number of athletes to the point that competitions became major events. As a result, judo and kendo faced challenges, as both sports sought other ways to reform in the post-war period.

The GHQ/SCAP policy initially removed *budo* from the Japanese educational experience, permitting *kyudo* to return in July of 1950 and judo the following October. Kendo did not resume until April 1953, after the U.S. occupation ended, because of the Far Eastern Commission's belief that 'Classical sports, such as kendo, which encouraged the martial spirit, should be totally abandoned'.[1]

It would be incorrect to conclude, however, that *budo* were never practiced during the occupation, as there were no restrictions prohibiting

---

1 Reiko Yamamoto, *Beikoku-Tainichi-Senryo-Seisaku to Budo-Kyoiku: Dainihon-Butokukai no Koubou* (U.S. occupation policy and *budo* education: The rise and fall of Dainihon-Butokukai) (Nihon-Tosho-Center, 2003), pp. 73–74.

individuals from practicing *budo* as a means of maintaining their health. In fact, it was not uncommon to see newspaper reports about GHQ/SCAP staff and family members vigorously practicing kendo or judo at local police stations. The effort against *budo* practices varied—some police precincts halted the practice of *budo* due to the military jurisdiction, while others held judo/kendo matches from the very early stage of the occupation, to which GHQ/SCAP staff members were invited.

Police periodicals published during the occupation reported on judo and kendo matches. These articles make it clear that such matches were not scheduled to reform police *budo* into a democratic sport, but were instead held to help Japanese individuals to overcome the hardship from the loss of the war by relying on spirit alone, just as they had done during the war, as well as to flatter members of GHQ/SCAP staff regarded as the new rulers. For example, the first post-war issue (December 1946) of *Keiko*, the periodical published by the Nagasaki Prefecture Police Association, contained an article that described a judo match between a police officer and fire-fighter. The article did not emphasize the sport as an example of 'sporting' *budo*. Rather, it conveyed the writer's excitement about seeing a sport that had long been banned. The writer also pointed out that, in order to reconstruct Japan, the country needed an 'indomitable spirit', arguing that policemen, as role models, were the leaders of the indomitable spirit which appears to be consistent with the reliance on spirit alone emphasized during the war.[2] Another article, this one published in *Kagaribi*, a periodical issued by the Ehime-Prefectural Police Department, offered the following spiritual argument:

> 'The police officers become confident when they train their mind and body with police *budo* and master *budo*. Police officers with enough confidence to show fortitude. Police officers with great fortitude gain trust from the citizens', said Mr. Engel of the Civil Information and Education Section, GHQ/SCAP. It is entirely true that when citizens truly trust police officers, they can focus on their work; and then, the citizens can appreciate the nation and achieve patriotism. Moreover, it will lead them to be wholesome citizens.

---

2 Matsuda, 'Tai-sho Budo Taikai' (*Budo* tournament among departments), *Keiko*, Vol. 24, No. 21, December 1946, Nagasaki-ken Kei-Min Kyokai, pp. 23–24.

> Police *budo* training which turns them into true police officers with fortitude and able to earn the citizens' trust must not only contend with the improvement of technique.[3]

The GHQ/SCAP official's words expressed the importance of police *budo*. The article also quotes a principal of the Central Police Academy stating the importance of democratizing the police system while reconstructing peace in Japan, assisted by a 'super-human feat' in the process. The article indicates the true face of the police kendo participants, which is entirely consistent with their attitude that relied solely on spiritualism during the war.

At the same time, the Kodokan, the headquarters of the judo society, seemed to be moving toward drastic revolution. The Kodokan published a periodical called *Judo*, and in the December 1948 issue, Kodokan Director Risei Kanou stated that judo must be popularized as a sport for a new age.[4]

The issue also contained two articles that were influenced by Risei's statement. One of the essays, written by Ichiro Moriwaki, declared that judo should not persist with the old customs, but should be transformed into a sport. Moreover, he declared that the idea that *budo*, as spiritual education, is superior to all other sports should be abandoned, and argued that judo should be a democratic sport supported by the spirit of fair play. Moriwaki, who quoted and was influenced by American philosopher John Dewey, demonstrated the internationalization of the Kodokan.[5]

The other essay was written by Heita Okabe, a promoter of the internationalization of judo. Okabe had been a pupil of the Kodokan who worked as chair of the board of directors of the Manshu (Manchuria) Sports Association during the war, and was later active in the general sports sphere where he was a training coach of the Japanese track and field team for the 1964 Tokyo Olympics. In his essay entitled 'The future of judo', Okabe offered a blueprint for the future of the sport, but his thesis may have been considered absurd from the standpoint of ordinary judo supporters in the late 1940s.

Fumio Adachi, 'Akarui Heiwa-Nihon no Saisei to Keisatsu-Budo' (Rebuilding glorious, peaceful Japan and police *budo*), *Kagaribi*, No. 5, May 1948, Ehime Prefecture Police Department, pp. 68–70.

4 Risei Kanou, 'Kaitaku subeki Judo no Nimensei' (Two aspects of judo to be developed), *Judo*, Vol. 19, No. 12, December 1948, Kodokan, p. 1.

5 Ichiro Moriwaki, 'Supoutsu toshiteno Judo' (Judo as a sport), *Judo*, Vol. 20, No. 1, December 1948, Kodokan, pp. 17–19.

I have discussed the plan with a few people that we should try to open up wrestling and judo matches internationally as a solution to govern the direction of judo. In other words, we would first discontinue the Japanese traditional-style uniform, and switch to a Western style. We will adopt the rules from wrestling requirements as much as we can. If we cannot have matches with America, we will try domestically with wrestlers like Kazama.[6] I would think that this would be interesting at a professional level as well as successful.[7]

Okabe's plan presented a future for judo in which the sport was reformed from a 'player's sport' to a 'spectator's sport'. Today, the history of judo in post-war Japan is well known. The adoption of symbolic colored judo uniforms was exactly what Okabe suggested seventy years ago. Judo (in kanji characters) has been transformed into 'JUDO' (described in Katakana characters used for foreign words). The sport has been internationalized, with Japan no longer recognized as its leader. During the final match of the heavyweight (+100kg) class at the 2000 Sydney Olympics, David Douillet, a French judoka, was declared the winner over Shin-ichi Shinohara of Japan due to a controversial split-decision by the referees.[8] For most people concerned with Japanese judo, it seemed apparent that Shinohara's '*uchi mata sukashi*' technique, which is the counter maneuver to the opponent's '*uchi mata*' attack, was effective enough, but the judge did not accurately see what happened and declared Douillet's *uchi mata* as '*ippon*' (a full point). Shinohara's loss seemed to represent the direction of Japanese judo in the post-war period.

During the post-war period, kendo was restricted more than judo or *kyudo*. Although the Kodokan worked hard to get judo accepted as a sport, no one in the mainstream of kendo was attempting to keep it alive by willingly accepting its transformation into an international sport. Sasaburo Takano, the leader of the Shuudou Gakuin, the governing body of kendo in Japan—just like the Kodokan represented mainstream judo under the

---

6 Eiichi Kazama became the champion of the lightweight class at the first All-Nippon Wrestling Match and then went on to achieve a total of ten championships in two classes.

7 Heita Okabe, 'Judo no Shourai' (The future of Judo), *Judo*, Vol. 20, No. 5, April 1949, Kodokan, pp. 17–19.

8 Takeshi Tsuchimoto, 'Mis-Jajji ni taisuru Nihon-Gata Taio: Olympic Danshi Judo 100 kg Cho-Kyu Kesshousen' (Japanese way of corresponding over misjudgment: Final match of the male judo over 100 kg class at the Olympics), *Sousa Kenkyu*, No. 590, 2000.

leadership of Jigoro Kanou — found his authority undermined by the war due to the fact that the Shuudou Gakuin building was destroyed for the purpose of compulsory relocation by government order. Takano passed away in 1950 without knowing whether or not kendo would be revived.[9]

In the end, kendo did not undergo transformation from a participatory sport into a spectator sport, and its rules and image remained the same. In an effort to protect the purity of kendo, the All Japan Kendo Federation continues to oppose the addition of kendo as an Olympic sport.[10] Today, Japan is recognized as the home of kendo, despite the fact that there are many kendo participants and fans all over the world.

Reform of the Japan Sumo Association

Japan's sumo world entered the post-war period with the retirement of Sadaji Futabayama, the Grand Yokozuna Champion, who had won an unprecedented sixty-nine consecutive matches. In his retirement address, Futabayama said, 'I believe that there is nothing like the *heya* system [stable system] that renders the way in which the seniors train and nurture their juniors or followers through their master's orders'. Futabayama, who headed a sumo stable called 'Futabayama-Dojo' while he was still an active wrestler (a practice forbidden today), warned that operating the system improperly 'would destroy it and the relationship between the master and his followers would become just like that of a capitalist and laborers'.[11]

The world of sumo had a pre-modern mechanism that GHQ/SCAP perceived as a problem. Following the war, pessimism surrounded sumo and the sport's very existence seemed to be in danger. Sumo survived, however, and today, as sumo, like other martial arts, is being internationalized, some wrestlers are unaware of its traditional discipline. Nevertheless, the *heya* system still exists in Japan with little fundamental change. In 2007, sixty-

---

9 Akihiko Domoto, *Kendo Shugyou: Shudou Gakuin no Seishun* (Kendo training: Young days at Shudou Gakuin) (Ski Journal Publisher Inc., 1985), pp. 412–414.

10 Tetsushi Abe, 'Kendo ni okeru Kokusaika no Shomondai' (Various problems of the internationalization of kendo), *Budo Ronshu, No.III,: 'Global Jidai no Budo'* (*Budo* in the global age) (Budo & Sports Science Research Institute, International Budo University, 2012), pp. 185–186.

11 Sadaji Fatabayama, 'Shin-Hossoku ni Atatte' (Facing the new start), *Sumo*, Vol. 11, Nos. 4–7, July 1946, Dai-Nippon Sumo Kyokai, pp. 8–9.

two years after Futabayama retired and became Tokitsukaze-Oyakata (Stable Master Tokitsukaze), the mysterious hazing death of a seventeen-year-old trainee in the same Tokitsukaze stable led to criticism of the *heya* system. In response to this incident, authorities charged the master and three of his senior followers with manslaughter. Since the scandal, authorities in the sport have been working hard to restore sumo's image, while critics continue to call for reform of the structure of the national sport.[12]

During his retirement, Futabayama became involved in Ji-u, one of the many cult-like religions that emerged in post-war Japan. Futabayama's interest in Ji-u took his attention away from the training of young wrestlers. In January 1947, Futabayama and the leader of the Ji-u cult, a woman named Nagako Nagaoka who called herself 'Jikouson', were arrested together in Kanazawa. Futabayama's association with Ji-u damaged sumo's image, as many saw him as being used by the cult to publicize and legitimate their cause. Yet, when Futabayama returned to the Japan Sumo Association, he was not excluded from the mainstream. In 1957, after the occupation ended, Futabayama became the chairman of the board of directors of the association. As chair, he attempted to establish the sixty-five years of age retirement system for sumo seniors and referees. He also sought to abolish the *chaya* system and introduce the *heya-betsu sou-atari* system, in which every wrestler was required to fight against every other wrestler who was not a member of his *heya* (stable).[13]

Sumo reforms actually began during the occupation period before Futabayama, known as Tokitsukaze in retirement, took over as chairman of the board of directors. By 1945, matches were infrequent because of air-raids. In June 1945, a seven-day private tournament was held at the Ryogoku Kokugikan, an arena that had lost its roof to American bombing. In November 1945, for the first time during the occupation, a ten-day sumo tournament was held. The tournament was staged to demonstrate to the occupation authorities that sumo was a 'spectator sport'. Tournament officials sought to make the event more spectator-friendly by creating more competitive matches. As a result, the inside diameter of the sumo ring was increased from fifteen *shaku* (4.55 meters) to sixteen *shaku* (4.8 meters), and the maximum length of time

---

12 On January 28, 2014, the Nihon Sumo Kyokai announced that it had been authorized by the Cabinet Office to be a Public Interest Incorporated Foundation after years of struggle to reform its structure in the wake of the 2007 scandal.

13 Taketoshi Takanaga, *Sumo Showa-shi: Gekidou no Kiseki* (History of sumo in the Showa Era: The track in convulsions) (Koubun-sha, 1982), pp. 151–162.

for preparation before the match was decreased from seven minutes to five minutes. The enlarged ring proved too wide for wrestlers undernourished by the war, and the ring was returned to its original size in 1946.[14] Officials from the Japan Sumo Association and writers who covered the sport debated which reforms to pursue, including the implementation of three tournaments per year, the revival of the fifteen-day tournament length, the separation into East and West sides and the round-robin tournament system (which is fought amongst *ichimon* rather than *heya*).[15]

In November 1946, the finance ministry, the Kangyo-Bank and the Japan Sumo Association implemented a sumo lottery to help Japan financially. Due to the lottery's unpopularity, however, it was quickly discontinued. Other reforms attempted to make sumo more spectator friendly. Starting with the June 1947 tournament, the scoring system was revised and a play-off was introduced. Until then, if more than one wrestler had the same score at the end of the tournament, the title would be awarded to the wrestler with the highest score who was ranked the highest. In November 1947, the East-West match system was abandoned in favor of a round-robin tournament. Starting that month, three new prizes were also awarded — for outstanding performance, for the best 'fighting spirit' and for the most accomplished skill. The three-tournament per year system was revived in January 1949, and the fifteen-day length was reinstated the following May.[16]

If sumo was to survive, however, it needed a venue in which matches could be watched by audiences. *Ozumo* (professional sumo) is very dependent upon an audience, and, without a suitable public venue, the sport would cease to exist. Despite the fact that the November 1945 tournament at the badly damaged Ryogoku-Kokugikan was staged for the occupation forces, GHQ/SCAP condemned the venue in 1946. In June, the building was renovated by GHQ/SCAP and renamed Memorial Hall. The upgraded multi-use facility featured a huge chandelier and ice-skating rink. Because

---

14 Showa no Ozumo Kankou Iinkai, ed., *Showa no Ozumo* (TBS Britannica, 1989), pp. 111–113.

15 Mutsuo Uemura, Motoi Soma, Saburo Hara, Koichi Yamaguchi, Tsuyoshi Kasugano, Hidemitsu Fujishima, Koichiro Sadogatake and Kozo Hikoyama, 'Sumo-kai Kikyoku Kokufuku Shin-Doukou Sakuan Zadankai' (Round table talk about overcoming difficulties and planning the new approach of the sumo world), *Sumo*, Vol. 11, Nos. 2–3, March 1946, Dai-Nippon Sumo Kyokai, pp. 26–47. *Heya* is the smallest unit of organization wrestlers belong to, and each *heya* belongs to an *ichimon*. There are several *ichimon* and the relationship between them is competitive.

16 Showa no Ozumo Kankou Iinkai, ed., op cit., pp. 116–123.

of the construction, the summer sumo tournament was cancelled. Instead, a temporary sumo ring was set up in the Abeno district of Osaka and at the Yasukuni Shrine in Kudan, Tokyo, for the next couple of tournaments. Although a thirteen-day tournament was finally permitted inside Memorial Hall in November 1946, the three tournaments held between June 1947 and May 1948 were staged at an open-air temporary sumo ring at the Jingu Gaien, now called Jingu Second Stadium, which meant that matches could not be held during inclement weather.[17]

In the post-war period, securing a location for a sumo tournament proved to be quite a challenge. In order to establish better communication, the Japan Sumo Association recruited Kaichiro Toyonishiki, an American-born sumo wrestler who had acquired Japanese citizenship after being promoted to '*sekitori*' (the name given to wrestlers at the '*juryo*' or higher position entailing privileges such as a high salary) to act as an interpreter between association officials and GHQ/SCAP staff. Eventually, the Japan Sumo Association, with the approval of GHQ/SCAP, selected a site in the Kuramae neighborhood of Tokyo to construct a new sumo stadium.[18]

As a concession to the occupying forces, the Japan Sumo Association changed its name. Originally, the Japanese name for the organization was Zaidanhojin Dai Nippon Sumo Kyokai. According to the description in colophon on the association's periodical, *Sumo*, during the post-war era, the organization went by the interim name, Zaidanhojin Nihon Ozumo Kyokai, out of concern that GHQ/SCAP would learn that the phrase 'Dai Nippon' also appeared in the name, 'Dai Nippon Teikoku', the war-time term for 'the Japanese Empire'. In 1958, after the occupation was over, the association adopted Zaidanhojin Nihon Sumo Kyokai (Japan Sumo Association) as its permanent name.[19]

The sumo world experienced a difficult time during the occupation. Futabayama's retirement ceremony was held following the Memorial Hall tournament of November 1946, and Setsuo Akinoumi, another *yokozuna* (grand champion), also announced his retirement. The new age created new heroes. Eigoro Maedayama, who had been in the *ozeki* (champion) rank for a long period of time, rose to become thirty-ninth *yokozuna* in November

17 Ibid., pp. 114–119.

18 Taketoshi Takanaga, p. 149.

19 *Sumo*, Zaidanhojin Nihon Ozumo Kyokai, Vol. 11, No. 1, Vol. 11, Nos. 4–7, Vol. 11, Nos. 8–9, Vol. 11, No. 10. Showa no Ozumo Kankou Iinkai, ed., op cit., p. 181.

1947. Maedayama was the first sumo wrestler to become *yokozuna* in the post-war period. Other young wrestlers appearing on the scene included Masanobu Chiyonoyama, who later became the forty-first grand champion, and Mitsuhiro Rikidozan. In January 1949, Kin-ichi Azumafuji became the sport's fortieth grand champion.[20]

The road for each new hero was tumultuous. The certificate that promoted a wrestler to *yokozuna* had been issued by the Yoshidatsukasa family under authority granted by Emperor Gotoba 750 years earlier. When the controversial Maedayama received the certificate, it contained a condition stating that it 'would be revoked if [he engaged in] any improper conduct'.[21] As will be discussed in Chapter Seven, Maedayama's name drew public attention when he was involved in a scandal caused by the visit of the San Francisco Seals in 1949. A year later, Mitsuhiro Rikidozan stunned the sumo world when, in the midst of a feud with his master, he cut his own topknot. The gesture imitated the symbolic ritual practice of sumo wrestlers who are announcing their retirement. Having turned his back on sumo, Rikidozan tried his hand at professional Western wrestling. In 1953, he established the Japan Pro Wrestling Alliance. As a member of the alliance, Rikidozan became one of the dominant professional wrestlers in the world. In 1953, Masanobu Chiyonoyama offered to return his status as grand champion to the Japan Sumo Association due to the fact that his scores at the January and March tournaments were unsatisfactory. The Japan Sumo Association did not accept his offer and instead encouraged Chiyonoyama as the youngest *yokozuna* at the time. In 1954, Kin-ichi Azumafuji, another grand champion, also left sumo to join the Japanese Pro-Wrestling Association. Rikidozan later convinced Masahiko Kimura, an undefeated judo player, to give up his sport for professional wrestling.

Growth of the two-league system for professional baseball

Professional baseball in Japan underwent a difficult period due to the post-war reforms. Before the war, Japan only had one professional league, the Nihon Yakyu Renmei (Japanese Baseball Association). Following the war,

---

20 Ibid, pp. 113–122.

21 Juzen Imada, *Dokankai: Harite Ichidai Maedayama Eigoro* (Get out of my sight: Eigoro Maedayama, 'Harite' sumo wrestler) (BAB Japan, 1995), pp. 179–180.

a second league, called the Kokumin Yakyu Renmei (People's Baseball Association), was born.[22] Daisuke Miyake, a former player and manager of the Dainippon Tokyo Yakyu Kurabu when it was established, wrote about the sport after the war and welcomed the new league, noting that the state of California, which had a smaller population than Japan, had several professional leagues.[23] Miyake later managed the Ohtsuka Athletics, one of the teams belonging to the Kokumin Yakyu Renmei.

Auto parts magnate Isao Utaka formed the Kokumin Yakyu Renmei at the suggestion of Ryuji Suzuki, the head of the Nihon Yakyu Renmei. Utaka had been denied an application for a team in the existing league. To appease Utaka, who also operated a sports equipment business, Suzuki recommended that he form an independent league, a suggestion he would later regret. Utaka assembled a team he called the Utaka Red Sox. To stock the roster, he attracted players from teams belonging to the Nihon Yakyu Renmei. Another independent team, called the Tokyo Cubs, also had its application to join the Nihon Yakyu Renmei rejected. In March 1947, the Utaka Red Sox and the Tokyo Cubs (renamed the Greenberg after Hank Greenberg, the Jewish-American star of the Detroit Tigers) established the new league, the Kokumin Yakyu Renmei,[24] and Utaka himself became its president.

Notwithstanding its ambitious start, due to its parent company's financial problems, the Greenberg was forced to sell to a construction material company in Yuuki City, Ibaraki Prefecture, and was promptly renamed the Yuuki Braves. These two teams—the Utaka Red Sox and the Yuuki Braves—became the nucleus of the new league, and two more teams were recruited.

The two other charter members of the league were the Ohtsuka Athletics, owned by Kounosuke Ohtsuka, an umbrella manufacturer in Matsudo City, Chiba Prefecture, and the Karasaki Crown(s), owned by a soda company in

---

22 The Kokumin Yakyu Renmei (People's Baseball Association) operated the Kokumin Yakyu League (People's Baseball League), just like the Nihon Yakyu Renmei (Japanese Baseball Association) operated the Japanese Baseball League.

23 Daisuke Miyake, 'Yakyu wo Kagaku seyo!' (Think about *yakyu* scientifically), *Baseball Magazine*, Vol. 2, No. 4, May 1947, Koubun-Sha, pp. 9–12.

24 Hank Greenberg was so popular in Japan because he hit fifty-eight home runs in 1938, the best record spanning more than three decades between Babe Ruth (sixty home runs in 1927) and Roger Maris (sixty-one home runs in 1961).

Osaka. The league scheduled two seasons in 1947 — a spring season in June and an autumn season in October.[25]

Immediately after its establishment, the Kokumin Yakyu Renmei faced hard times. The Japanese sports media paid little attention to the new league, and because few stars played on its teams, game attendance was light. Then, tax problems compelled Isao Utaka to give up the Red Sox. The franchise was purchased by Kumagai Gumi, a large Japanese construction company, which renamed the team the Kumagai Red Sox, and Kounosuke Ohtsuka replaced Utaka as the head of the league. During the 1947 season, Ohtsuka took over financial responsibility for the undercapitalized Karasaki Crown(s) when that franchise could no longer financially support itself. The final nail in the league's coffin occurred when the bankrupt Kinsei Stars of the Nihon Yakyu Renmei approached Ohtsuka for help. Ohtsuka, recognizing the opportunity, obtained a stake in the Kinsei Stars and then merged what remained of his Athletics into the Nihon Yakyu Remei team in February 1948. The People's Baseball League was over after only one year.[26]

Although the Kokumin Yakyu Remnei quickly disappeared into the darkness of history, expectations for creating an American-style two-league system in Japan remained high. Maj. Gen. William F. Marquat, whom Gen. Douglas MacArthur had authorized to manage Japanese baseball under the U.S. occupation, was a strong proponent of the two-league system. In April 1949, Matsutaro Shoriki, the president of the *Yomiuri Shimbun*, issued the 'Shoriki Proclamation', declaring that the Nihon Yakyu Renmei was to expand by four teams and divide into two six-team leagues. While still reeling from the 'Shoriki Proclamation', Japanese baseball would later be heavily influenced by the visit of the San Francisco Seals of America's Pacific Coast League.[27]

▌ Boxing as a scientific sport

The novel, *Setouchi Shonen Yakyu Dan* (MacArthur's children), was written by Yu Aku, who passed away in August 2007. He was one of Japan's leading

---

25 Kyushi Yamato, *Shinsetsu Nihon Yakyuu-shi: Showa hen sonogo* (True history of Japanese Baseball: Showa Era Vol. 5) (Baseball Magazine-Sha, 1979), pp. 139–144.

26 Ibid., pp. 139–144.

27 Ibid., pp. 293–302.

songwriters in the post-war period, and was nominated for the Naoki Award for this novel. In the book, there is a character nicknamed 'Baraketsu'[28]—a roughneck boy who is a close friend of the main character. The main character is a schoolboy who was modeled on the writer himself. Baraketsu's dream of becoming a naval captain is shattered due to Japan's defeat in the war. Since his dream is unrealizable, he thinks the best thing that a real man can do is to join a Yakuza organization. The movie remake of the novel was a great hit, and a sequel entitled *Setouchi Shonen Yakyu Dan Seishunhen: saigo no Rakuen* was released in 1987. In this movie, Baraketsu has grown to be a youth who practices to become a boxer, symbolizing Japan's boxing fever that actually existed during the occupation era through the 1950s.

Baraketsu brags in the movie, 'My father is a black marketeer, my older brother is a swindler and my older sister is a prostitute, then I'll have to shoot for something bigger'. His goal is to become a boxer like Yoshio Shirai, who became the first Japanese world champion boxer. Although Baraketsu talks big and enthusiastically, saying, 'I'm going to be Yoshio Shirai', he is beaten in his debut match. Yoshio Shirai embraced Japan's post-war recovery and gave hope not only to Baraketsu, but to the Japanese people who lost confidence in their future as a result of the defeat. However, Yoshio Shirai did not appear out of nowhere to the boxing world of the post-war period.

Boxing in Japan dates back to 1922, when the first match was held in the country. One of the pioneers of boxing in Japan was a man named Yujiro Watanabe, who opened a training gym after studying the sport in the U.S. Although it was not until 1922 that an actual boxing match was held in Japan for the first time, Japanese audiences had previously enjoyed watching boxing in motion pictures like the popular Charlie Chaplin film, *The Champion*, produced in 1915 and released in 1916, which featured a scene of two pugilists sparring.[29]

Among the early boxers in Japan were White Gypsies from Russia, who not only boxed among themselves but also fought against judo players in sideshows. By the beginning of the Showa period, the *Yomiuri Shimbun* started to arrange large-scale international boxing matches. At the time, *Yomiuri* was a small company competing against the larger *Tokyo-Asashi* and *Tokyo-Nichinichi* newspapers. The most notable of these matches was

---

28 '*Baraketsu*' literally means 'bad boy' or juvenile delinquent.

29 Ginga Kyokai, ed., *Chaplin no Sekai* (The world of Chaplin) (Eichi Shuppan, 1978), p. 35.

the 1933 Japan-France match, in which three top-level French boxers fought against Japanese boxers. Prior to this match, *Yomiuri* had also sponsored the pre-match tournament to select Japanese boxers to fight against the French. The match became profoundly popular among the Japanese audience. Tsuneo 'Piston' Horiguchi, the only Japanese boxer to defeat a French boxer in the competition, acquired national fame and recognition from the event. Horiguchi had earned the nickname 'Piston' from his unorthodox fighting style. Instead of utilizing a defensive tactic, Horiguchi was always on the offensive, with his arms punching continuously like pistons moving up and down in an internal combustion engine.[30]

The boxing industry started afresh after the war, yet it seemed to return to the sideshow business of the Taisho period, before Hirohito became emperor. The *Yomiuri Shimbun* and the Nihon Kento Kyokai, which was established in June 1946, organized a two-day championship match to mark the twenty-fifth anniversary of boxing in Japan on September 19–20, 1947. The event was held as an official championship match by authentic promoters, but the match was somewhat unusual: fought between a light-heavyweight boxer and a bantamweight boxer, it involved two different weight classes.[31] Perhaps potential participants in many weight classes were casualties of the war, or perhaps malnourishment caused by the war and occupation made the weight class meaningless.

In the case of the lowest level matches in provincial regions, irresponsible matches were common where a proxy boxer was used despite the fact that the promoter announced the name of a different boxer on promotional posters. Boxing columns in pugilist magazines indicated that the boxing industry was in chaos:

> The recent provincial shows are disorderly: the program schedule change was done shamelessly; proxy boxers are used shamelessly. Do they care about the fans? They are not boxing matches, but circus sideshows. They shouldn't show them to us if they think they are theatrical plays. If they are to just make money by using boxers, get out of the business. They hurt innocent,

---

30 Mitsuo Yamazaki, *Rashhu no Ouja: Kensei Piston Horiguchi Den* (King of rush: Biography of Piston Horiguchi, a holy boxer) (Bungeishunju, 1994), pp. 45–54.

31 Chiyohiko Asama, 'Bokushingu Zuiso' (Essay on boxing), inaugural issue of *Boxing Digest*, December 1947, Boxing Digest-Sha, p. 6.

hardworking boxers, and poison the boxing industry. Get rid of all the bosses to create clean sports in Japan.[32]

Boxing officials understood that, if the boxing industry was to thrive as a sport, it needed to establish a commission system with a clean, fair and regulated organization. Several GHQ/SCAP staff members echoed these points in a column in a boxing magazine.

> I would like to express my view on the recent boxing industry situation that I cannot ignore. I also wish that it will progress towards a healthy and sound future.
>
> I suggest that the Japanese boxing industry needs to immediately establish an effective commission system like the one in New York. An institution that has absolute authority and is a deliberative body should be founded. Everyone in the boxing industry, including boxers and judges, must obey it. Anyone purged by this institution can no longer remain in the service of the boxing industry. The members belonging to the institution should be highly respected people like the superintendent-general of the metropolitan police. Essentially, it would regulate the industry both legally and functionally […]. In conclusion, my word to the boxing industry is this, 'clean up the corruption'.[33]

It is clear that the boxing industry, including both professional and amateur boxing, wanted to develop boxing as a sport, not a roadshow. This viewpoint was often presented in boxing magazines. The Nihon Kento Kyokai, Japan's professional boxing association, was established in 1946 as a consolidated organization for the professional boxing industry. It worked tirelessly and sent observers nationwide to eliminate fixed matches and end disreputable roadshows.[34]

Under the occupation, recreational boxing matches were often held with the occupation forces. Japan's boxing industry may have seen this as a great opportunity to popularize the sport by taking advantage of the strict

---

32 Matsuoka, 'Bosu no Issou' (Removal of bosses; in the 'Voices from the fans' section), *Kento Fan*, Vol. 2, No. 2, December 1946, Kento-Fan-Sha, p. 14.

33 Frank B. Haggins, 'Nihon-Kento-kai ni Ata'u' (Giving to the Japanese boxing world), *Kento Gazette*, Vol. 22, No. 5, October 1946, Kento-Gazette-Sha, p. 3.

34 'Nihon no Bokushingu ha Moukarunoka?' (Does Japan's boxing make a profit?), *Gekkan Kento* (Boxing), Vol. 10, No. 2, February 1948, Kento-Sha, p. 8.

regulations on judo and kendo. During the occupation, a growing number of magazines appeared, boxing periodicals among them. One such boxing magazine was the *Kento Gazette*. Nobuo Gunji was editor-in-chief and it was published by Gazette Shuppan Sha. Gunji was convinced that it was the era for boxing. In the pre-war period, boxing was commonly called '*kento*', the Japanese term for the sport. As time went by, however, and more and more Japanese people increasingly interacted with members of the occupation forces, the name *bokushingu* (boxing) eventually replaced *kento* as the term for the sport. In line with this trend, in 1947 the *Kento Gazette* renamed itself the *Boxing Gazette*.[35]

If the boxing industry was going to survive in post-war Japan, it needed to attract more fans, and that meant the sport needed champion boxers. At the time, the most popular boxer in Japan was Piston Horiguchi, who, since his debut in 1933, had amassed an undefeated record of forty-seven consecutive wins with five draws. In February 1946, with Japan's boxing industry still recovering from the war, Horiguchi issued a retirement statement. This was around the same time that Futabayama, the Sumo Grand Champion, who had established a record of sixty-nine consecutive wins during the war, released his retirement statement. At age thirty-one, Horiguchi was past his prime. He announced that he intended to remain in the sport as a promoter to assist his four younger brothers who had followed him into boxing. Horiguchi obtained the necessary permits from GHQ/SCAP to schedule a boxing match featuring Hiroshi Horiguchi, one of his younger brothers, at Hibiya Kokaido Hall. During the fight, Hiroshi Horiguchi suffered an injury to his ear and was scratched from his next scheduled bout. As a result, Piston Horiguchi ended his retirement to take his brother's place in the ring.[36]

Horiguchi's comeback was big news and many boxing fans as well as Horiguchi himself were excited. Soon, however, it was revealed that this comeback was in fact ill-advised. Horiguchi, himself, recognized his weakness. On January 1, 1948, in a journal discovered by biographer Mitsuo Yamazaki at the Piston Horiguchi Dojo, which still exists in Chigasaki, Kanagawa Prefecture, Horiguchi wrote:

---

35 Tatsuo Shimoda, *Bokushingu Kenbunki* (A record of personal experiences in boxing), Baseball Magazine-Sha, 1982, pp .75–78; *Boxing Gazette*, Vol. 23, No.5, Gazette Shuppan Sha, June 1947.

36 Mitsuo Yamazaki, p. 78.

Thinking about the past five years, I spent meaningless time. In the past five years, my physical ability was declining somewhat every day; my boxing skills didn't just stop improving. I once almost prepared myself to die due to the Daitoa War—a great obstacle, and I did not feel like working on the mastership of boxing as a Japanese citizen back at that time. Then the surprising defeat, the occupation, etc., with these unexpected incidents, I was not able to jeep myself up as a professional boxer and wasted precious time while busying myself with this and that. Eventually, I was able to become a foremost popular boxer in the post-war era during the industry's recovery, but it was too late. Since then, for two whole years of 1946 and 1947, I did not practice at all, only bragging about my fifteen-year career. I had a reckless boxing life, and was beaten seven times during the first two years after the war.[37]

Although Horiguchi was unbeaten in the pre-war years, his return to boxing hurt his record and damaged his reputation. Many observers blamed his fighting style due to its lack of a defensive mechanism. Others suggested that he fought too frequently, taking on as many as ten matches per month. Still others criticized Horiguchi's tactics for not being scientific. Although he was able to win a middleweight championship in Japan in March 1948, after his comeback, ultimately, his record worsened to 176 matches with 138 wins, including eighty-two knock-outs, twenty-four losses and fourteen draws. Horichuchi retired from boxing in April 1950. Six months later, at the age of thirty-six, Horiguchi was killed by a train while walking along the Tokaido rail line in the middle of the night.[38]

While Piston Horiguchi's career was waning, another boxer's star was rising. Although Yoshio Shirai made his professional debut in 1943, his career was soon interrupted when he was drafted into the navy. As a maintenance man in the navy, Shirai suffered an injury to his buttocks. After the war, Shirai returned to boxing, but his injury continued to trouble him. Shirai was training at a gym located in the Ginza Kobikicho district of Tokyo in July 1948 when he happened to encounter an American named Dr. Alvin R. Cahn. Cahn was researching fish and shellfish for the Natural Resources Section (NRS) of GHQ/SCAP. Cahn, a fan of the sport, became intrigued with the boxer. When he learned through a translator that Shirai did not have a manager or coach, Cahn volunteered to become his coach. Although Cahn

---

37 Ibid., pp. 210–211.
38 Ibid., pp. 22–23, 200.

had experience as a college tennis coach while teaching at the University of Illinois, he had no experience in coaching boxing. Cahn helped Shirai with the basics. He also managed his physical condition and diet, which made him a better athlete. Cahn's method is referred to as 'Scientific Training'.

Cahn's efforts were successful. Shirai entered the All Japan Flyweight Champion Match in January 1949. He defeated defending champion Yoichiro Hanada with a knock-out in the fifth round. Before his fight with Hanada, most Japanese sports fans hadn't even heard of Shirai. After the bout, he was famous across the country. The fact that he was discovered by an American working for GHQ/SCAP who helped him to become a champion fascinated the Japanese people. Shirai's rise became a popular Cinderella story throughout Japan, and he was looked up to as a hero by the Japanese people.

In early March, barely a month after Shirai defeated Hanada, the editors and writers of *All Sports* met to prepare the magazine's fifteenth issue. The discussion turned to the contrasting styles of Shirai and Horiguchi. Horicuchi represented the old-school, offensive-minded approach, while the American-trained Shirai, with his emphasis on logic and defense, seemed to represent a new way to fight. Those present at the discussion praised Shirai as capable of fighting based on the logic of sports science, and spoke of how he benefited from being scientifically trained to maximize his condition.[39] As Cahn himself wrote, 'Shirai's defense position could block an opponent's punch and then immediately respond with a crushing blow'.[40]

In summary, the key point of the debate was to praise Shirai's fighting capability based on logical sports science as well as how he was being trained to scientifically maximize his physique.

In comparison with Horiguchi with his 'Piston Tactics', Shirai was markedly different. These contrasting styles symbolize Japanese mentality under the U.S. occupation. When Japan faced a supply shortage during the war, the Japanese said, 'We'll win with our courage'. When Japan lost the war to the U.S. and its allies, America became an example for Japan to strive towards. As a result, the Japanese people attempted to learn America's scientific stance. I believe that these two popular yet contrasting boxers

---

39 'Boxing Champion Shirai Yoshio wo Kakonde' (Round-table talk with Yoshio Shirai, a champion of boxing), *All Sports*, No. 15, June 1949, All-Sports-Sha, pp. 18–19.

40 Alvin R. Cahn (Kaneo Nakamura), 'New Champion Shirai Yoshio wo Kataru: Kaan-Hakase no Shuki' (Talk about the new champion, Yoshio Shirai: Dr. Cahn's essay), *Yomiuri Sports*, Vol. 2, No. 4, April 1949, Yomiuri Shinbun-Sha, pp. 42–46.

from Japan's boxing world can be taken to symbolize the mentality of the Japanese who lived during this period.

In September 1951, the San Francisco Peace Treaty was signed, and the American occupation of Japan officially ended when the treaty took effect on April 28, 1952. Exactly three weeks later, on May 19, Shirai met American boxer and defending World Flyweight Champion Salvador 'Dado' Marino in a title fight in front of 40,000 fans in Tokyo. Shirai and Marino went the entire fifteen rounds. When the fight was over, Shirai was declared the winner, becoming the first-ever Japanese World Boxing Champion.

The Suppression of Kendo

During the occupation, the U.S. implemented policies to 're-educate' the Japanese people with the intention of creating a relationship in which Japan would become a privileged ally in the Far East that would support U.S. political and ideological agendas. Chief among the tools used to foster positive views of the U.S. were films, particularly American feature films, and sports. While subsequent chapters will address the use of baseball to promote democratization and re-education, here the origins of GHQ/SCAP's sports policy are explored with emphasis on the prohibition of native sports, particularly kendo.

Under the occupation, GHQ/SCAP banned certain Japanese films, among them those of the Chushingura genre, the 'national story' of Japan, because it was perceived as promoting feudalism.[1] Such extreme vigilance also led to the banning of revenge and so-called 'sword-play' films (*chanbara*). In the sports world, *budo* (martial arts) was severely restricted because GHQ/SCAP believed its connection with Shintoism had exerted a negative influence during the war.

It is widely believed in Japan that GHQ/SCAP eliminated kendo from among the *budo* sports. It is important to note, however, that few reliable studies have been conducted on the U.S. occupation's policy regarding kendo, and these studies examine the history of this period from the mainstream perspective which holds that the post-war period was an age of oppression for kendo. A small number of neutral studies, such as those conducted by Yasuhiro Sakaue and Reiko Yamamoto,[2] have questioned this thesis.

---

1 In the U.S., the story, part historical and part folktale, with its themes of honor and revenge, is better known as 'The Forty-Seven Ronin'.

2 See Yasuhiro Sakaue, 'Kendo-Yougu to Sono Rekishi: Hitotsu no Kenkyuu Josetsu toshite' (Kendo equipment and its history: An introduction), *Supoutsu-Yougu-shi-Kenkyu no Genjou to Kadai to* (The situation and the subjects in studies of sports equipment) (Mizno Sports Shinkoukai, Research Report of the 1999 Research Grant, 2000); and Reiko Yamamoto, *Beikoku-Tainichi-Senryo-Seisaku to Budo-Kyoiku: Dainihon-Butokukai no Koubou* (U.S. occupation policy and *budo* education: The rise and fall of the Dainihon-Butokukai) (Nihon-Tosho-Center, 2003).

The question is, were the occupation policies regarding sports, like those regarding films, based on Americans' positive and negative perceptions of the various traditions?

Kendo as the continuation of *bushido*

This chapter will argue that, like *jidaigeki* (costume dramas or period films) in the film industry, kendo in the sports industry was strictly controlled and deemed undesirable by the occupying authorities. Kyoko Hirano has shown that *chanbara* films were disliked by GHQ/SCAP,[3] while my own research has revealed the fact that prior to the establishment of GHQ/SCAP occupation policies, the U.S. Department of State was involved in an examination of potential regional issues in Japan. As a result, the Inter-Divisional Area Committee on the Far East issued a document on Japan's mass media entitled 'Japan: Occupation: Media of Public Information and Expression' (the PWC-288 series). GHQ/SCAP's ban on *chanbara* films appeared in the second draft, CAC-237 Preliminary a, dated July 7, 1944. The draft contained the following statement: 'Films and plays dealing with everyday life in a setting of the last two or three centuries are for the most part unobjectionable'.[4] This sentence implies that there were perceived problems with films set in the earlier, feudal era, in which the privileged warrior class was depicted.

On November 19, 1945, after the implementation of GHQ/SCAP occupation policies, each of Japan's film companies received a notification identifying 'contents that must be banned in film production'. The notice, issued by David W. Conde, the director of the film division of the Civil Information and Education Section (CIE), consisted of thirteen themes that could not be depicted in Japanese films. Although the notice did not use the term 'ban', the restrictions prohibited films from 'showing revenge as a legitimate motive' or 'portraying feudal loyalty or contempt of life as desirable and honorable'. As a result, Japanese film companies understood that they would not be allowed to produce *jidaigeki* during the post-war era.[5]

---

3 Kyoko Hirano, *Mr. Smith Goes to Tokyo: Japanese Cinema under the American Occupation, 1945-1952* (Smithsonian Institution Press, 1992), pp. 66–70.

4 Takeshi Tanikawa, *America-Eiga to Senryou Seisaku* (American films and occupation policy) (Kyoto University Press, 2002), pp. 25–34.

5 Tanikawa, *America-Eiga*, pp. 197–204; Kyoko Hirano, *Mr. Smith Goes to Tokyo*, pp. 44–45. Original source: Press release from GHQ/USAFPAC, CIE, November 19, 1945.

The Press, Pictorial, and Broadcasting Division (PPB) of the Civil Censorship Detachment (CCD) banned all Chushingura-related stories from film and theater, believing them to promote revenge or feudal loyalty.[6] When the PPB permitted the revival of the distribution of one of the pre-war films, *Enoken no Kuramatengu* (1939, Toho), they received complaints from the CIE on the basis that the film was set in the time of the samurai, despite the fact that the film satirizes samurai values.[7] The underlying issue behind the Western opposition to these films was the fear of the Japanese sword, which could be a highly effective and violent assault weapon that could not only kill enemies but could also be used for *seppuku* (honorable suicide).[8] In the year 1943, *Life* magazine published a special issue on Japan as the enemy, analyzing the Chushingura mindset — feudalistic Japanese loyalty — in an attempt to understand the Japanese mentality.[9] As noted above, the intention of the thirteen themes of the 'contents that must be banned in film production' must be understood in light of *bushido* (way of the samurai) principles. As such, it was logical for the CIE to issue a ban on *chanbara* films that were closely tied to Japanese swords and their uses.

As far as the meaning of having a metal sword is concerned, it seems clear that for Japanese athletes, it shows their determination to face the duel risking their own life, rather than having a weapon which can take their opponent's life. In Japanese, a metal sword with a blade is described as '*shinken*', and the meaning of the kanji characters of '*shinken*' is 'seriousness'.

For example, Sadaharu Oh, known as the all-time home-run king of Japanese baseball, is remembered for the fact that he practiced swinging with a metal sword instead of a baseball bat. This can be explained as his method of practicing hip action and a downward swing by using a heavier object than a baseball bat, but it also symbolizes Sadaharu Oh's strong will to face each pitcher in earnest.

---

6 Takeshi Tanikawa, 'Chushingura wo tsuujite miru Senryo Shitamono to Saretamono no Mentality' (The mentality of occupier and occupied people through observing Chushingura), *Bungaku*, September–October 2003, pp. 39–42.

7 Memorandum for Record: Motion Pictures Section of the CIE policy on sword-fighting scenes in pictures (Memo by WYM), 2 March 1948, Box 8579, Folder 26 'Movie Films (Censorship) 1948' file, CIE, GHQ/SCAP, RG 331, NARA.

8 Comment made by Faubion Bowers in an interview with the author on November 1, 1999, in New York City.

9 '"The 47 Ronin": The Most Popular Play in Japan Reveals the Bloodthirsty Character of Our Enemy', *Life*, November 1, 1943, p. 52.

Kendo means 'the way of the sword', but while it relates to *bushido*, it utilizes a bamboo foil, or *shinai*, and poses little risk of injury relative to a metal sword. The issue, however, is whether or not GHQ/SCAP believed kendo to be as threatening as *jidaigeki*—whether GHQ/SCAP considered kendo a continuation of *bushido* and monitored it accordingly.

▌ *Budo* policies during the occupation

To determine whether kendo was completely prohibited, like *jidaigeki* in the film industry, it is useful to review Reiko Yamamoto's research, which includes a timeline of events associated with *budo* from the occupation period through to early 1954.[10]

The Ministry of Education issued all of the notifications listed in Table 3.1. This is because, unlike in the mass media including the film industry, an indirect sovereignty was employed as part of the fundamental framework of the occupation policies. However, this does not mean that all notifications were issued under the strong direction of GHQ/SCAP. It was clear that the first two notifications, issued by the end of 1945, although voluntarily announced by the Ministry of Education, were consistent with GHQ/SCAP intentions.[11] Also, it is necessary to note that the notification issued on November 6, 1945 specified a total ban on 'school kendo'. In other words, the ban did not apply to all kendo practice. Kendo, in both the pre- and post-war periods, had been divided into three categories: (1) school kendo, (2) dojo kendo and (3) police kendo. Only school kendo was the subject of this particular ban.

Compared with other forms of *budo*, kendo was the most controversial, as evidenced by the number of years before its return. More than sixteen months after *kyudo* and judo were revived, the practice of kendo was finally allowed on April 10, 1952. Even at that time, the term 'kendo' was still avoided. Instead, under the authority of the Ministry of Education at the behest of

---

10 Yamamoto, *Beikoku-Tainichi-Senryo-Seisaku to Budo-Kyoiku.*

1945/11/06	Complete ban on school kendo.
1945/12/26	Notification of the disposal of *budo* equipment.
1946/10/31	Declaration of voluntary dissolution of the Dainippon Butoku Kai (The Greater Japan Martial Virtue Association).
1946/11/09	Order from the Ministry of Internal Affairs (Naimu-sho) issued by the Government Section (GS) of GHQ on the confiscation and forfeiture of assets of the Dainippon Butoku Kai.
1946/12/13	Kendo demonstrations requested by the CIE (at the Hibiya Kokaido).
1947/03/27	Far Eastern Commission defines kendo as a 'classical sport which should be eliminated from educational facilities'.
1948/05/23	Regional Friendship Tournament featuring fencing and kendo held at the Tokyo Kanto Hatsuden Arena.
1949/05	*Budo* demonstrations permitted for the sake of revival.
1949/09	Tokyo Kendo Club established.
1949/10/30	First All-Japan Kendo Kyougi Tournament, held at the Toutetsu Dojo in Harajyuku, Tokyo.
1950/03/05	Establishment of the All-Japan Kendo Kyougi Federation. (Soon renamed the All-Japan Shinai Kyougi Federation.)
1950/07	Notification of the revival of *kyudo*.
1950/10	Notification of the revival of *judo*.
1950/10/29	First All-Japan Shinai-Kyougi Tournament (at the Nagoya Dentetsu Honsha Kodo).
1951/05/04	The first All Japan Selective Shinai-Kyougi Championship Tournament (at the Hibiya Kokaido).
1952/04/10	The practice of *shinai-kyougi* allowed at junior high school level and above.
1952/08/18	All Japan Kendo Tournament (in Nikkou City, Tochigi Prefecture).
1952/10/14	Establishment of the All Japan Kendo Federation.
1953/04	Notification of kendo revival.
1953/05/4–5	The first Kyoto tournament of the All Japan Kendo Federation.
1953/11/06	All Japan Police Department Kendo Tournament (at the gym of the police headquarters).
1953/11/08	The first All Japan Kendo Tournament (at the Kuramae Kokugikan, Tokyo).
1954/03	All Japan Shinai-Kyougi Federation merged with the All Japan Kendo Federation.

Table 3.1 Events associated with *budo* from the occupation period to early 1954

GHQ, it was replaced by the unfamiliar term, '*shinai kyougi*'.[12] Although the CIE translated it as '*shinai* game', the All-Japan Shinai Kyougi Federation cannily changed the translation. According to a handwritten letter from Junzo Sasamori, a representative of the All-Japan Shinai Kyougi Federation and a former cabinet official under prime minister Tetsu Katayama, the federation translated '*shinai kyougi*' as 'pliant staff play'.[13] The new definition sounded unthreatening and gave the impression that it was an enjoyable game to play. While *kyudo* and judo were also removed from the school curriculum during the occupation, these sports were reinstated before kendo, which wasn't revived until the end of the occupation. Although the word 'kendo' was avoided, it was understood that the term '*shinai kyougi*' meant 'kendo'. Furthermore, efforts to preserve kendo continued throughout the occupation era. It is impossible to determine whether or not GHQ/SCAP's policies were based on the perception that the practice of kendo was taboo in its entirety without examining dojo kendo and police kendo.

School kendo ban and the Dainippon Butoku Kai dissolution order

The confiscation and forfeiture of assets of the Dainippon Butoku Kai on November 9, 1946, represented a significant development in the GHQ/SCAP *budo* policies. With the school *budo* ban and the disposal of school *budo* equipment, the notifications were issued by the Ministry of Education, which was acting out of what it thought to be the goals of GHQ/SCAP. In the case of the Dainippon Butoku Kai, on the other hand, GHQ/SCAP invoked its power to enforce the order. This meant that GHQ/SCAP rejected the volunteer dissolution of the Dainippon Butoku Kai and instead instituted the confiscation and forfeiture punishment. According to Yamamoto, *budo* was discussed twice during the review process conducted by the Department of

---

12 The author graduated from Tokyo Toritsu Komaba High School and is one of the board members of the alumni of its kendo club. Fujio Cho, CEO of Toyota Motor Corporation and one of the founders of the Komaba High Kendo Club, recalls that they had to name it 'Shinai Kyougi Club' instead of 'Kendo Club' when it was founded, though it was allowed to launch immediately after the Ministry of Education approved the revival of the sport.

13 Letter from Junzo Sasamori, the representative of the Shinai Kyougi Association, to the CIE, dated March 29, 1950, Box 5725, 'Shinai Game' Folder, Education Division, Physical Education & Youth Affairs Branch Topical File 1945–51, CIE, GHQ/SCAP, RG 331, NARA.

State on the occupation policies. The first occasion was during the Inter-Divisional Area Committee on the Far East in its discussion of political parties and political organizations, the results of which were published in the PWC-113 series documents. The Dainippon Butoku Kai was identified as a nationalistic organization, and the occupation authorities were determined to eliminate it along with other organizations it deemed dangerous.[14]

The second discussion occurred in October 1945. A document was prepared for a meeting of the Advisory Committee on the Far East, which was set up under the Subcommittee for the Far East established by the State-War-Navy Coordinating Committee (SWNCC). Called 'Re-education of Japanese: Unofficial Preliminary Notes', the document was prepared and submitted by the Australian Legation in Washington, D.C. It not only addressed the 'ban of *budo*', but noted other issues, such as thought control, treatment of the Imperial Rescript on Education and the issue of Japanese textbooks. The document suggested that 'classical sports such as Judo and Kendo should be redirected so as not to revive the martial spirit. Western sports should be encouraged and the competitive spirit of the individual rather than the mass developed'. Furthermore, the document continued, 'Physical training should no longer be associated with the so-called *Seishin Kyoiku* [Spiritual Training]'.[15]

Many of the measures discussed at the SWNCC were preliminary, requiring further development before the occupation policy was to be enforced. The document itself was not an official directive, nor was it communicated to GHQ/SCAP as a command. Rather, it was a way to send human resources to the CIE from the Department of State, which was regarded as a direct channel to GHQ/SCAP. In the document, the Australian government asserts that judo and kendo, both of which are forms of *budo*, encourage the 'martial spirit'. The CIE viewed *budo* in the same way. Perhaps because of the recommendations of the Australian government, the Advisory Committee on the Far East, after it

---

14 Yamamoto, *Beikoku-Tainichi-Senryo-Seisaku to Budo-Kyoiku*, pp. 14–15.

15 Ibid., pp. 15–16. Original source: 'Re-education of Japanese: Unofficial Preliminary Notes, October 1945', included in a Department of State memorandum of a conversation from October 29, 1945, with its subject identified as 'Interest of Australian Government in Formulation of a Plan of Reeducation in Japan'. (Documents of State-War-Navy Coordinating Committee Files Microfilm frame No. 458.)

was renamed the Far Eastern Commission (FEC), designated kendo as a classical sport to be eliminated from the Japanese education system.[16]

GHQ/SCAP believed the Dainippon Butoku Kai to be at the center of the *budo* connection with nationalistic and spiritual education. Before the war, however, that organization, founded in 1895, was neither nationalistic nor spiritual. In 1941, the Dainippon Butoku Kai was reorganized as a tool of state control. The prime minister was assigned as chairman, and the secretaries of the army and navy were given important posts in the organization. Thus, Hideki Tojo was the head of the Dainippon Butoku Kai when the Department of State began planning its occupation policies.[17]

At the time the occupation of Japan began, the argument that the Dainippon Butoku Kai was similar to another nationalistic association, the Taisei Yokusan-Kai (the Imperial Rule Assistance Association), was beyond doubt. The fact that, on October 31, 1945, the Government Section (GS) of GHQ/SCAP ordered the Dainippon Butoku Kai to dissolve while rejecting the organization's own voluntary dissolution did not mean GHQ/SCAP intended to suppress *budo* or kendo. The difference between dissolution by order and a voluntary dissolution is that under the former, confiscation is involved and officials are displaced. In this sense, the GHQ/SCAP's action against the Dainippon Butoku Kai had a positive outcome in that it removed the nationalistic cornerstone from the organization.

With the order to ban school kendo and the dissolution of the Dainippon Butoku Kai, it is certain that dojo kendo and police kendo also faced difficulties. School kendo was banned if taught in the context of nationalistic and spiritual education (it was also banned as an extracurricular activity), and the Dainippon Butoku Kai was dissolved because of its link to nationalism. GHQ/SCAP, however, did not prohibit individuals from practicing kendo according to their own initiative. In this regard, GHQ/SCAP handled kendo differently from *chanbara* films, where films were banned simply because some characters held swords.

---

16 Yamamoto, *Beikoku-Tainichi-Senryo-Seisaku to Budo-Kyoiku*, pp. 15–16; SWNCC Document, No. 458, Modern Japanese Political History Materials Room, National Diet Library.

17 Yamamoto, *Beikoku-Tainichi-Senryo-Seisaku to Budo-Kyoiku*, p. 114.

▌ Assessing 'dojo kendo' and 'police kendo'

Practicing kendo 'according to an individual's will' can mean either dojo kendo or police kendo. Thus, GHQ/SCAP did not believe that there was a problem if the public practiced these forms of the sport. Col. Kermit R. Dyke (later promoted to Brig. Gen.), the first chief of the CIE, addressed this issue on November 1, 1945 saying that judo and kendo would be removed from school education programs, but that the practice outside of school would not be banned, nor would the occupation authorities interfere with individual practice.[18] According to *budo*-related articles in police periodicals found in the Gordon W. Prange Collection located at the University of Maryland, College Park, the practice of police kendo varied by region. Below is a chronological list based on a keyword search of 'kendo' or '*budo*' in 'The database of Newspapers and Magazines Published during the Post-War Occupation Period from 1945 to 1949'.[19]

From the chronological list presented in Table 3.2, it is clear that, for example, judo-kendo matches were often held within the Tokyo Police Department between May 1946 and September 1948, presumably as traditional events. The Ibaraki Prefectural Police Department, on the other hand, did not hold its first post-war kendo match until May 1948. The Gunma Prefectural Police Department was also late, restarting in March 1949, and the Hyogo Prefectural Police Department delayed its first match until September 1949. In the case of the Tochigi Prefectural Shudou-kai, even with permission from the occupation forces, the initial match was not held until October 1948. These facts indicate that there were significant local variations in the reintroduction of kendo because the regional occupation forces adopted policies that were very different from those applied in Tokyo.[20] Alternatively, there is a possibility that these variations were merely caused by the differing interpretations of GHQ/SCAP's attitude toward police kendo made by each prefectural police department.

GHQ/SCAP staff members and family were often invited guests at kendo or judo matches held by prefectural or regional police departments. Some Americans even started taking judo or kendo lessons. For example, the Special Services Office of GHQ/SCAP submitted a request to the

---

18 Yamamoto, *Beikoku-Tainichi-Senryo-Seisaku to Budo-Kyoiku*, p. 29; and *Stars and Stripes*, November 17, 1945, p. 4.

19 20th-Century Media Information Database (accessed May 30, 2015), 20thdb.jp/.

20 'Yomigaetta Kendo: Fencing-Kisoku wo Kami' (Revived kendo: Adding fencing regulations), *Seinen-Fukushima*, Fukushima-Minpo-Sha, December 1948, p. 12.

1946/05/6–7	*Budo* competitions by the inspectors of the police department (Tokyo) (at the police practice gym).
1946/06/29	Nagasaki Prefectural Police and Fire Department inter-divisional judo match (at the Tamazono Yamashita Butoku Palace).
1946/09/13	Kyoto Prefectural Yamashina Police Station *budo* match (at the Yamashina Police Station Dojo).
1946/10/16	Saga Prefectural police officer judo and kendo match (the first match in Saga Prefecture in the post-war era).
1946/10/27	Nagano Prefectural Police Department judo match.
1946/11/01	Kanagawa Prefectural Police and Fire Department *budo* match (at the Nakamura-cho fire fighter practice gym, Minami-ku, Yokohama city).
*1946/12/04	Hiroshima Prefecture Regional Judo-Kendo Tournament.
*1946/12/07	Central Hiroshima Prefectural Judo-Kendo Tournament.
1947/01/11–31	Kanagawa Prefectural Police and Fire Department winter practice and the first *budo* practice of the new year.
*1947/08/04	Kanagawa Prefectural Fourth Block Judo Match (preliminary) (at the Kamakura Police Station).
1947/08/13	Kanagawa Prefecture inter-divisional invitational judo competition (at the fire department gym).
1948/05	The First Ibaraki Prefecture Police Judo-Kendo Match.
1948/09/8–11	The police department inter-division, section, unit judo-kendo competition (at the Seinei House of the Imperial Household).
1948/10/17	Kendo practice hosted by Shudou-kai in Tochigi Prefecture (at the Nikko Seidoujyo Dojo).
*1948/10/27	The Yamaguchi Prefecture Police Officer Autumn Judo-Kendo Match (at the Old Butoku Den).
1948/11/11	The First Six City Police Officer Judo Match (at the Seinei House of the Imperial Household).
1948/12/01	The Second Ibaraki Prefecture Police Judo-Kendo Match (at the Ibaraki Prefecture Police Academy Gym).
1949/03	The Gunma Prefecture Police Judo-Kendo Tournament (kendo was revived in Gunma Prefecture as a sport).
1949/05/26	The Kagoshima Prefecture Shinsei (reborn) Kendo Club was established.
1949/09/01	The Hyogo Prefecture Police Staff Kendo Match (at the National Police Academy second gym).
1953/11/06	All Japan Police Department Kendo Tournament (at the gym of the police headquarters).

*Note: Items marked with an asterisk are events to which GHQ/SCAP staff members were invited.

Table 3.2 The reality of kendo and *budo* as depicted in post-war print media

Mitsubishi Yowa Kai (an affiliate organization of the Mitsubishi *zaibatsu*, the conglomerate that, among other things, manufactures aircraft and automobiles) asking to rent the organization's gym three times a week for judo and *kyudo* practice. Mitsubishi Yowa Kai not only agreed to the request, it also provided instructors for the Americans.[21]

Evidence that matches were sanctioned by GHQ/SCAP can be found in an article on the Hiroshima Regional Judo-Kendo Tournament that stated, 'although judo and kendo were diminishing after the loss of World War II, with the understanding of the Allied nations and effort of the chief of the police department, a regional tournament was held in each district on December 4 […]. In the department of Hiroshima, there was an occupation forces visit, jazz was played, etc. This seems to suggest that this is the way of a new generation of judo-kendo'.[22] Regarding the Central Hiroshima Prefectural Judo-Kendo Tournament, the article indicated, 'The tournament's opening ceremony began, the police department chief gave an address, followed by Lieutenant Col. Tamson's congratulatory address as a representative of the guests, and exciting matches were held'.[23]

Another article reported on the Yamaguchi Prefectural Police Autumn Judo-Kendo Tournament. According to the article, 'The assembly was at 9:30 a.m., and the brass band and prefectural police chorus played. An address by the police department chief followed, and then the tournament was opened. The audience of the occupation forces and the public were thrilled, as each match was simply marvelous'.[24]

As noted earlier, each region's tournament was held at a different time from the others until the autumn of 1949, around the time when CCD magazine censorship ended. During this period, police kendo and dojo kendo eliminated past malpractice, and kendo (or *budo*) was reborn as a new sport akin to Western fencing. During the occupation, kendo and judo were practiced throughout Japan. Although there were reports of minor incidents in which members of local occupation forces ordered the destruction of kendo equipment or penalized certain individuals for having

---

21 'Shinchu-Gun ga Budo Keiko' (Occupation troops officer practicing *budo*), *Yowa Kai Shi*, Mitsubishi Yowa Kai, No. 174, p. 32.

22 Akira Ooki, 'Judo-Kendo Kyougi-Taikai Ki' (Note on a judo-kendo match), *Izumi*, Hiroshima Police Association Branch, No. 2, February 1947, p. 39.

23 Ibid.

24 Tahara, 'Shuuki-Ju-Kendo-Taikai Ki' (Note on the autumn judo-kendo match), *Boucho-Keiyu*, Yamaguchi Prefecture Police Department, 1949 New Year Issue, p. 26.

such equipment, it would be wrong to interpret these incidents as GHQ/ SCAP efforts to suppress the sport.[25]

Transfer of confiscated kendo equipment to baseball

During the occupation, there was an unexpected exchange between kendo, which had a negative image and had been completely eliminated from the education system, and baseball, which had a positive image and was strongly promoted by GHQ/SCAP to re-establish the Japan-U.S. friendship. Baseball equipment, which was in high demand during the occupation, was provided in exchange for the kendo equipment confiscated by the Ministry of Education on December 26, 1945.

In an article that appeared in the first issue of *Sports*, a periodical published by Taiiku-Nihon-Sha, Tokyo, Major John W. Norviel of the CIE wrote:

> The shortage of and damage to the sports equipment in Japan makes it difficult to promote democracy [through sports]. To overcome these conditions, I am pleased to lead the effort to produce sports equipment [...]. Conventional kendo equipment, for example, has been converted for baseball, and much of the military equipment has been modified for use as sports supplies.[26]

Maj. Norviel was in charge of physical education, and he served in this position until at least the end of 1947.[27] Maj. Norviel also acted as a liaison in negotiations with the Ministry of Education, which was trying to avert the dissolution of the Dainippon Butoku Kai. According to Yamamoto, Norviel stated that the issue was whether or not individuals were capable of letting go of their wartime mindset. If this were possible, there would

---

25 Zen-Ken-Ren 30 Nen Kinenshi Editing Committee, ed., *30 Nen-Shi* (30 years) (Zaidan-Hojin Zen-Nihon Kendo Renmei, 1982), pp. 19–20.

26 Maj. John Norviel, 'Nihon Sports Hatten no tame ni' (For the development of Japan's sports), the inaugural issue of *Sports*, Taiiku-Nihon-Sha, June 1, 1946, p. 8.

27 Hideo Sato, ed., *Sengo Kyouiku Kaikaku Shiryou 2: Rengoukaku Saiko-Shireikan Soushireibu Minkan Jouhou Kyouiku Kyoku no Jinji to Kikou* (The staff rosters and organization charts of C.I. & E. Section, GHQ/SCAP: Compiled from 'GHQ/SCAP telephone directory') (National Institute for Educational Research of Japan, 1984).

be no need to abolish *budo* itself. Therefore, steps had to be taken to rid the people of their military imprint.[28] Eventually, Norviel agreed with the voluntary dissolution of the Dainippon Butoku Kai. The Government Section of GHQ/SCAP, however, opposed it. Thus, on November 9, 1946, GHQ/SCAP issued an order to dissolve the Dainippon Butoku Kai and confiscate its assets. Maj. Norviel did not take a strict approach toward kendo, remarking that the military government officials had the discretion to allow it at the individual level.[29]

It is unclear whether the CIE was behind the decision to turn banned kendo equipment into baseball equipment. Either way, Norviel's statement is symbolic because he was dealing with both positive and negative policies— the promotion of baseball and the removal of *budo* from the education system.

Discussion on the conversion of kendo equipment into baseball equipment was not confined to the sports world. The January 1, 1947 edition of *Shufu no Tomo* (Housewives' companion), a periodical that did not normally feature sports or law enforcement, carried an article that promised housewives they could earn 'three hundred yen per month by dismantling kendo equipment':

> This kendo equipment was mass produced during the war by women and female students, but now it is going to be reworked into sports equipment. The job is to disassemble the mask, barrel and gloves into pieces of fabric, metal, etc. It is so easy that anyone can do it; just be careful not to damage them.[30]

The article presented an example that featured an Osaka housewife who disassembled the kendo equipment after being directed to do so by the Kita City Hall of Kita Ward. It seemed from the article that municipalities handled the disassembly, but it is not yet possible to establish beyond doubt that they were involved with the Ministry of Education upon CIE instruction and therefore as part of GHQ/SCAP policies.

---

28 Yamamoto, *Beikoku-Tainichi-Senryo-Seisaku to Budo-Kyoiku*, pp. 35–37.

29 Ibid., p. 41.

30 Kimi Kuwabara, 'Kendo-gu no Hodoki de Gesshuu Sanbyaku-en Zengo' (Earning three hundred yen per month by unfastening *kendo* equipment), *Shufu no Tomo*, Shufu-no-Tomo-Sha, January 1947, p. 97.

According to Sakaue, when baseball appeared in the Meiji period in Japan, kendo's *mengane* (the metal part of the kendo mask) were reused as catchers' masks.[31] Although confiscated school kendo equipment was converted to baseball equipment during the occupation, the literature on the histories of baseball and kendo has largely ignored this fact.

▌ 'Severe suppression of kendo' as an illusion

Police periodicals conserved at the University of Maryland's Gordon W. Prange Collection consist of materials published through October 1949, the only period in which the CCD engaged in censorship. During this time, depending on the region, it is clear that police kendo continued to be practiced. The literature on the history of kendo, however, implies that police kendo was temporarily restricted after that period. According to *Kendo Jiten: Gijutsu to Bunka no Rekishi* (Kendo dictionary: History of its skills and culture), written by Tamio Nakamura, the following notifications were issued:

> 1949/11/10: Notification of the suspension of police kendo
> (the 55th Notification)
> 1953/05/11: Notification of the resumption of police kendo
> (the 103rd Notification)[32]

As noted above, at the end of World War II, GHQ/SCAP removed kendo from the school curriculum and issued a dissolution order to the Dainippon Butoku Kai. GHQ/SCAP, however, placed no restrictions on individuals, who were free to practice according to their will. Given these facts, it is difficult to understand why GHQ/SCAP, having demonstrated its tacit approval of the sport, suddenly banned police kendo for four years after the end of the war. The date for the notice of the ban is in doubt, with some sources indicating that it was issued in November 1949 and others specifying a date six months earlier.

---

31 Sakaue, 'Kendo-Yougu to Sono Rekishi: Hitotsu no Kenkyuu Josetsu toshite', p. 62.

32 Tamio Nakamura, *Kendo-Jiten: Gijutsu to Bunka no Rekishi* (Kendo dictionary: History of its skills and culture) (Tokyo: Shimazu-Shobou, 1994), p. 270.

It was around May 20, 1949. The exact date is not certain. The Chuo-Ku branch of the police department reserve corps (now 'riot control') was planning and preparing a judo-kendo match. With the idea of demonstrating how the police officers were trained and introducing Japanese national sports, we decided to invite the police-related officers of GHQ/SCAP, like Col. Puliam and Mr. Angel. We visited GHQ/SCAP, suspecting nothing, and politely delivered the invitation card. Surprisingly, the reply was, 'It is inexcusable to keep practicing kendo. Suspend it immediately!' It was more than a bolt from the blue—something more akin to a bucketful of ice water being poured on us while we were basking in the sun. To be sure, we cancelled the judo-kendo match immediately, as well as notified every branch of the suspension of kendo. This problem seemed to apply not only to the police department reserve corps, but to kendo at the police department itself, and we finally put our *shinai* [a bamboo sword-like weapon] away in its case.[33]

Keishicho Budo 90 Nen-Shi (Ninety years of *budo* at the police department) also introduces an article published in the *Tokyo Nichi-Nichi Shimbun* dated May 22, 1949, titled 'Suspension of kendo at the police department':

Since the war ended, the police department continued practicing kendo as one of the official subjects of physical education, but on May 21, it decided to abolish kendo. The reason for the abolition of kendo is due to the fact that it was defined as a militaristic sport, but whether it should be continued or not had long been controversial. Moreover, only Tokyo and a couple of other prefectures' police kept practicing kendo after the war. Kendo teachers and 100 sports instructors of the Tokyo Metropolitan Police Department will be converted to teach arresting techniques and handling nightsticks, and the adoption of boxing as a new physical education subject is under consideration. Besides, judo will be encouraged more than ever.[34]

Thus, 'police kendo' was prohibited three years and nine months after the start of the occupation, and the prohibition continued until May 1953, long after the occupation was over. The idea of teaching boxing instead of banned kendo refers to the strategy taken by the boxing world at that time

---

33 *Keishicho Budo 90 Nen-Shi* (Ninety years of *budo* at the police department) (Tokyo: Education Section of the Metropolitan Police Department, 1965), pp. 205–206.

34 *Tokyo Nichi-Nichi Shimbun* (newspaper), May 22, 1949.

which was introduced in Chapter Two. Takichiro Yoshida, the chief of the education section of the Tokyo Metropolitan Police Department who was in charge of the practice of kendo at Tokyo police departments, visited GHQ/ SCAP after the ban on police kendo to ensure he understood the official view on the sport. Yoshida was informed that, while practicing kendo inside any police building was prohibited, anyone could practice it outside of a police facility as a civilian, even if that person was a police officer.[35]

The common perception that GHQ/SCAP oppressed kendo during the occupation is rooted in the prohibition of kendo in schools, the forced dissolution of the Dainippon Butoku Kai and the ban on police kendo. Yet, after thoroughly examining the banning of police kendo, it seems apparent that simply defining the occupation era as an oppressive period for kendo would be overly emotional, on par with insisting 'The Constitution is one-sidedly imposed by GHQ/SCAP without giving the Japanese any chance to discuss its legitimacy, and a revised Constitution that upholds Japanese defense forces is necessary as an independent nation'. Such a view is misleading. While many GHQ/SCAP officials may have felt that Japanese police departments misunderstood 'tacit approval' for 'permission', and some believed that kendo should have been banned from the beginning of the occupation, not all American officials felt that way. As shown above, some key officers of the CIE, like Col. Kermit R. Dyke, the first CIE chief, and Maj. John W. Norviel, who served as the officer in charge of handling physical education, did not take a negative stance toward the sport. Rather, they stressed that only 'school kendo' should be banned and there was no problem with any individual wishing to practice kendo on their own.

There were significant differences among the attitudes of GHQ/SCAP officers. There were also notable local variations towards kendo among the regional occupation forces that varied from the attitudes of GHQ/SCAP officials in Tokyo. As a result, it would be misleading to argue that 'the occupation era was a period in which GHQ/SCAP oppressed kendo', because there was no unified GHQ/SCAP kendo policy.

The fact that 'police kendo' was banned for four years, from May 1949 to May 1953, indicates that practicing kendo at police departments was never officially prohibited during the first half of the occupation period. If only police-related GHQ/SCAP officers had not been invited to the judo-kendo match of the police department reserve corps in May 1949, Japan's

---

35 *Keishicho Budo 90 Nen-Shi*, p. 206.

mainstream kendo historians may have been able to claim, thanks to GHQ/ SCAP, that 'despite the fact that school kendo was strictly prohibited, police kendo as well as dojo kendo were allowed to continue throughout the occupation period'.

There are some articles that indicate that kendo continued to be practiced regionally, even at police stations, after May 1949. Such articles emphasize that the 'new kendo' was a form of physical and mental training as well as a healthy sport to play.

An article in the magazine *Ayumi* about the Hyogo Prefectural Police-Staff Kendo Match held on September 1, 1949, stressed, 'although the police kendo was assumed to become confined to memory and a historic sport immediately after World War II ended, it just made a new start after more than four years' absence with the profound understanding of the occupation forces'.[36]

Moreover, in May 1949, an article in the *Kagoshima-ken-Kyoiku-Iinkai Geppou* declared 'the creation of new kendo as a sport'. This report, which announced the establishment of the Kagoshima-ken Shinsei-Kendo-Dokokai (Kagoshima Prefecture Newborn Kendo Club) on May 26, took a hard look at the kendo referee outfit with its white *tabi* (traditional Japanese socks) and formal crested kimono-vest, and examined the entry bow that celebrated Shintoism. Furthermore, it indicated that kendo should not be practiced at schools or any facilities where banned, and stressed that kendo 'must be practiced only at an individual level as a sport, and it must be improved as part of the physical refinement of society'.[37]

In addition, a column entitled 'Rotary' in the *Shukan Asahi*, published on May 29, 1949, analyzed the details of the circumstances of kendo in the period.

> Kendo practice has been popular through the pivot of the police department. It has become semi-legalized in Tokyo, Chiba, Ibaraki and Fukushima as well as Osaka and Kyoto in the Kansai region, and Yamaguchi. It seems that kendo has been understood as a graceful sport as it has been revised,

---

36 'Gyouji-Nisshi: Kenka Keisatsu-Shokuin Kendo-Taikai' (Event diary: Kendo match for prefectural police officers), *Ayumi*, Kobe-City Police Department, October 1949, p. 79.

37 'Kagoshima-ken Shinsei-Kendo-Dokokai ni Nozomu' (Anticipating the Kagoshima Prefecture Newborn Kendo Club), *Kagoshima-ken Kyoiku-Iinkai Geppou* (Kagoshima Prefecture Education Committee Monthly Report), inaugural issue, 1949, p. 20.

rather than violent as was thought earlier. This is how kendo has been understood externally.

In the post-World War II era, judo was permitted, but kendo was banned. That is because the kendo sword gave the impression that it was a bloody sport (this is funny in the sense of the modern age) and that it was an assault weapon. Moreover, the fact that most chiefs of local Butoku Kai branches were local governors, profoundly engaging in politics, gave a bad impression. The Butoku Kai was dismissed as of November 8, 1945, and all the executives were purged [...]. At schools, judo and kendo still remain banned. In the April of two years ago, the order of the Far Eastern Commission on Japan's education system especially noted, 'Classical sports, such as kendo, which encourage the martial spirit, should be totally abandoned'. A notification from the physical education department of the Ministry of Education was sent to the private sectors in August 1946, which stated that 'kendo in its traditional way, should not be taught or encouraged'; overall, kendo seems not to be permitted.

However, kendo has recently begun a process of reform in order to adapt to the modern era. Its new rules include the following: violent behavior and loud yells are banned; a three-referee system has been adopted; if a sword touches others this would be a point-one, if it touches efficiently; the size of the court is fixed at 6m by 7m.[38]

The common theme running through these three articles is the description of 'kendo reborn as a sport'. This was the only way in which kendo could survive. It is important to understand that some regions simply took the 'Notification of the suspension of police kendo' in May 1949 to mean only the suspension of 'conventional kendo', which meant that practicing the newly revised kendo as a sport was not a problem at all.

In October 1952, the Zen Nihon Kendo Renmei (All Japan Kendo Federation) was established as a new national kendo organization to replace the Dainippon Butoku Kai. The new organization was created after the Ministry of Education allowed the practice of *shinai kyougi* (meaning 'sport which uses *shinai*' with a change in the wording) at junior-high school level and above. Kendo practices were resumed at schools the following year and have continued to this day.[39]

---

38 'Kendo', in the column 'Rotary', *Shukan Asahi*, May 29, 1949, p. 19.

39 *30 Nen-Shi*, pp. 37–40.

In summary, the presumption that kendo was strictly controlled in the field of sports while *jidaigeki* was completely banned is incorrect. Generally, the occupation era is considered as a period of the severe oppression of kendo. However, this impression is derived from the differing actions taken in regions, rather than part of the organized policies of GHQ. The CIE, as an agency that controlled sports in Japan, separated kendo from the nationalistic or spiritual sentiment, while taking the position that it was up to the individuals who love practicing kendo as to whether the future development of the sport would be guaranteed or not. Furthermore, converting kendo equipment into baseball equipment was both a symbolic and actual example of the GHQ/SCAP's negative and positive influences on sports in Japan.

Promotion of Sports Through CIE Films

Sports as the contents of U.S. film policies in occupied Japan

In this chapter I analyze films as media, examining how the focus on sports supported the occupation policies of 'democratization through baseball' to 'reorient' and 're-educate' (these words were used by GHQ/SCAP, the Department of State and the War Department, as policy makers) the Japanese people. I also examine how baseball was utilized as a tool in the cinematic context and treated as a media source.

American film policies in occupied Japan pertained to a variety of levels and formats, including feature films, news films, documentaries and public relations films. Films were divided into theatrical and non-theatrical and classified according to film stock (black and white or color, called '*so-ten-nen-shoku*' in Japan at the time) and gauge (8mm, 16mm, 35mm and so forth).

Many of the films released in post-war Japan highlighted baseball or other sports. Hollywood-made feature films distributed in Japan by the Central Motion Picture Exchange (CMPE) included biographical films on professional athletes such as *Gentleman Jim* (Warner Bros., 1942, released in Japan in July 1947), *The Pride of the Yankees* (Samuel Goldwyn, 1942, released in Japan in March 1949), *The Babe Ruth Story* (Allied Artists, 1948, released in Japan in October 1950) and *The Stratton Story* (MGM, 1949, released in Japan in October 1949), as well as works of fiction that featured the baseball world like *The Kid from Cleveland* (Republic, 1949, released in Japan in April 1950) and *It Happens Every Spring* (20th Century Fox, 1949, released in Japan in April 1950).[1] Moreover, the ZM Production Company, a Japanese documentary film company, produced and released a documentary

---

1 Information about the date of release of each film in Japan is based on Arihiro Hazumi et al. ed., *Sengo Kokai America-Eiga Daihyakka* (Encyclopedia of American films), Shiryou-Hen PART2 45-78 Nihon-Koukai-Zensakuhin-Jiten (Vol. 11: Data PARTII 45-78 Dictionary of All Films Distributed in Post-War Japan) (Nihon Book Library, 1979).

film about the San Francisco Seals prior to their 1949 tour of Japan, to be discussed in greater detail in Chapter Seven.[2] Furthermore, the United Newsreel, news films distributed through the CMPE, frequently screened news on the baseball drills and game results of the American major leagues. Overall, the intent was to expose the Japanese audience to the visual images of American professional athletes, to promote physical and mental health through sports and to establish proper images of sportsmanship.

This chapter will focus on CIE films—films distributed by the Civil Information and Education Section that strongly adhered to the U.S. film policies promoted by GHQ/SCAP. If their aim in giving the Japanese audience certain images of sports was to guide or reorient them toward American values—and these images were used to support the efficacy of the provision of actual participant sports and spectator sports—it would be more effective to target the images toward Japanese people who lacked the opportunity to actively participate in sports or attend live sporting events.

Along this line, CIE films, along with the components of movie projectors—called 'NATCO' by the Japanese audience due to the logo on the projectors made by the National Company of Chicago—were sent to isolated fishing villages and mountainous regions where there were no movie theaters and outdoor cinema was common (see Photo 4.1 & Figure 4.1). As these audiences did not have the opportunity to watch professional sports, GHQ/SCAP took the initiative and educated them through film media.

| Outlines of CIE films

The CIE was the GHQ/SCAP division that dealt with the occupation policies that promoted democratization to the Japanese people through media and education. It was similar to the public relations department of a corporation. The Educational Film Unit operated under the Motion Picture and Theatrical Branch of the CIE's Information Division. The films referred to here were the short educational films shown in every prefecture of Japan via NATCO film projectors. The structure of the CIE varied throughout the occupation era. The Educational Film Unit was previously the Educational Film Exchange, an independent organization like the CMPE.

---

2 ZM Production 'The San Francisco Seals' (Memorandum for record), 1 October 1949, 'Relation with CI&E' File, PPB Division Central File, Box 8579, RG 331, NARA.

Photo 4.1
Outdoor showing
of a CIE film
*Source: Beatrice
Duke Collection.*

Figure 4.1
Outdoor showing
of a CIE film,
frontispiece of *USIS
Film Catalog for
Japan 1953*
*Source: ©American
Embassy, Tokyo
(Takeshi Tanikawa
Collection).*

57

In the beginning of the occupation, there were only nine movies issued as CIE films.[3] These films were originally prepared by the Office of War Information (OWI) and distributed to theatres by the CMPE along with feature films. The list of films was expanded during the occupation. Occasionally, the CIE purchased films made by a Japanese documentary film company. As a result, the number of CIE films increased to more than 400.

After February 1948, CIE films were shown by NATCO mobile projectors throughout Japan. Although the NATCO projectors showed 16 mm films, starting in May 1948, 35 mm films of the same CIE films were prepared and shown at Toho, Shochiku and Daiei movie theaters free of charge.[4] CIE films were transferred to the film collection of the United States Information Service (USIS) after the occupation. During the transfer, the CIE logo and the War Department logo that appeared in films' opening credits were replaced with a logo representing the United States International Information and Education Program Service (USIE).[5]

The above summarizes CIE films in Japan. However, CIE films were not only prepared for occupied Japan. The educational and informational films prepared by the Department of State were also part of the U.S.'s international cultural policies. Below, I first examine the outline of the situation in Japan by providing detailed findings on how CIE films during the occupation depicted baseball and other sports, and explore how the Japanese audience received the contents of these films. Later in the chapter I discuss the baseball and sports films in the context of U.S. international cultural diplomacy policies and look at how the CIE films were developed in Japan.

---

3 The titles and numbers of the first nine CIE films are as follows: (1) *Hymn of the Nations—Toscanini*; (2) *A Better Tomorrow*; (3) *Tuesday in November*; (4) *Freedom to Learn*; (5) *Northwest U.S.A.*; (6) *Electricity and the Land*; (7) *Steel Town*; (8) *Winged Scourge*; (9) *Trees to Tame the Wind*. The document stating that these first nine CIE films were transferred from the OWI to the Department of State is as follows: Report on January to June, 1946, Period, International Motion Picture Division, Office of International Information and Cultural Affairs, Box 164, 'Program Report FY 1946' File, Records Relating to International Information Activities 1938–53, State Department Lot File (Public), RG 59, NARA.

4 *Jijitsushin Nikkan Eiga-Geinou-Ban* (*Jijitsushin* daily movie and entertainment issue), May 18, 1948, p. 680.

5 Letter from Dean G. Acheson to Saxton Bradford via Herbert T. Edwards, IMP, March 7, 1952, State Department Central File 1950–54, 511.945, RG 59, NARA.

The position of sports in CIE films

It is difficult to accurately determine the number of film titles released as CIE or USIS films. Research has revealed that more than 400 CIE titles were shown in provincial regions in Japan during the occupation.[6] In addition, according to USIS catalogs, by 1958 at least 220 other titles were shown as USIS films, making a grand total of 620 titles.[7] It can be assumed that every newly released title would have been added to the catalogs. At the same time, titles with expired copyrights or with damaged and unusable film would have been removed from the catalogs. Therefore, the catalogs issued in 1953 and 1959 provide comprehensive information about CIE films from March 1946 — when its films were first shown — to January 1959. Regarding the titles of CIE films excluded from the 1953 catalog, I have relied on the studies derived from Japanese materials conducted by Akira Abe as well as research based on GHQ/SCAP materials housed in the National Archives conducted by Takeshi Tanikawa and Yuka Tsuchiya.[8]

6　Akira Abe, *Sengo Chihou-Kyouiku-Seido Seiritsu Katei no Kenkyu* (A study on the developmental process of the post-war regional education system) (Kazama-Shobou, 1983); Takeshi Tanikawa, *America-Eiga to Senryou Seisaku* (American films and occupation policy) (Kyoto University Press, 2002); Hideyuki Nakamura, 'Senryouka Beikoku-Kyouiku-Eiga nitsuite no Oboegaki: "Eiga-Kyoushitsu" Shi nimiru Natco (Eishaki) to CIE Eiga no Juyou nitsuite' (Memorandum of American educational films under the occupation: Demands for NATCO projectors and CIE films through observing 'Eiga-Kyoushitsu'), *CineMagaziNet*, No. 6, 2002, http://www.cmn.hs.h.kyoto-u. ac.jp/CMN6/nakamura.htm (Last date of access: May 31, 2015); and Yuka Tsuchiya, *Shinbei-Nihon no Kouchiku: America no Tainichi Jouhou-Kyouiku Seisaku to Nihon-Senryou* (Constructing a pro-U.S. Japan: U.S. information and education policy and the occupation of Japan) (Akashi-Shoten, 2009).

7　This number has been calculated from information included in the following two catalogs: *USIS Film Catalog for Japan 1953* and *USIS Film Catalog for Japan 1959*. These catalogs are equivalent to the stock list of an ordinary film company listing its films available to be shown. Moreover, according to Misaki (Tomeko Misaki, 'GHQ/CIE Kyouiku-Eiga to sono Eikyou: Sengo Minshushugi to Dining Kitchen' (GHQ/CIE films and their influence), *Image and Gender*, Vol. 7, March 2007), there are multiple USIS film catalogs, including 1955, 1957, 1963 and 1969 issues. Adding these to the abovementioned lists results in 1,125 titles. This book explores 620 titles published in up to the 1959 issue. The 1955 and 1957 issues are excluded because the 1953 and 1959 issues provide overall information. See *USIS Film Catalog for Japan 1953*, and *USIS Film Catalog for Japan 1959*, prepared by Distribution Section, Motion Picture Branch, American Embassy, Tokyo. Information on the location of other years' catalogs is referred to in Misaki (2007).

8　Akira Abe, *Sengo Chihou-Kyouiku-Seido Seiritsu Katei no Kenkyu*; Takeshi Tanikawa, *America-Eiga to Senryou Seisaku*; Yuka Tsuchiya, *Shinbei-Nihon no Kouchiku: America no Tainichi Jouhou-Kyouiku Seisaku to Nihon-Senryou*.

CIE film titles are numbered 1 through 406. USIS films issued before 1957 start at number 501 and continue to 605. However, for titles numbered from the 520s to 550s, an additional twenty-three USIS films have duplicate numbers, but contain the suffix 'S' (for instance, film number 520 and film number 520-S are different titles). After these titles, the numbering resumes at 5701 — a four-digit number system — and continues up to title number 5750. At this point, the title number jumps up to 5801, continuing on up to 5910. I assume that when the year changed a more appropriate numbering system was implemented in place of the consecutive numbering system — it seems rational that films from 1957 are numbered 5701 through 5750, and those from 1958 begin with the number 5801, but there is no proof of this rule. As noted earlier, the grand total is approximately 620 titles. When a title number skips consecutive numbers, the missing title number was removed due to a contract-related issue. To discuss my argument further, I use a tentative number, 620, as a denominator. With this denominator, I will substantiate some ideas about the subjects and genres as well as the numbers of films — whether baseball or its related subject, sports in general, how many of these films existed and so forth.

Table 4.1 presents a summary of a total of forty-five out of the 620 film titles including the film titles of fifteen baseball subject films (including those only partially about baseball) and thirty sports subject films, excluding baseball (including those only partially about sports). The table also includes CIE film numbers, the original titles in English (there are no English titles in the *USIS Film Catalog for Japan 1959*, but the English titles were sourced from Tsuchiya's and Misaki's research), the edition (1953 or 1959) in which the film was cataloged and the Japanese release dates. In addition, the English title of production number 12, *Baseball Instructions*, was verified by prior research. Although it was removed from the list in the 1953 catalog, I include it in the above list due to the fact that it is clearly about baseball.

The two USIS film catalogs include an index showing each film's genre. Because the 1959 edition differs slightly from the 1953 edition, I include films from either edition provided they are classified as 'sports' in at least one edition. Production number 213, entitled, *Let's Square Dance*, is classified as a sports film in the 1959 edition of the catalog, but not in the 1953 edition. Square dance is a form of folk dance and may or may not be classified as a sport. This film was also included in the 1950 showing data, analyzed for the CIE's film records, and is among the films shown in the four prefectures, which will be discussed in the next section. Because it had been categorized

#	Title	1953 catalog	1959 catalog	B/S	Release date
12	*Baseball Instructions*	×	×	B	5/26/48
14	*Let's Play Baseball*	○	○	B	2/15/48
113	*Baseball Swing King*	○	○	B	5/6/49
125	*Topics of America*	○	○	B	6/24/49
129	*Sports Revue* (USIS Film Sketch No. 15)	○	○	B	8/26/49
140	*Sports' Golden Age*	○	×	B	2/24/50
182	*Television Workshop* (USIS Film Sketch No. 28)	○	○	B	5/19/50
206	*Boys' Baseball League*	○	○	B	7/14/50
305	*World Series of 1949*	○	○	B	5/4/51
340	*World Series of 1950*	○	×	B	9/21/51
536-S	*Tokyo Giants in the U.S.*	×	○	B	8/7/53
549-S	*Learning from Three Baseball Experts*	×	○	B	8/2/54
551	*Sealion Baseball Team*	×	○	B	3/26/54
592	*Baseball's Goodwill Ambassadors*	×	○	B	3/28/56
5909	*The Cardinals Visit Japan*	×	○	B	1/??/59
16	*White Carnival*	○	○	S	3/5/48
132	*Vacation Sports* (USIS Film Sketch No. 17)	○	○	S	9/30/49
154	*Glimpses of America* (USIS Film Sketch No. 19)	○	○	S	12/2/49
174	*Views of America* (USIS Film Sketch No. 26)	○	○	S	4/21/50
213	*Let's Square Dance*	△	○	S	7/21/50
295	*Briefs From America* (USIS Film Sketch No. 32)	○	○	S	4/20/51
298	*Views of America* (USIS Film Sketch No. 35)	○	○	S	7/13/51
301	*Notes From America* (USIS Film Sketch No. 36)	○	○	S	8/10/51
302	*News From America* (USIS Film Sketch No. 37)	○	△	S	9/7/51
320	*News From America* (USIS Film Sketch No. 38)	○	○	S	4/25/52
321	*News From America* (USIS Film Sketch No. 39)	○	△	S	5/23/52
335	*News From America* (USIS Film Sketch No. 40)	○	○	S	6/20/52
336	*News From America* (USIS Film Sketch No. 41)	○	○	S	7/18/52
338	*News From America* (USIS Film Sketch No. 43)	○	○	S	9/19/52
509	*The Appalachian Trail*	○	△	S	2/20/53
535-S	*Victory in Boston*	×	○	S	8/12/53
542-S	*USIS Screen Magazine* No. 4	×	○	S	10/30/53
543-S	*USIS Screen Magazine* No. 5	×	○	S	11/17/53
599	*USIS Screen Magazine* No. 8	×	○	S	6/5/55
5701	*USIS Screen Magazine* No. 9	×	○	S	7/16/56
5704	*USIS Screen Magazine* No. 10	×	○	S	8/30/56
5724	*Our Times* 4–25	×	○	S	2/17/57
5728	*Our Times* 6–27	×	○	S	3/6/57
5739	*Our Times* 8–20	×	○	S	5/22/57
5740	*Our Times* 9–31	×	○	S	6/4/57
5747	*Our Times* 12–34	×	○	S	7/16/57
5802	*Our Times* 13–35	×	○	S	8/10/57
5821	*USIS Screen Magazine* No. 11	×	○	S	6/19/58
5819	*Althea Gibson—Tennis Champion*	×	○	S	4/4/58
5822	*USIS Screen Magazine* No. 12	×	○	S	6/24/58

Note: the triangle indicates that the film is in one edition of the catalog but is not categorized as sports in the other edition.

Table 4.1 Films featuring baseball (B) and sports (S) out of 620 CIE (USIS) films

as a sports film in either one of the USIS film catalogs, it is automatically classified as a sports film.

Out of the 620 CIE/USIS films, forty-five (7.3%) are sports related, of which fifteen (2.4%) focus on baseball. In addition to sports, other genres include politics, economics, religion, history, topography and science—literally every possible category of genre. Therefore, the number of films about sports is rather significant.

Based on the contents of each film from the *USIS Film Catalog for Japan 1959*, the list below (Table 4.2) classifies them into thirty subjects. The number of films is indicated for each subject. If one film includes multiple subjects, it is counted multiple times under each relevant subject.[9] For instance, *Television Workshop*, production number 182, is classified into subject number fifteen (Newspapers, Broadcasting, Communication) in the below list, but it also falls into the 'Sports' category, number sixteen, because it deals with baseball as a content of television. The list numbering one through thirty is used for the convenience of our purpose here

Among these thirty subjects, only nine have significantly more film titles than the subject of sports. Six subjects have roughly the same number of film titles as the subject of sports. In the process of re-educating and reorienting the Japanese people during the occupation, CIE/USIS films were used as a vehicle to spread information about a variety of fields. It is clear that the film genre of 'Sports' was recognized as a worthwhile subject, on par with the United Nations, youth activities, the agriculture, forestry and fishing industries, health insurance and medicine and labor issues.

Analysis of CIE films showing in 1950 in four prefectures

Questions surround the 620 CIE/USIS films. How often were these films shown? How many people viewed them? Yuka Tsuchiya published statistical data on the number of viewers who watched CIE films during July 1951 based on data from each prefecture recorded in GHQ/SCAP documents.[10] According to her research, 330 productions were shown, and a total of 945,053,007 people

---

9 *USIS Film Catalog for Japan 1953*, p.113

10 'Democracy and Educational Film Audience Report' (25 July 1951), RG 331, GHQ/ SCAP, CI&E, Box 5088, NARA.

Subject and Number		Number of Films
1	Eisenhower	9
2	Carriers and Transportation (including railways, ships and vessels)	19
3	# Science and Industries (including energy, power, inventions, dams and construction)	52
4	Climate	5
5	# Education and Schools (including various training institutions, specialized facilities, students, foreign students, English language and debates)	77
6	Communism	20
7	# Communes (including social life, public enterprises, social institutions and cooperatives)	59
8	# Art (including theaters, fine arts, music, movies and photography)	62
9	Nuclear power	20
10	Aviation	10
11	# International relations (including international diplomacy, international cooperation and peace corps)	97
12	*The United Nations	35
13	*For Children	37
14	Religions	7
15	Newspapers, Broadcasting, Communication (including postal services, telecommunications and television)	15
16	Sports (including no. 182; 45 if those in the 1953 list are added)	39
17	Politics and Governments (including elections, police and fire departments, securities, laws and proceedings)	27
18	*Youth Activities	38
19	# Topography (cities, historic sites, customs and manners)	65
20	Libraries, Museums (including books and art museums)	21
21	Biographies (words, deeds and productions by eminent individuals)	31
22	# Japan (including movies concerning Japan and domestic productions)	91
23	# Agriculture, Forestry, Fishing Industries (including village lives of farmers, mountaineers, fishermen and livestock farmers)	27
24	For Women	20
25	*Health Insurance, Medicine	40
26	# Democracy (including liberalism)	56
27	History	15
28	Recreation	38
29	*Labor (including the lives of laborers and factory workers and the activities of labor unions)	40
30	*Color Movies	40

Notes: Subjects marked with '#' have a significantly greater number of film titles than the subject of sports. Subjects marked with * have roughly an equal number of film titles (30–40) as the subject of sports.

Table 4.2 Film subjects in the *USIS Film Catalog for Japan 1959*

watched these films that month. Considering the population of Japan in 1950 was approximately 83,000,000, it can be assumed that each individual viewed more than ten CIE films over that time. This estimate includes people of all ages — from babies to elderly Japanese. This data, however, does not accurately portray CIE film operations. A better understanding can be derived from the monthly GHQ/SCAP prefectural reports that document the number of times baseball or sports-related films were shown and how many people attended each showing throughout the year.

I now analyze the 1950 data from the following prefectures: Tokyo, Ibaraki, Niigata and Fukushima.[11] Eight of the targeted productions are about baseball — *Baseball Instructions* (film no. 12), *Let's Play Baseball* (film no. 14), *Baseball Swing King* (film no. 113), *Topics of America* (film no. 125), *Sports Revue* (film no. 129, USIS film sketch no. 15), *Sports' Golden Age* (film no. 140), *Television Workshop* (film no. 182, USIS film sketch no. 28) and *Boys' Baseball League* (film no. 206). Five other targeted productions are sports related — *White Carnival* (film no. 16), *Vacation Sports* (film no. 132, USIS film sketch no. 17), *Glimpses of America* (film no. 154, USIS film sketch no. 19), *Views of America* (film no. 174, USIS film sketch no. 26) and *Let's Square Dance* (film no. 213). I now briefly outline each film listed above based on descriptions in the USIS film catalog. I also analyze some archival records on these productions, and, where possible, viewed any available films in order to present an outline or synopsis using the CIE/USIS film informational retrieval database of the University of Tokyo Interfaculty Initiative in Information Studies.

As far as *Baseball Instructions* (film no. 12) is concerned, there is no description of the film in either the 1953 or 1959 USIS film catalog. Further, there is unfortunately no film or videotape of it available, and thus I can't discuss any details here. Its Japanese title, *Yakyuu no Dageki / Toukyuu Shidou*, which means 'Coaching baseball batting / pitching', suggests its contents well, however.

Let's Play Baseball (film no. 14) and *Baseball Swing King* (film no. 113) were created in partnership with the Boston Red Sox. *Let's Play Baseball* shows Joe Cronin, the then manager of the Red Sox, giving baseball instructions to a team of children, while *Baseball Swing King* features lectures on hitting techniques by Red Sox slugger Ted Williams. The latter

---

11 'Monthly Consolidated Report of Showings', Tokyo, Jan–Dec 1950, Ibaraki Prefecture, Feb–Dec 1950, Niigata Prefecture, Jan–Dec 1950, Fukushima Prefecture, Jan–Nov 1950, RG 331, GHQ/SCAP, CI&E, Box 5270, NARA.

film also includes clips from Red Sox games from the 1946 season, focusing on Williams' return from the war and culminating with his selection as the 1946 American League Most Valuable Player. In Japan, *Baseball Swing King* was retitled *Dageki-Ou* ('The batting champion'). In March 1949, two months before the release of *Dageki-Ou* in Japan, the 1942 Hollywood film, *The Pride of the Yankees*, a movie about New York Yankees first baseman Lou Gehrig, was released in Japan under the same name, *Dageki-Ou*. It is likely that the CIE informational film was given the same title in order to capitalize on the popularity of the Gehrig biopic.

Topics of America (film no. 125) consists of two sections: the first is an introduction to the New York Public Library, and the second is about the World Series and its enthusiastic audience. This CIE film was shown in June 1949.[12] Two other CIE films which featured the World Series, film no. 305 (*World Series of 1949*) and film no. 340 (*World Series of 1950*), would later be released. It is possible that they were issued as a result of the popularity of *Topics of America*.

Sports Revue (film no. 129, USIS film sketch no. 15) consists of four segments—'"Pirogue Race": A Race in a Pirogue (a long, flat-bottomed, dug-out canoe)'; '"Bowling, The Focus of Popularity": One of the most popular indoor sports in America'; '"Prize Horses": Specially trained horses do tricks'; and '"Women's Baseball": A professional girls' team in America'. The fourth segment includes scenes of the Grand Rapids Chicks practicing as well as scenes featuring the game between the Rockford Peaches and Grand Rapids Chicks from the All-American Girls Professional Baseball League, teams that would later appear in the 1992 Hollywood film, *A League of Their Own*. *Sports Revue* may have inspired the promoters who launched the short-lived Japanese Women's Baseball Association in 1950.

The 1953 USIS film catalog describes *Sports' Golden Age* (film no. 140) as 'A panorama of sports in present-day America'. Unfortunately, the contents cannot be determined solely from that description. The film organizer's feedback, however, was noted in the CIE report of Fukushima

---

12 The informational retrieval database is based on the films discovered at Kiryu City, Gunma Prefecture. Unfortunately, the database for this film lacks the second session. Therefore, it is impossible to determine which World Series is featured in the film. It may have been the 1948 World Series between the Cleveland Indians and the Boston Braves, but, considering the amount of time it took to create a CIE adaptation (dubbing in the Japanese language or adding Japanese subtitles), it is more likely that it features the 1947 World Series between the New York Yankees and the Brooklyn Dodgers. See http://kirokueiga-hozon.jp/cie/.

Prefecture, which states that it is commentary about America's latest sports technology, including women's baseball.[13]

Television Workshop (film no. 182, USIS film sketch no. 28) analyzes U.S. television broadcasting mechanisms and technology at a time when television's popularity was rapidly expanding. It includes actual television productions created by New York University students. During the initial three minutes, live baseball coverage was introduced as the most popular contents of the new media.

Boys' Baseball League (film no. 206) focuses on Little League Baseball, a non-profit youth baseball league for boys between the ages of eight and twelve. The film features footage of a team from Lock Haven, Pennsylvania, defeating a team from St. Petersburg, Florida, by a score of 6 to 5 in the 1948 Little League World Series at Williamsport, Pennsylvania. The film, which was dedicated to the memory of Babe Ruth who had passed away earlier that year, begins with an introduction to the National Baseball Hall of Fame and closes with credits indicating that Little League had the support of both the American and National Leagues. The below statement is included in the opening credits.

> Little League Baseball is a non-profit organization which is composed of a number of boys' baseball teams from a variety of cities, towns and villages throughout the USA. The players are boys between the ages of eight and twelve. The size of their playing fields is two thirds of the normal size and the rules are slightly different from those of the adult version, but the uniform style and equipment are the same. The headquarters is located in Williamsport, Pennsylvania. The teams first play each other locally, then regionally, and finally at the national level. Little League Baseball advances to realize the vision and goals of founder Carl Stotz, under the appropriate leadership and guidance of his followers. His vision and goals are to teach boys sportsmanship and teamwork and lead them to become good citizens who are physically and mentally healthy.[14]

---

13 'Educational Film Attendance Report' (From: Nippon Cultural Association, To: Lt. I.B. Miller, Educational Film Exchange, CIE, GHQ, SCAP, APO500), RG 331, GHQ/SCAP, CI&E, Box 5269, NARA.

14 This statement (in Japanese) appears in the film's opening credits. The film can be viewed by entering the title or CIE film number into the Search Data System for CIE/ USIS Movies of the University of Tokyo Interfaculty Initiative in Information Studies— http://www.kirokueiga-hozon.jp/cie/.

The concept of 'vision and goals' noted in the statement above resembles the contributory statement made by the GHQ/SCAP staffer of the headquarters of the Maebashi military government in the first issue of *All Sports* introduced in Chapter One.[15] This is because baseball is a sport that emphasizes and relies on teamwork. Moreover, central to the spirit of teamwork and the philosophy driving it is an understanding of the principles of democracy. The virtues one would expect to gain from baseball as a sport were the same regardless of whether the policymaking authority was the local military government, CIE physical education coordinators or CIE film staff members.

Next, I examine five sports-related CIE productions.

White Carnival (film no. 16) shows students enjoying a variety of winter sports, including skiing and skating, at the Dartmouth College winter carnival.

Vacation Sports (film no. 132, USIS film sketch no. 17) consists of three sections. The first section is titled 'Opening of the Fishing Season' and portrays trout fishing as one of the favorite sports of Americans. The second is 'Sportsman's Show', which depicts the sports equipment fair, an annual event held every spring at the Grand Central Palace in New York City. The segment includes footage of a seal show and their handlers, as well as scenes of canoe tumbling and log rolling competitions open to all entrants. The final section, 'Water Sports', features footage of waterskiing performances shot in Florida by high-speed cameras.

Glimpses of America (film no. 154, USIS film sketch no. 19) contains three segments. The first, 'A Trip from Chicago to Los Angeles', shows a forty-hour, super-express train ride from Chicago to Los Angeles. The second section is titled 'The Plastic Lung: A Godsend by Science for Polio Patients', and the final segment is called 'To the Mountains in Winter: Sun Valley in Idaho and Its Winter Sports, Including Sledge Race, Bobsledding, and Skiing'.

Views of America (film no. 174, USIS film sketch no. 26) has two parts. The first part is titled 'Foreign Sports in America: Different Foreign Sports as Played in America', while the second is 'Central Park: Views of the Famed Central Park in New York City'. The first part of the film focuses on non-mainstream sports such as hurling (an Irish game similar to field hockey), cricket, bocce (an Italian boules game), Sokol gymnastics (a parallel bar sport developed by the Czechs), fencing and Gaelic football (an Irish game similar to soccer).

---

15 'Undou-Kyougi no Minshushugi ni Oyobosu Eikyo' (Effects of democracy on adaptation to sports), *All Sports*, October 15, 1946, p. 5.

Let's Square Dance (film no. 213) was produced by the Tokyo Eiken Company and revised by the Riken Film Company. The film's contents are exactly what the title implies—an introduction to square dancing, an American form of folk dance, with dance lessons filmed by a high-speed camera.

Table 4.3 indicates the number of screenings and viewers of each baseball-related film, while Table 4.4 shows the figures for sports-related films. Of Japan's forty-six prefectures, Tokyo, Ibaraki, Niigata and Fukushima were chosen because the reports from these prefectures included nearly a full year of data for 1950.[16] Although this data is somewhat imperfect, the below is a brief list of the numbers of film showings and viewers from the four prefectures in Eastern Japan.

As noted above, CIE films were primarily distributed in order to bring the content to people who lived in remote areas of the occupied nation where there were no movie theaters. The Tokyo, Ibaraki, Niigata and Fukushima prefectures are all in Eastern Japan, not too far apart. However, this was during the U.S. occupation when there were no Shinkansen (bullet trains) running. As a result, many people in Japan may have felt at the time as if each prefecture was located far from the next. In the Niigata and Fukushima

---

16 The original data, Appendix 1: Number of Film Showings and Viewers of Eight Baseball-Related CIE Films (Prefectural Monthly Report from Jan. 1950 to Dec. 1950) and Appendix 2: Number of Film Showings and Viewers of Five Sports-Related CIE Films (Prefectural Monthly Report from Jan. 1950 to Dec. 1950), are shown on pages 176–185. I explain the items marked with 'N/A' in Appendices 2 and 3. 'N/A' refers to either 'Not Available' or 'Not Applicable', depending on the case. First, in cases where monthly data does not exist, it means 'Not Available'. March and December reports of Fukushima Prefecture as well as the December report of Ibaraki Prefecture, for example, are relevant here. Next, when the concerned production was not scheduled to show in the month, it is listed as 'Not Applicable'. In other words, as it appears in Table 4.1, there is data that documents the opening date for each production. The opening date indicates the first showing of the production after the adaptation of the concerned production. Therefore, the productions with dates of months prior to the opening dates are not included in the list. In the case of Tokyo, it seems that adaptation work was carried out there, and perhaps some films were shown before nationwide opening days. As a result, no productions were marked with 'N/A'. The following are examples of this situation: no. 206, *Boys' Baseball League*, actually opened on July 14; no. 140, *Sports' Golden Age*, was first shown on February 24; no. 174, *Views of America* (USIS film sketch no. 26), first appeared on April 21; no. 182, *Television Workshop* (USIS film sketch no. 28), was shown on May 19; and no. 213, *Let's Square Dance*, was first shown on July 21. In the reports, each production was marked '0' as recorded. Moreover, no. 16, *White Carnival*, in the Ibaraki report in February is shown as (??48), which means the first two digits were unclear in the monthly report. For this reason, the number of the grand total of CIE sports-related films is indicated by '+*'.

prefectures there are a number of areas that receive heavy snowfall. It is unlikely that movie theaters operated in those regions. Notwithstanding, it is possible that the above numbers may reflect data collected from regions where CIE film showings were not very active—for example, in Tokyo, movie theaters were commonplace. As a result, there is no guarantee that these numbers indicate a national average.

It seems likely, however, that all titles, with the exception of *Baseball Instructions* (film no. 12), were screened between 200 and 1,000 times. In the case of *Baseball Instructions*, it appears that it was shown in Tokyo in February and March before its copyright expired. Furthermore, because the collected data represents only four of Japan's forty-six prefectures, we can assume that the total nationwide audience for these films was around ten times larger than the numbers above. It is clear that this was not a minor

No.	Title	Screenings	Viewers
140	*Sports' Golden Age*	998	390,621[a]
113	*Baseball Swing King*	628	325,871
129	*Sports Revue*	685	321,940[w]
014	*Let's Play Baseball*	699	319,801
182	*Television Workshop*	489	254,148[b]
206	*Boys' Baseball League*	539	236,258[c]
125	*Topics of America*	193	75,743
012	*Baseball Instructions*	15	3,740

Notes: (a) numbers are for ten months only; (b) numbers are for seven months only; (c) numbers are for five months only.

Table 4.3 CIE baseball-related films

No.	Title	Screenings	Viewers
132	*Vacation Sports*	913	460,722
174	*Views of America*	549	262,585[a]
213	*Let's Square Dance*	552	252,716[b]
154	*Glimpses of America*	622	243,762
016	*White Carnival*	398	163,078[a]*

Notes: (a) numbers are for eight months only; (b) numbers are for five months only.

Table 4.4 CIE sports-related films

movement. Within the four prefectures examined above, at least 75,000 people, and as many as 460,000, saw each film. Taken together, more than 3,307,000 people attended the films in the four prefectures in 1950. The average number of viewers per film was slightly higher than 275,000.

It can be assumed that newly released titles would have been shown more frequently than previously released films. Thus, new releases like *Sports' Golden Age* (film no. 140), *Views of America* (film no. 174, USIS film sketch no. 26), *Boys' Baseball League* (film no. 206) and *Let's Square Dance* (film no. 231) had more screening opportunities. Other, older films, however, were also screened frequently. *Topics of America* (film no. 125) was shown frequently in February, April, July and September in Fukushima Prefecture, but it did not open in the Tokyo, Ibaraki and Niigaka prefectures until July. Once released in these three prefectures, it was shown frequently. Another example was *Baseball Swing King* (film no. 113), which was not shown in Tokyo until March, but was screened forty-four times there in April, and frequently after that. Some films were shown many times over a short period.[17]

Ideally, all four prefectures would have been stocked with all the available films. Consequently, the practice of showing a package of films frequently over a short period before moving on to another package made it possible for a single film to be screened in many different regions of the same prefecture. Likewise, delays in the copying process at the film developing facilities meant that not all prefectures received a particular film at the same time. As a result, the opening date for a film sometimes varied from prefecture to prefecture. In addition, the content of a film may have influenced when it was shown. For instance, both *White Carnival* (film no. 16) and *Glimpses of America* (film no. 154, USIS film sketch no. 19) contain footage of winter activities, making the winter season a suitable time to show these films.

---

17 See Appendices 1 and 2: Number of Film Showings and Viewers of Eight Baseball-Related CIE Films (Prefectural Monthly Report from Jan. 1950 to Dec. 1950) and Number of Film Showings and Viewers of Five Sports-Related CIE Films (Prefectural Monthly Report from Jan. 1950 to Dec. 1950).

Fukushima Prefecture CIE film showing report

The 'Educational Film Attendance Report' issued for Fukushima Prefecture for the period of June through November 1950 contains information on the opening date of each film, the name of the town or village where the film was screened and the number of viewers of each film (The original data, Appendix 3: 'Educational Film Attendance Report', are shown on pages 186–193).[18] The report was compiled by the Fukushima branch of the Nippon Culture Association with the addressee of Lt. I.B. Miller, Educational Film Exchange, CIE, GHQ, SCAP, APO500.[19]

The Fukushima branch of the Nippon Culture Association organized the screening of CIE films in Fukushima Prefecture. The films were likely shown in public places, such as the playgrounds of elementary or middle schools and community squares. In some cases, films were shown in hospitals, storage facilities and even private lots. In addition to screening location, the data shows the fact that the same package of films was screened at the same location for as long as one month. Films were sent to their screening locations in either pairs or sets of four. Films were rotated between several locations in a prefecture, but a specific film did not necessarily play in every location in that prefecture. It is not clear whether the handwriting on the records was done by one individual. Other details include the following: the duration of one title was approximately one month; two or four titles of CIE films were sent together; the titles of the films were rotated productively, traveling from one location to another (for example, around Minami-Aizu-Gun, or around Yama-Gun, etc.), and the rotation was repeated if necessary. In other words, CIE films were shown on a once per several months basis at random, so that in this rotation system there was no guarantee that every single production went to all the locations.

Information from the Fukushima branch of the Nippon Culture Association indicates that these films were not included in the monthly reports that the Fukushima Prefectural Education Office submitted to the CIE (Appendices 1 and 2). It is apparent that these films were shown in the prefecture, however, because in some cases, the monthly report marks these films as 'no showing' despite of the fact that information from the Fukushima branch of the Nippon Culture Association reveals that there were, in fact, showings. For example,

---

18 The handwritten report is A5 size and printed on *senka-shi* (recycled, poor-quality paper).

19 'Educational Film Attendance Report' (From: Nippon Culture Association, To: Lt. I.B. Miller, Educational Film Exchange, CIE, GHQ, SCAP, APO500), RG 331, GHQ/SCAP, CI&E, Box 5269, NARA.

June showings of *Sports Revue* (film no. 129, USIS film sketch no. 15), September showings of *Sports' Golden Age* (film no. 140), October showings of *Boys' Baseball League* (film no. 206) and October showings of *Vacation Sports* (film no. 132, USIS film sketch no. 17) were not recorded on the monthly report, but were screened in Fukushima Prefecture by the Fukushima branch of the Nippon Culture Association.[20]

The discrepancy doesn't just affect baseball- and sports-related films. According to data from the Fukushima branch of the Nippon Culture Association, *Panama Canal* (film no. 53) and *Beware of Fire* (film no. 39) were shown with *Sports Revue* (film no. 129, USIS film sketch no. 15); *Northern Ireland* (film no. 130) was shown with *Sports' Golden Age* (film no. 140); and *Burroughs Newsboy Foundation* (film no. 172) and *Floating Theater* (film no. 176) were shown with *Boys' Baseball League* (film no. 206) and *Let's Square Dance* (film no. 213). Yet, none of these additional films were listed as having been shown in the monthly report. The monthly report records the showing of three other films—*New Traffic* (film no. 149), *The Care Story* (film no. 128) and *Lobster Town* (film no. 134)—but there is no indication as to whether or not this means that the Fukushima branch of the Nippon Culture Association had the opportunity to show *Vacation Sports* (film no. 132, USIS film sketch no. 17).[21]

A likely explanation for the discrepancy is that the newly released CIE films were sent to the Fukushima Prefectural Education Office where they were made into a package that included several other films—new releases and formerly released titles. The Education Office then organized and screened some of these films. Later, the package was lent to the Fukushima branch of the Nippon Culture Association for one month. Thus, the association also showed these films with grassroots dedication. It is also possible that subsidiary organizations of the Imperial Rule Assistance Association (Taisei Yokusan-Kai) were transformed into a small unit of the Nippon Culture Association to show CIE films.

---

20 See Appendices 1 and 2: Number of Film Showings and Viewers of Eight Baseball-Related CIE Films (Prefectural Monthly Report from Jan. 1950 to Dec. 1950) and Number of Film Showings and Viewers of Five Sports-Related CIE Films (Prefectural Monthly Report from Jan. 1950 to Dec. 1950).

21 Appendix 3: Educational Film Attendance Report (From: Nippon Culture Association, To: Lt. I.B. Miller, Educational Film Exchange, CIE, GHQ, SCAP, APO500).

As a result, the number of viewers in Tables 4.3 and 4.4 are not quite accurate. By simply adding the numbers from the Fukushima branch of the Nippon Culture Association, the total number of screenings and viewers increases significantly. The report on educational films submitted by the Fukushima branch of the Nippon Culture Association is also important because it includes feedback on each film that summarizes viewers' opinions. This feedback seems to have been collected by the organizer, but it is possible that the bureaucrat putting the report together may have manipulated or modified it to suit their purpose. In another words, it is possible that they believed there might have been an advantage in pleasing GHQ/SCAP by presenting the feedback in a positive light. Keeping such a possibility in mind, below I introduce some typical feedback contained in the reports on each film.

Comments on Sports Revue *(film no. 129)*

Women baseball from *Sports Revue* was very interesting. I was impressed with the special technique of pitching. I would like to apply it myself. If there is any film taken by a high-speed camera showing basic movements, please give us an opportunity to view it. (Kawara-Machi, Wakamatsu-Shi)[22]

Sports Revue was very interesting to a sports man. Watching these sports while staying in a remote farming area is a great pleasure, and hope for tomorrow seems shining. I would like to ask you to give us more sports films. (Arakai-Mura, Minami-Aizu-Gun)[23]

The youthful farmers of our remote village had a very enjoyable time with the movie screening of sports in the USA. Surrounded by mountains, there are almost no leisure activities in the village; only magazines, newspapers and radio can sometimes be found. Rarely, once a year or two, only young or special people can see a movie. Most farmers here, however, have not seen even a talkie movie. Thus, this movie screening opportunity was greatly appreciated; I cannot say enough thankyous. I'd deeply appreciate other opportunities to screen movies such as views of the oceans, the South Pole and the North Pole, especially in color. (Oosugo, Higashiyama-Mura, Kita-Aizu-Gun)[24]

---

22 'Educational Film Attendance Report' (From: Nippon Cultural Association, To: Lt. I.B. Miller, Educational Film Exchange, CIE, GHQ, SCAP, APO500), RG 331, GHQ/SCAP, CI&E, Box 5269, NARA.

23 Ibid.

24 Ibid.

Comments on Sports' Golden Age *(film no. 140)*

I was very interested in the movie from the title alone. [In] Recent years, sports have become popular, so that was informative. Every participant including children was excited to see women's baseball. (Tateiwa-Mura, Minami-Aizu-Gun)[25]

I enjoyed very much seeing a glimpse of some sports from an advanced nation. I wish that you could provide us with other opportunities to see movies of this kind. (Ookawa-Mura, Minami-Aizu-Gun)[26]

Comments on Vacation Sports *(film no. 132)*

I was impressed with the incredible technique of the water sports as well as their thrills. I am grateful for the opportunity. It would be impossible to see them in Japan. I could never express the extent of my desire for another opportunity to see movies of this kind. (Kitakata-Cho, Yama-Gun)[27]

I express my astonishment at and praise for *Vacation Sports*. I was particularly excited with the skills and thrills of the waterskiing. It's truly wonderful! (Matusyama-Cho, Yama-Gun)[28]

Comments on Boys' Baseball League *(film no. 206)*

The Boys' Baseball League wouldn't appear in Japan anytime soon. The film well depicts the affairs of the boys' baseball teams, and I became interested. I respect the advanced nation—the U.S.A.—and learned profoundly many points from it. (Aza Kamimiyori, Ooto-Mura, Kita-Aizu-Gun)[29]

Baseball nurtures us with teamwork spirit and sportsmanship. It's also a great sport to train physically. Thus, boys are big fans of baseball without exception. The movie was fantastic in teaching how to play baseball properly. (Doujima-Mura, Kawanuma-Gun)[30]

Baseball has become very popular among children. The movie was very interesting and the boys' baseball is truly welcome! (Aza-Itozawa, Aragai-Mura, Minami-Aizu-Gun)[31]

---

25 Ibid.

26 Ibid.

27 Ibid.

28 Ibid.

29 Ibid.

30 Ibid.

31 Ibid.

Baseball teaches sportsmanship and deepens teamwork, so that playing it should be encouraged. The movie taught villagers of each household to understand these aspects of baseball and is a wonderful movie! (Inamura, Minami-Aizu-Gun)[32]

Comments on Let's Square Dance *(film no. 213)*

The movie was cheerful and enjoyable, so that it made me feel like dancing! It was also interesting to see the young people dancing with the festival music of drums and flutes at the riverside with the mountains behind. (Aza-Kuraga, Ooto-Mura, Kita-Aizu-Gun)[33]

The square dance can be enjoyed in mountains and fields! It became so popular because it's simple, easy and fun. All the students know about it. It was very interesting. (Niitsuru-Mura, Oonuma-Gun)[34]

Despite the phrases that may have been inserted to flatter GHQ/SCAP, these comments reveal how CIE films were received by the Japanese people. It is also evident that baseball films, and other films about sports, were viewed very positively by the Japanese people. The comments also tell us that baseball was very popular among Japanese children, even in remote regions where no leisure activities existed. Of special significance is the fact that the Fukushima Prefectural Education Office report indicated that at least one film on baseball or other sports was screened at all showing opportunities during the period examined above.

These comments point to the fact that film organizers understood the tendency of potential Japanese viewers to prefer sports-related films. GHQ/SCAP's plan to re-educate and reorient the Japanese people through sports was well received in Japan. The Educational Film Exchange, CIE Information Department/Unit of Educational Films, and the Fukushima branch of the Nippon Culture Association coordinated their efforts to apply the CIE agenda to movie viewers. Demand and supply were well-matched.

---

32 Ibid.

33 Ibid.

34 Ibid.

Informational/educational films within U.S. cultural diplomacy policies

The 1950 data from the four prefectures in Eastern Japan indicate that the screening of CIE sports-related films, especially baseball films, had a significant impact on Japanese society. This media was developed as an effective tool to re-educate and reorient the Japanese people. The use of such films in occupied Japan was actually part of a broader American policy agenda—the U.S. was using informational and educational films as part of its worldwide cultural diplomacy. Documents from the International Motion Picture Division (IMP) of the Office of International Information and Cultural Affairs, Department of State, the International Motion Picture Services (IMS), which was the successor of the IMP, and the United States Information Agency (USIA), which took over the role of using film in foreign policy from the Department of State, indicate the fact that other films with baseball content existed besides those shown in Japan by the CIE/USIS.[35]

These films are found in the film list titled 'Movie Scripts: 1942–1965' issued by the USIA. Many of the films on the list were CIE/USIS productions, but some were produced for other parts of the world than Japan. Some of the films can easily be identified as baseball films from their titles. For example, the scripts of *Baseball Today* (1950) and *The Ballplayers* (1953) are recorded in the document.[36]

The Ballplayers was directed by Jack Delano, a photographer for the New Deal's Farm Security Administration (FSA). It should be noted that some of the first nine CIE films prepared by the Office of War Information were produced and directed by individuals such as Willard Van Dyke, the director of *Northwest U.S.A.* (1944) and *Steel Town* (1944), and producer John Houseman and director Nicholas Ray of *Tuesday in November* (1945), who are well known as New Deal devotees.

Delano was born in Kiev, Ukraine, and migrated to the U.S. as an infant. He first visited Puerto Rico in 1941 for his work with the FSA and became a resident of that island in 1946. *The Ballplayers* was produced by the Puerto Rican government's Department of Instruction. The USIA purchased the film, overdubbed it in English and distributed it around the world to further

---

35 'Movie Scripts: 1942–1965', Records of the U.S. Information Agency, RG 306, NARA (Entry 1098, Location 230/47/17/1-).

36 All scripts are arranged alphabetically and housed in fifty-nine boxes of 'Movie Scripts: 1942–1965'.

its own diplomatic policy agenda. As the director, Jack Delano, was raised in the U.S., this film, like the CIE films shown in Japan, effectively spread American democracy, values and virtues through baseball.

The Ballplayers is a film about poor Puerto Rican villagers who want to build a school but do not have enough money to construct one. A man named Momo suggests they can build it themselves. The other villagers think Momo is crazy, until he tells them the story of his childhood. When Momo was a boy, families in his neighborhood were poor. Boys in Momo's neighborhood passed the time by playing baseball every day. Momo explains that Don Pepe, a former baseball player (played by Ramon Rivero) who had been shunned by the other villagers, taught the boys how to play the game. The boys want baseball uniforms, but because their fathers are poor (Momo's dad had lost his job), they cannot afford them. Pepe suggests to the children that they could earn money for uniforms by helping the townsfolk. Momo and the other children begin working and give their money to Pepe to mind. But, Pepe is also poor, and so his wife, Lolita (played by Miriam Colon), suggests that he use the children's money to buy a suit for job hunting. Pepe insists that he cannot steal from children, but Lolita responds that they will pay them back after he finds a job. Pepe eventually uses the money. When Momo and the other boys eventually learn that Pepe has used the money, they are very hurt. Driven by his conscience, Pepe decides to sell his precious pet pig to the butcher and uses the money to replace what he took from the uniform fund. As an adult, Momo uses this story to convince the villagers that they can build a school.[37]

The theme of *The Ballplayers* suggests moral and ethical principles derived from baseball that can nurture teamwork and sportsmanship while preventing humiliation and degradation. The film even hints that baseball can provide a meaningful life, even if one is poor. The statement in the opening credits of the CIE film *Boys' Baseball League* (film no. 206) makes virtually the same argument.

Filmed in 1950, *Baseball Today* is a short film believed to have been produced by the Atlas Film Corporation. The existing script has a mark indicating that some portion was removed. The film was modified for the USIA, which subsequently purchased it.

Baseball Today is very similar to *Baseball Swing King* (film no. 113). While the latter examines Boston Red Sox star Ted Williams, the former features hard-throwing Cleveland Indian pitcher Bob Feller. Despite the fact

---

37 'The Ballplayers' Folder, RG 306, USIA, 'Movie Scripts: 1942–1965', Box 4, NARA.

that his career was interrupted by four years of naval service during World War II, Feller, also known as 'Rapid Robert', won 266 games for Cleveland. He also led the Indians to the 1948 World Series championship. The film also includes footage of Chicago White Sox shortstop Luke Appling sharing the secrets of his success with high school players. Appling, who was playing in his final season when the movie was filmed, amassed 2,749 hits in his career. The film also contains details on different circumstances that might arise in a game, including where the umpire should stand in specific situations and what would constitute interference.[38]

The document indicates that advertisements embedded in the film—one for baseballs and gloves manufactured by Wilson Sporting Goods and a scene featuring Luke Appling eating Wheaties, a breakfast cereal produced by General Mills—should be deleted. It is likely that these two scenes were originally placed in the film in exchange for a financial contribution to the Atlas Company. The last scene in the film concludes with the following statement:

> Baseball is a grand old game… filled with infinite opportunities for dazzling action, superb strategy, magnificent teamwork, splendid sportsmanship and courageous play. Through the years, thousands have devoted their lives to it… their fans are numbered in millions. A knowledge of the basic rules and fundamentals contribute to a full measure of appreciation of the fine points of the sport. On baseball diamonds all over our land there are potential champions, who will maintain the great traditions of this national game. They will contribute, through play, to a strong, healthy and happy America.[39]

Like the above statement, 'an homage of love for baseball' is the theme of *The Ballplayers* and *Baseball Today*, and it shares a common interest with the various materials introduced in this chapter. The principles of democratizing Japan and establishing American values there existed not only as the U.S. film and sports policies in occupied Japan, they also followed the general guidelines of American cultural diplomacy. Moreover, these fundamental elements were also used by other media, such as radio, and are evident in the delegation of Major League athletes who visited Japan from the U.S.

---

38 'Baseball Today' Folder, RG 306, USIA, 'Movie Scripts: 1942–1965', Box 4, NARA.

39 'Baseball Today', ATLAS Film Corporation, January 17, 1950, p. 33. 'Baseball Today' Folder, RG 306, USIA, 'Movie Scripts: 1942–1965', Box 4, NARA.

5
The Use of the Image of Jackie Robinson in VOA Radio Programs

Breaking the racism barrier through U.S. Major League Baseball

U.S. authorities believed baseball to be the most effective way to democratize Japan and re-educate and reorient the Japanese people and saw it as a valuable tool in the war against communism. Baseball was viewed as a clear example of why the U.S. was superior to the Soviet Union. This chapter focuses on Jack Roosevelt 'Jackie' Robinson, the first African American in mainstream U.S. sports (except boxing)[1] to circumvent the racism imbedded in athletics and rise to stardom.

Robinson's presence in the game ushered in a turning point in baseball history. This chapter not only examines how Robinson's story was used to convey a positive image of the U.S. in the context of the Cultural Cold War, but also how it was actively used in Japan during the occupation. In terms of practice, this chapter focuses on the use of radio, which had a huge influence in the mass media and which had been the major instrument of communication in the second quarter of the twentieth century alongside motion picture, which I examined in the previous chapter. Specifically, I look at how baseball and other sports, especially the positive image of racial integration exemplified in Jackie Robinson, was used effectively as the contents of Voice of America (VOA) broadcasts, one of the most famous tools of U.S. cultural diplomacy policy. Before examining the above, I first briefly introduce the career of Jackie Robinson.

Born on January 31, 1919, in Cairo, Georgia, Jackie Robinson became the first African American to play Major League Baseball (MLB) in the twentieth century in 1947. For a decade, the fleet-footed Robinson was a star player for the Brooklyn Dodgers. He played first base in his 1947 rookie season, spent most of his career as second baseman and played third baseman and outfielder before retiring in 1956. Prior to Robinson crossing the 'color

---

1 Joseph 'Joe' Louis Barrow, who knocked out Max Schmeling at Yankee Stadium on June 19, 1936, became a national hero before Robinson made his debut.

line', organized baseball in the U.S. had refused to sign African Americans. Instead, African American ballplayers found their opportunities limited to an all-black institution called the Negro leagues and internationally in countries like Canada, Mexico, Cuba and eventually Japan.

Robinson was a gifted athlete. After graduating from the University of California, Los Angeles, where he became the first UCLA athlete to earn varsity letters in four sports—baseball, basketball, football and track and field—Robinson played semi-professional football with a team called the Honolulu Bears. In April 1945, after serving in the military, Robinson signed a $400-per-month contract to play as shortstop for the Kansas City Monarchs of the Negro American League.[2] That year, Branch Rickey, co-owner and general manager of the Brooklyn Dodgers, took notice of Robinson, who appeared in the Negro League All-Star Game. In August, Rickey offered Robinson a $3,500 bonus to sign a $600-per-month contract with the Montreal Royals of the Class AAA International League, the top farm club of the Dodgers. Robinson joined the Royals in 1946, becoming the first African American to play for a white team since the color line was drawn in the late nineteenth century.

Playing second base, Robinson excelled in Montreal. He batted a league-leading .349, while scoring 113 runs and posting a .985 fielding average. Robinson's play earned him the International League's Most Valuable Player award, as he led his team to a four-games-to-two victory over the American Association's Louisville Colonels in the post-season Junior World Series.[3]

Shortly before the start of the 1947 season, the Dodgers announced Robinson's promotion to Brooklyn. On April 15, at Ebbets Field in Brooklyn, he made his Major League debut, becoming the first African American to play in an MLB game since Moses Fleetwood Walker in 1884.

Robinson's talent and Rickey's vision made this breakthrough possible. The obstacles in Robinson's way were not insignificant. At an owner's meeting before the start of the 1947 season, the Major League teams voted fifteen to one to bar Robinson from the big leagues, with the Dodgers being the only team in dissent. The result of the vote, however, was overturned by Baseball Commissioner Albert 'Happy' Chandler, who supported the Dodgers' decision. Those unconvinced of the morality behind the decision

---

2 Jackie Robinson (As told to Alfred Duckett), *I Never Had It Made* (G. P. Putnam's Sons, 1972), p. 35.

3 Jonathan Eig, *Opening Day: The Story of Jackie Robinson's First Season* (Simon & Schuster Paperback, 2007), p. 33.

to admit Robinson to the Major League were won over by his play on the field. Playing his Major League season at first base, Robinson hit .297, with twelve home runs and twenty-nine stolen bases. Robinson won the National League Rookie of the Year award, despite the fact that opponents and their fans taunted him with racial slurs and often boycotted the games in which he participated.[4]

For his second year with Brooklyn, Robinson was switched to second base. The Dodgers renewed his contract, paying him $12,500 for the season. In 1949, Robinson earned the National League's Most Valuable Player award, hitting .342, having 124 RBI and stealing thirty-seven bases. That year, Robinson became the first African American player selected by fans to participate in the Major League All-Star Game. He would go on to play in the All-Star Game for six consecutive years. Soon Hollywood came knocking. Robinson portrayed himself in the 1950 biopic *The Jackie Robinson Story*, a film that appealed to baseball fans and others who did not have the chance to see Robinson play in person.

As a pioneer, Robinson not only opened the door for other African American players, he also earned the respect of many white fans who viewed him as an individual who achieved the American Dream despite the obstacle of prejudice and racial discrimination. Many other African Americans, however, continued to struggle against the hardship of racism. In April 1949, in a speech before the communist-led World Congress of the Partisans of Peace in Paris, African American singer Paul Robeson contrasted race relations in the U.S. with those in its Cold War enemy, the Soviet Union. 'It is unthinkable', Robeson said, that American Negroes 'would go to war on behalf of those who have oppressed us for generations against a nation'. Three months later, the House Committee on Un-American Activities (HUAC) summoned Jackie Robinson to Washington to hear his opinion of Robeson's speech. In his testimony before the HUAC, Robinson said Robeson's statement 'sounds very silly'. Robinson assured the committee that he and 'other Americans of many races and faiths have too much invested in our country's welfare for any of us to throw it away'.[5] Robinson's remarkable performance before the committee led many white Americans to admire his baseball career.

---

4 *Jackie Robinson, The Official Website*, Stats page. http://jackierobinson.com/stats.html (last date of access: July 26, 2020).

5 Martin Bauml Duberman, *Paul Robeson* (Knopf, New York, 1989), p. 342; *New York Times*, April 21, 1949; *New York Times*, July 19, 1949.

Robinson became a hero not only because he broke racial barriers through baseball, but also because he served in the military. Robinson was a proud patriot, announcing that the U.S. was a great country that provided tremendous opportunities. For many whites, Robinson created the perfect image of a black man, demonstrating that an African American could accomplish much despite the country's deep-seated racism. The fact that Robinson was court-martialed for failing to move to the back of a bus in 1944 did not hurt his reputation as a great American.

The U.S. Department of State recognized that the Jackie Robinson story could persuade the rest of the world that American society was determined to overcome a variety of social problems. By spreading the story, the U.S. government sought to convince Japan and the rest of the world that American society was superior to that of the Soviet Union.

After his death at the age of fifty-three in 1972, the Los Angeles Dodgers retired Robinson's uniform number, forty-two. In 1997, on the fiftieth anniversary of his debut with the Brooklyn Dodgers, MLB retired his number throughout baseball in its entirety. The few active players who wore the number were exempted and allowed to continue wearing it. New York Yankees all-star relief pitcher Mariano Rivera became the last Major League player to wear the number forty-two when he retired in 2013. However, each season since 2007, on April 15, all MLB players can wear number forty-two to honor the pioneer who broke baseball's color line. Robinson is a baseball legend, and in the 1950s the U.S. used his positive image in Japan for the purpose of its international cultural diplomacy policy via the Voice of America radio program and other media.

▌ A history of VOA and its development in Japan

The U.S. government began to use radio as an instrument of propaganda in 1941, when, at the urging of New York-based lawyer William J. Donovan and American playwright Robert Sherwood, President Franklin Roosevelt created the Office of the Coordinator of Information (OCI). Roosevelt appointed Donovan, a classmate of the President from Yale University, to head the office despite the fact that he was a Republican and a political opponent. Donovan handled military intelligence while Roosevelt named Sherwood, who had been his speechwriter, as head of the OCI's Foreign Information Service, which would disseminate foreign propaganda.

A number of intellectuals worked for the OCI, including playwright Thornton Wilder and stage producer and later actor John Houseman, who also founded Mercury Theater with Orson Welles, both recruited by their friend Sherwood.[6]

In June 1942, FDR established the Office of War Information (OWI), a temporary agency designed to disseminate wartime information. Roosevelt appointed Elmer Davis, a journalist and former radio commentator, to manage this agency. Ten months later, Roosevelt issued an executive order defining the OWI as the organization in charge of spreading U.S. propaganda to the world except South America. The definition expanded the authority of the OCI, still directed by Donovan, and renamed it the Office of Strategic Services (OSS), which would become the precursor of the modern Central Intelligence Agency. The same order also removed the Foreign Information Service from the OCI and placed it at the center of the foreign division of the OWI. Sherwood remained its director. A couple of months earlier, in February 1942, using a transmitter borrowed from the British Broadcasting Company, the Foreign Information Service had begun broadcasting news and information programs to occupied Europe under an operation Sherwood called 'Voice of America'. Original VOA programs were produced in a New York studio under the supervision of John Houseman. By January 1943, the operation was expanded to twenty-three transmitters broadcasting in a total of twenty-seven languages. By 1944, VOA was transmitting hundreds of programs in more than forty languages.[7]

When the war ended in 1945, it seemed like there was no longer a need for VOA. The agency suffered a significant reduction in staff when the OWI was dissolved. Eventually, the Department of State took over the administration of VOA, cutting its broadcasts to twenty-three languages. With the outbreak of the Cold War, however, the U.S. government once again saw the need for a propaganda agency. In January 1948, President Harry S. Truman signed the U.S. Information and Education Exchange Act of 1948, better known as the 'Smith-Mundt Act', into law. The act set the terms in which the U.S.

---

6 Takeshi Tanikawa, 'Beikoku Seifu Soshiki to Hollywood Eiga-Sangyoukai tono Sougo-Izonkankei' (Interdependence of the U.S. government and the Hollywood motion picture industry), in Toshihiko Kishi and Yuka Tsuchiya, *Bunka-Reisen no Jidai; America to Asia* (De-centering the Cultural Cold War: The U.S. and Asia) (Kokusai-Shoin, 2009), pp. 54–55; http://www.insidevoa.com/content/a-13-34-beginning-of-an-american-voice-111602684/177526.html (last date of access: July 27, 2020).

7 Ibid.

government could engage global audiences. Five months later, the Soviet Union sealed off West Berlin, an enclave occupied and governed by the U.S., the U.K. and France 160 km from the border of the Soviet-dominated nation of East Germany. With the escalation of the Cold War, Truman initiated the 'Campaign of Truth' in April 1950.[8]

In 1951, under the Campaign of Truth, VOA was expanded to 400 broadcast hours per week in forty-five languages. Two years later, control over VOA was transferred to the newly established United States Information Agency (USIA). In 1999, under the William Jefferson Clinton administration, the USIA was dissolved and control over VOA reverted to the State Department. Under Robert Sherwood, VOA was located in New York City, but in 1954, it was relocated to Washington, D.C., where it still resides today.[9]

The Japanese-language VOA broadcast began in 1942, in the midst of World War II. By December 1944, VOA programs were relayed to the main islands of Japan on medium wave from Saipan Island. When the war ended, however, the Japanese broadcasts ended as well. In 1950, during the implementation of the Campaign of Truth, proposals to revive VOA in occupied Japan originated from within the State Department and the United States Political Advisor in Tokyo (USPOLAD). A test broadcast of a music program was first aired on August 26, 1951. On September 3, 1951, just five days before the signing of the Treaty of San Francisco which ended hostilities between the U.S. and Japan, shortwave VOA broadcasts resumed in Japan.[10]

Generally, VOA was broadcast in Japan from 6:30 to 7:00 p.m., but the time varied according to season. To gauge its influence, the USIA often conducted listener surveys. A USIA survey of Tokyo in 1968 determined that VOA did not draw an audience in Tokyo comparable with those of Voice of Russia and Radio Peking. In February 1970, the USIA discontinued VOA broadcasts in Japan.[11] Voice of America, however, did have an impact

8 Yuka Tsuchiya, 'The USIA and the privatization of overseas information activities', pp. 35–38.

9 http://www.insidevoa.com/content/a-13-34-2007-reorganizing-us-international-broadcasting-in-the-1990s-111602649/177524.html (last date of access: July 27, 2020).

10 Mitsuo Ikawa, 'Sengo VOA Nihongo-Housou no Saikai' (Resumption of VOA Japanese broadcasts after World War II), *Media History*, Association for Studies of Media History, Vol. 12, 2002, p. 53.

11 Mitsuo Ikawa, 'Reisen-ki niokeru VOA Risunā Chousa: Nihongohousou wo Rei ni' (VOA listener survey during the Cold War era: A case study of VOA Japanese language broadcasts), *The Journal of Applied Sociology*, Rikkyo University, No. 51, 2009, pp. 24–25.

on Japan. It provided the Japanese Broadcast Company (Nihon Housou Kyoukai, or simply 'NHK') and other commercial radio stations with a variety of materials and package programs, and its influence was not insignificant in the overall sphere of international diplomacy.

A study by Mitsuo Ikawa determined that, with the resumption of VOA broadcasts in Japan, the Major League World Series was broadcast by VOA as part of the NHK package deal. From October 4 to October 10, 1951, all six games of the 1951 World Series played between the New York Yankees and New York Giants were broadcast by NHK. The games were called by Minoru Okada and Shirou Nose, two popular Japanese announcers, who were temporarily transferred to VOA.[12] The 1951 World Series was the first played between the Yankees and Giants in fourteen years.

The games of the 1951 World Series were not broadcast live in Japan— NHK recorded the broadcasts through VOA and aired them on a tape-delay rebroadcast. Although the games were not aired in real time, the time lag was not significant. The games started at 1:00 p.m. in New York, which was 3:00 a.m. in Tokyo. According to the U.S. military newspaper, *Pacific Stars and Stripes*, English language coverage of the series was broadcast live on shortwave in Japan from 2:15 a.m. and rebroadcast at 3:05 p.m.[13] It seems apparent that the Japanese language broadcast was delayed until 4:00 p.m., because, after the broadcast was over, NHK sent a comment to VOA in which they stated that the games should be broadcast at 8:00 a.m. instead of 4:00 p.m. as the results would already be available in the afternoon newspapers. Notwithstanding the disadvantages of the broadcast delay, according to a report from the U.S. Embassy, six million people listened to the VOA World Series coverage in Japan. Therefore, it is fair to claim that baseball was well-received and played an influential role in post-war Japan on par with that of CIE films.[14]

---

12 Mitsuo Ikawa, 'Sengo VOA Nihongo-Housou no Saikai' (Resumption of VOA Japanese language broadcasts after World War II), pp. 55–56.

13 'World Series re-broadcasts in Japan', State Department Decimal File, 511.944/10-2551, RG 59, NARA and *Pacific Stars and Stripes*, Vol. 7, No. 276, Thursday, October 4, 1951, p. 16.

14 From Bradford to Foy, State Department Decimal File, 511.944/10-951, RG 59, NARA.

Baseball broadcasting programs published in VOA press releases

Among the USIA documents preserved in the National Archives and Records Administration (NARA) are copies of press releases issued by VOA between 1951 and 1953, before it fell under the authority of the USIA. These records, filed in 847 folders, fill fifteen boxes. The records are divided into geographic regions: 236 folders are labeled 'The Far East' (including one folder marked 'South Asia and the Far East'), 192 folders are labeled 'The Near East', 206 folders are labeled 'South America' and 198 folders are labeled 'Europe' (including three folders marked 'Europe and South America', one marked 'Europe and the Near East', one marked 'Europe and the Far East/Near East', one marked 'Europe and the Far East' and one marked 'Europe and South America/the Far East'). An additional fifteen folders are simply labeled 'World'. Each file presents the content of the radio news and programs broadcast into a particular country. The folders labeled 'World' may contain programs without a specific geographic focus. After categorization by region, the files are sorted by nation and then by program title.[15] Table 5.1 indicates how much baseball and other sports content was broadcast by VOA, and in which countries or regions it was broadcast.

It is unlikely that the 847 files represent every program broadcast by VOA between 1951 and 1953. Rather, it is probable that they are the files that survived, by accident, when the State Department transferred control of VOA to the USIA.

From the data in this table, it is clear that baseball and other sports were not popular topics for VOA radio news programs in the Near East, South America, Europe or most of the Far East. Of the 800 folders dedicated to the Near East, South America, Europe and the Far East, with the exception of Japan, only ten are sports-related and three are baseball-related. Notwithstanding this fact, it is remarkable that out of the forty-seven folders dedicated to Japan, one was dedicated to sports and seven were baseball related. Boxing seems to have been the focus of programming in South America, while skiing and soccer were the focus in Europe. Only three files for the rest of the world featured baseball, but in Japan, seven files are concerned with baseball. The only other sports-related file in Japan was about African American football coach and player Frederick D. 'Fritz' Pollard. Although no records exist indicating what

---

15 'VOA Radio News Press Release 1951–1953' (Entry 1095), 350/78/12/05, RG 306, Records of the USIA, Box 1–15.

Region	Nation	Number of Folders	Number of Folders and Titles of Baseball-Related (B) and Sports-Related (S) Folders	
Far East	Australia	1	0	B: Casey Stengel,
	Burma	14	0	Yankees' manager
	Indonesia	8	0	S: Frederick D. Pollard
	Japan	47	7 + 1	(Football Hall of Famer)
	Korea	28	0	B: Sports Show: Joe DiMaggio
	Malaya	5	0	B: Bobby Shantz (pitcher)
	The Philippines	70	0	B: World Series
	Thailand	13	0	B: All-Star Game
	Vietnam	1	0	B: Baseball Game
	India	1	0	**B: Jackie Robinson**
	Others (not nations) or empty folders	48	1 + 0	**B: Jackie Robinson**
	Subtotal	236	8 + 1	
Near East	Israel	23	0	
	Pakistan	25	0	
	Turkey	44	0	
	Greece	17	0	
	India	14	0	
	Iran	6	0	
	Others (not nations) or empty folders	63	1 + 0	**B: Jackie Robinson**
	Subtotal	192	1 + 0	
South America	Argentina	9	0 + 1	S: Two Boxing Experts
	Brazil	76	0	
	Chile	5	0	
	Colombia	5	0	
	Costa Rica	2	0	
	Cuba	2	0	
	Dominican Republic	2	0	
	Ecuador	1	0	
	Guatemala	1	0	
	Haiti	2	0	
	Mexico	5	0	
	Paraguay	2	0	S: Pancho Segura (tennis player)
	Uruguay	5	0	S: Louis Angel Filippo (boxer)
	Venezuela	1	0	S: Bob Allison (sports round up)
	Others (not nations) or empty folders	88	1 + 3	**B: Jackie Robinson**
	Subtotal	198	0 + 6	
Europe	Austria	25	0 + 2	S: Olympic Stars
	Belgium	1	0	S: Ski Champions
	Czechoslovakia	1	0	
	Denmark	1	0	S: Indianapolis Auto Race
	Finland	42	0 + 2	S: Boston Marathon
	France	40	0	S: Heinz Ulmeier (athletics)
	Germany	28	0 + 2	S: Soccer Player in Stuttgart
	Others (not nations) or empty folders	60	0	
	Subtotal	198	0 + 6	
World	Not Nations	15	0	
Grand Total		847	10 + 11	

Table 5.1 USIA documents: VOA radio news press releases (1951–1953)

types of programs were the most popular in each country or region, music-related shows appear to top the list, especially in South America.

While all three of the baseball files for the rest of the world focus on Jackie Robinson, just one out of the seven baseball files for Japan feature the Dodger legend. Table 5.2 contains a list of the seven Japanese baseball-related files, along with their broadcast dates, where known.

The first three folders listed in Table 5.2 do not have numbers, as those files concerned live sporting events, which were not assigned file numbers. Only pre-recorded programs, such as those containing interviews with athletes, were assigned file numbers.

The first file listed is a broadcast of a baseball game played between the Washington Senators and the New York Yankees. The game, which was the opening game of the season for both teams, was played on April 18, 1952 at Yankee Stadium in the Bronx, New York. According to the press release, the game was called by NHK announcers Minoru Okada and Shirou Nose, the same pair who announced the Japanese-language broadcast of the World Series the previous October. The broadcast, which only featured the highlights of the game, was aired from 6:30 to 7:00 p.m., Tokyo time.[16] As VOA was based in New York City at the time, the three clubs that then represented New York City in the Major League — the New York Yankees, the New York Giants and the Brooklyn Dodgers — offered a geographical advantage for live VOA broadcasts. Although all three New York teams were very good during the post-war period, the Yankees were especially successful, having won pennants in 1947, 1949, 1950, 1951, 1952, 1953, 1955, 1956, 1957 and 1958. During this period, the Yankees won the World

Subject	Broadcast date	File No.
Baseball Game	Apr. 19, 1952	N/A
All-Star Game	July 7, 1952	N/A
World Series	Oct. 2–8, 1952	N/A
Bobby Shantz (pitcher)	Oct. 19, 1952	C-152
Joe DiMaggio (outfielder)	Nov. 16, 1952	C-180
Casey Stengel (manager)	Apr. 16, 1953	C-780
Jackie Robinson (infielder)	Unknown	B-221

Table 5.2 Japanese baseball-related files and their broadcast dates

16 Box 1, 'Japan—Baseball Game—gl' Folder.

Series eight times with only two exceptions—1955 (lost to the Brooklyn Dodgers) and 1957 (lost to the Milwaukee Braves). Thus, the Yankees were a popular radio attraction. Also, seven out of ten World Series which featured the Yankees, with the exception of 1950 (vs. Philadelphia Phillies), 1957 and 1958 (vs. Milwaukee Braves), were the so-called 'Subway Series', games fought between the Yankees and the New York Giants or Brooklyn Dodgers.

The second file listed is a broadcast of the 1952 MLB All-Star Game, which was played on July 8, 1952 at Shibe Park in Philadelphia. Again, NHK announcers Minoru Okada and Shirou Nose handled the broadcast duties for VOA. The broadcast was taped, and then edited down to two hours at VOA's New York studio. The edited program was relay-broadcast by NHK on middle wave on July 9 at 1:00 p.m., Tokyo time.[17] The 1952 All-Star Game remains the only Major League All-Star Game to be cut short due to rain. Only five innings were played before the game was called off. Jackie Robinson hit a home run in the first inning, as the National League defeated the American League by a score of five to three.[18]

The third file listed is a broadcast of the 1952 World Series between the New York Yankees and the Brooklyn Dodgers. Once again, NHK announcers Nose and Okada called the games. For Japanese-speaking listeners, the broadcasts were taped and edited down to one-hour before they were rebroadcast in Japan. During the course of the World Series, the English-language program, *America Calling the People of Japan*, was aired each morning at 7:30. In addition to the program, the ordinary news program during the course of the World Series included a segment called 'The Player of the Day'.[19] The program, *America Calling the People of Japan*, featured VOA sports editor Bob Allison interviewing a player from both teams. Allison was a New Yorker who handled all VOA sports programs, but especially those featuring baseball. Prior to joining VOA as an events coordinator in 1950, he worked as a sports commentator for New York radio stations WNYC and WNEW, and as a producer for CBS educational programs.[20]

The fourth file listed is an interview with pitcher Bobby Shantz of the Philadelphia Athletics. At the end of the fifth inning of the 1952 All-Star Game, Shantz had struck out Whitey Lockman, Jackie Robinson and Stan

---

17 Box 1, 'Japan—All-Star Game—gl' Folder.

18 Ibid.

19 Box 1, 'Japan—[World Series]' Folder.

20 Box 7, 'Latin America: Bob Allison—Sports Round Up' Folder.

Musial in order, which put him in a position to tie or break Carl Hubbell's eighteen-year-old record of striking out five consecutive batters in an All-Star Game. Shantz, however, never got the opportunity to achieve that record, as rain ended the game before he was able to take the mound in the sixth. The interview conducted by Bob Allison, which was included in the program *America Calls the Japanese People*, was probably recorded on September 19, 1952 at Yankee Stadium before Shantz took the mound against the Yankees.[21] The program aired in Tokyo at 5:30 in the afternoon on Sunday, October 19.[22]

Bobby Shantz was a member of the team of Major League players that toured Japan in 1951. In the interview conducted by Allison, he spoke about his memories of Japan and his pitching technique. As it is not clear that Shantz was particularly popular with the Japanese people as was Babe Ruth, Joe DiMaggio and Bob Feller, it is likely he was selected for the interview not only because he had visited Japan a year earlier, but also because he had gained attention by striking out three consecutive batters in the 1952 All-Star Game, which had been broadcast in Japan on VOA.

Shantz's folder also contained a press release about Yankees pitcher 'Steady Eddie' Lopat, who was listed as a guest of Bob Allison on *America Calls the Japanese People*. There is, however, no independent file for Lopat.[23] It is possible that Lopat, along with Shantz, was interviewed by Allison prior to the Athletics-Yankees game, but that VOA chose to air only the interview with Shantz.

The folders mentioned above contain press releases, photographs and mailing lists that indicate the number of press packages to be sent and the name of countries and cities to which they should be sent. There were no photographs in the folder concerning the 1952 opening game between the New York Yankees and Washington Senators, nor were there photos in the file concerning the 1952 All-Star Game. However, the folder labeled 'Bobby

---

21 Though in the document the date of the interview not mentioned, it could not possibly have been October 19 as MLB had a rule prohibiting teams that were in the World Series from participating in post-season exhibition games. Instead, the Athletics played at Yankee Stadium on Friday, September 19. Shantz started, and won, that game. My conclusion is that the date is a typographical error, and the interview was recorded on Friday, September 19 and broadcast on Sunday, October 19.

22 Box 1, 'Japan—Bobby Shantz, Baseball Pitcher' Folder.

23 'Eddie Lopat to be heard on Voice of America', Box 1, 'Japan—Bobby Shantz, Baseball Pitcher' Folder.

Shantz' indicated that there were originally forty publicity photos of Shantz with Bob Allison (see Photo 5.1). Thirty-five were sent to Japan in press packages, but the remaining five are still in the file.[24]

The fifth file listed is about Joe DiMaggio, the 'Yankee Clipper'. The Japanese-language version of *America Calls the Japanese People*, which aired on Sundays at 7:30 p.m., encouraged listeners to request their favorite athletes as future guests of the program. Listeners could send their requests to either the U.S. Embassy in Tokyo or to the VOA office in New York.[25] The popular DiMaggio appeared on the program about one month after Bobby Shantz's appearance. Though there is a lack of evidence, it is likely that DiMaggio's appearance was negotiated because many in the Japanese audience named DiMaggio as their request, considering the fact that the VOA press release of October 17, which encouraged Japanese listeners to request future program guests, was included in DiMaggio's folder.

DiMaggio was almost certainly the most popular baseball player in Japan. Not only had he been the biggest star in the New York Yankees, the greatest team in the history of baseball, he also had professional connections with Japan. As a Minor League for the San Francisco Seals

Photo 5.1
Bobby Shantz
with Bob Allison

Source: National Archives and Records Administration (VOA publicity photos).

---

24 Box 1, 'Japan—Bobby Shantz, Baseball Pitcher' Folder.

25 'VOA radio news: Audience Requests and Queries Answered on VOA's Sports Show', Box 1, 'Japan—Sports Show: Joe DiMaggio (C-180)' Folder.

in 1935, DiMaggio played for Lefty O'Doul. When O'Doul visited Japan in 1950 for the purpose of giving technical advice to Japanese ballplayers, he brought DiMaggio with him.[26] As will be discussed in Chapter Seven, DiMaggio returned to Japan as a member of a visiting U.S. baseball team in 1951. Even after his retirement from the sport, DiMaggio astonished Japanese fans by returning to Japan for his honeymoon with Marilyn Monroe in February 1954.

During DiMaggio's first visit to Japan in 1950, the Japanese Baseball Association was divided into two leagues—the Central League and the Pacific League. Thus, for the first time in history, a 'Japanese World Series' was held between the pennant winners of each circuit. Japanese baseball authorities staged an elaborate ceremony for the opening of the first Japanese World Series. In a mock ceremonial first pitch, O'Doul was the pitcher, Major General William F. Marquat was the catcher and DiMaggio was the batter.[27] A year later, DiMaggio returned to Japan as the player-manager and outfielder of an American baseball team that played against Japanese teams. The Americans played a sixteen-game schedule against Japanese professional baseball teams, starting with the Yomiuri Giants at Korakuen Stadium in Tokyo on October 20. The second game was held at Korakuen against the Mainichi Orions, before the tour held games at Sendai, Utsunomiya, Toyama, Osaka, Koshien (two games), Shizuoka, Narumi (see Fig. 5.1) and Nishinomiya, and then again in Tokyo at Jingu Stadium on November 10 with an All-Central league team, and ending with four more games at Jingu Stadium, Okayama, Korakuen and again at Jingu Stadium. The team played sixteen games in total with the last game held on November 19 at Jingu Stadium. DiMaggio himself did not complete the tour, however. After hitting an eighth-inning home run off Nagoya Dragons' ace Shigeru Sugishita on November 10 at Jingu Studium, the Yankees called their slugger home. The home run against Sugishita would be DiMaggio's last hit. One month later, on December 11, 'Joltin' Joe' announced his retirement.[28]

One year after his retirement, DiMaggio appeared on VOA, speaking to Japanese fans about the 1952 baseball season and giving his take on how his former rivals performed during the previous season. According to a document

26 Masaru Hatano, *Nichibei Yakyu no Kakehashi: Suzuki Sotaro no Jinsei to Shoriki Matsutaro* (Bridge over Japan-U.S. baseball: The life of Suzuki Sotaro and Shoriki Matsutaro) (Fuyo Shobo Shuppan, 2013), pp. 199–200.

27 Masaru Hatano, *Nichibei Yakyu Shi:Major wo Oikaketa 70 Nen* (History of U.S.-Japan baseball: 70 years chasing the Major League) (PHP, 2001), pp. 207–208.

28 Ibid., pp. 213–215.

in the folder dated October 22, 1952, fifty copies of a photograph of DiMaggio in a suit standing in front of a VOA microphone (see Photo 5.2) were sent to Japan along with ten copies of a press release promoting the program.[29]

The sixth file listed is on an interview with Yankees manager Charles Dillon 'Casey' Stengel. Perhaps the greatest baseball manager of all time, in his twelve years with the Yankees, Stengel led New York to ten American League pennants and eight World Series championships, including five in a row (1949 to 1953). Stengel was the Yankees manager during DiMaggio's last three seasons, 1949 through 1951. The entire text of the press release, dated April 15, 1953, promoting the program with Stengel is included below:

Yankee Manager Talks it over with VOA Sports Editor

NEW YORK— 'If only Cleveland weren't in the league…!'

In an exchange interview with VOA sports editor Bob Allison, Casey Stengel, manager of the New York Yankees, thus summed up his team's chances of becoming the first in baseball history to win five pennants in a row. The famous baseball pilot added that he considered his outfield the best he's had in four years.

The interview, held in Stengel's office in the Yankee Clubhouse, took place just before the opening of the baseball season, and introduced VOA's 1953 baseball news reports.

In addition to Allison's Sunday Sports Show, the Voice presents baseball news coverage each day, with complete scores, at 7:30 PM Tokyo time, on its English language broadcast, and each Monday at 6:30 PM on its Japanese language broadcast.

C-780

4/16/53 RAG[30]

A publicity photograph of Stengel in his uniform with Bob Allison holding a VOA microphone was attached to the press release (see Photo 5.3). On April 17, fifteen sets of this material were sent to Tokyo by airmail. The word, 'Cleveland', in the article refers to the Yankees' chief rivals, the Cleveland Indians of the American League. The Yankees did win their fifth

---

29 'Joe DiMaggio to be heard on Voice of America', Box 1, 'Japan—Sports Show: Joe DiMaggio (C-180)' Folder.

30 'Yankee Manager Talks it over with VOA Sports Editor', Box 1, 'Japan—Yankee Manager Interview (C-780)' Folder.

Figure 5.1 1951–52 U.S.-Japan baseball games pamphlet (selected MLB team)
Source: Takeshi Tanikawa Collection.

Photo 5.2 Joe DiMaggio
Source: National Archives and Records Administration (VOA publicity photos).

straight pennant in 1953, setting a new Major League record that still stands. Casey's comments about Cleveland were prophetic, however, as Cleveland would win the 1954 American League pennant, keeping the Yankees from winning a sixth-straight pennant (and, potentially, keeping the team from winning ten-straight pennants, as the Yankees would win another four consecutive pennants, starting in 1955).[31]

VOA—'Jackie Robinson: Leading Baseball Star'

The seventh and final folder listed in Table 5.2 is the one featuring Jackie Robinson. The radio special, 'Jackie Robinson: Leading Baseball Star', was produced in February 1951, earlier than the six other baseball programs, and prior to the resumption of Japanese-language broadcasts on September 3, 1951. The press release contained in the file does not state the broadcast date, but a handwritten note found in the margins indicates that fifteen copies of the package were sent to Japan on February 4, 1951. It is possible that the package was sent to Japan that year, but the fact that the same kind of package was sent to the Near East on February 4, 1952 raises the likelihood that the date was recorded in error.[32] The folder entitled 'Japan: Jackie Robinson' contained no photographs, nor did it include information on the

Photo 5.3
Casey Stengel with Bob Allison
Source: National Archives and Records Administration (VOA publicity photos).

---

31 Joseph Durso, *Casey & Mr. McGraw* (The Sporting News, 1989), p. 319.

32 'Jackie Robinson, Leading Baseball Star, Broadcast to Japan over the Voice of America', Box 1, 'Japan—Jackie Robinson' Folder.

delivery schedule or the number of press releases and photographs sent to Japan, or even the addresses to which they were sent.[33] If the package was sent to Japan in 1951, it is possible that such information was not collected early on in that year. Perhaps because VOA had not yet started its Japanese-language partnership with NHK, this information was not yet needed.

As we saw above, Japanese-language broadcasting programs, in the case of baseball games, were provided to the Japanese audience with a short time lag. The selection of which athletes to interview was based on the familiarity and popularity of each athlete among the Japanese people. VOA sought athletes who would entertain Japanese audiences.

The programs about Jackie Robinson, however, were not only designed to entertain. VOA created these programs at the State Department's direction to impact listeners all over the world. Because the initial broadcasts were in English, there were not many VOA listeners in Japan when VOA broadcasts started in that country. The intention of this broadcast is clear, however, based on the inclusion of Robinson's comments that he knows about baseball in Japan, and even knows the names of baseball stadiums there, which would be pleasing to the Japanese people. Below is the press release regarding the broadcast on Robinson:

JACKIE ROBINSON, LEADING BASEBALL STAR BROADCAST TO JAPAN OVER VOICE OF AMERICA

NEW YORK—'It would be a great thrill for me if I could visit Japan this year', says Jackie Robinson, leading American baseball star, who recently discussed 'Baseball in the United States' in a special broadcast to Japan, over The Voice of America.

Mr. Robinson, second baseman for the famous Brooklyn 'Dodgers' and recipient of many major awards, broadcast during the ceremonies marking the Japanese-American Citizens League Installations.

'I've heard a great deal about baseball in Japan from friends, from reading newspaper articles, and from my fans', Mr. Robinson told Japanese listeners. 'I hope soon to be able to watch baseball from the Kormkuen [sic; Korakuen] Stadium in Tokyo'.

---

33 Ibid.

On the VOA broadcast Mr. Robinson also discussed growing interest in baseball in other overseas areas, gave 'Big League' advice to young athletes, and analyzed how professional athletes spend their off-season in the United States.

Voted the 'most valuable player in the National League in 1948' [sic], Mr. Robinson also received the George Washington Carver medal for 'contributions to race relations'.

B-221[34]

With the end of World War II, baseball-related periodicals and magazines resumed publication in Japan. These publications not only offered articles about professional baseball in Japan, they also carried information about the American Major League. The coverage of American baseball in Japanese publications proves that both those affiliated with baseball in Japan and Japanese baseball fans had more than a passing interest in baseball in the United States. As the emergence and success of Jackie Robinson was one of the biggest stories in U.S. sports, Japanese publications carried all sorts of stories about the Brooklyn infielder. The VOA press release not only described Robinson as a superior athlete, it also emphasized that his success represented a significant blow to racial discrimination.

Prior to Jackie Robinson taking the field for the Brooklyn Dodgers, one of the most famous African Americans in the U.S. was a botanist named George Washington Carver. Born into slavery in 1864, before the end of the Civil War, Carver had urged rotating cotton crops with legumes such as peanuts or soybeans to replenish depleted soil. Carver's work made a significant contribution to American agriculture. When Carver died in 1943, Franklin D. Roosevelt, then president of the United States, made a $30,000 contribution toward the building of a monument to commemorate his accomplishments. Soon after that, the George Washington Carver Memorial Institute Race Relations Award was established to honor his scientific endeavors. In 1949, Jackie Robinson was selected as the recipient of that award.[35] The image of Jackie Robinson was perfect as an American role model that the Department

---

34 Ibid.

35 John Vernon, 'An Archival Odyssey: The Search for Jackie Robinson, Federal Records and African American History', *Prologue Magazine*, Vol. 29, No. 2, Summer 1997; http://www.archives.gov/publications/prologue/1997/summer/jackie-robinson.html (last date of access: July 28, 2020).

of State wished to spread all over the world. Utilizing his image was a means to display the racial unification of the United States of America.

On February 3, 1952, exactly one year after the handwritten date on the press release, the VOA sent a press release regarding a radio program with a similar title to the Near East. The contents of the radio program probably included some of the same material that aired in Japan, but the contents of the press release differed considerably. Below is the text of the VOA press release sent to the Near East:

JACKIE ROBINSON, LEADING AMERICAN BASEBALL STAR, BROADCASTS OVER THE VOICE OF AMERICA

NEW YORK—'Sportsmanship—being able to lose as well as win—is the most important thing in athletics', says Jackie Robinson, leading American baseball star, who recently discussed athletic standards in the United States, in a special interview over The Voice of America.

Mr. Robinson, second baseman for the famous Brooklyn 'Dodgers' and recipient of many major sports awards, broadcast from a Boy's Recreational Club in New York's 'Harlem' district. During his seasonal vacation from professional baseball, Mr. Robinson gives sports instruction to young club members.

On the VOA broadcast Mr. Robinson discussed growing interest in baseball in overseas areas, gave 'Big League' advice to young athletes, and analyzed the life long importance of early sports training.

Voted the 'most valuable player in the National League in 1948' [sic], Mr. Robinson also received twice the George Washington Carver medal for 'contributions to race relations'.

B-221[36]

As the recording location of the interview differed from that announced in the press release sent to Japan, it is likely that, after multiple VOA interviews, the interviews were edited for specific regions. Furthermore, a separate press release seems to have been created for each broadcasting location. The press release included a publicity photograph of Robinson wearing a suit and tie and standing in front of a VOA microphone (see Photo 5.4). Table 5.3

---

36 'Jackie Robinson, Leading American Baseball Star, Broadcast over the Voice of America', Box 5, 'Near East—Jackie Robinson' Folder.

presents a list, broken down by country and city, of the number of copies of VOA press packages sent to the Near East, Africa and South Asia. The numbers in parenthesis indicate that the original number was crossed-out and a new number was handwritten alongside it.

By including the countries and cities that did not receive any press packages, Table 5.3 provides a clue as to how the State Department divided the material by region in order to pursue its international cultural diplomacy policies. A total of 120 copies of the photo were originally sent to seventeen cities, and the press release was originally sent to the same seventeen cities. In addition to three more, a grand total of 123 photo prints were developed and sent by airmail on February 4, 1952. This was recorded in a handwritten note in the margins.[37]

It seems likely that the South American version of the broadcast was aired at around the same time that the program was broadcast in the Near East. Although the broadcast date for the Near East is not included in the

Photo 5.4 Jackie Robinson (publicity photo for Special Program for the Near East)

Source: National Archives and Records Administration (VOA publicity photos).

37 Ibid.

Near East, Africa, South Asia	Copies Sent
Afghanistan: Kabul	6
Algeria: Algiers	4 (10)
Belgian Congo: Leopoldville	5 (5)
Ceylon: Colombo	10
East Africa: Nairobi	8
Egypt: Alexandria	0
Cairo	4
Ethiopia: Addis Ababa	10
French West Africa: Dakar	8
India: Bombay	0
Calcutta	0
Lucknow	0
Madras	0 (7)
New Delhi	8
French West Indies: Martinique	8
Gold Coast: Accra	8
Iran: Meshed	0
Tehran	6
Iraq: Baghdad	4
Israel: Tel Aviv	0
Jordan: Amman	0
Lebanon: Beirut	0
Liberia: Monrovia	10
Libya: Tripoli	8
French Morocco: Casablanca	6
Morocco: Tangier	7
Pakistan: Dacca	0
Karachi	0
Lahore	0
Saudi Arabia: Jidda	0
Syria: Damascus	0
Tunisia: Tunis	0
Turkey: Ankara	0
Istanbul	0
Izmir	0
Union of South Africa: Johannesburg	0
Pretoria	0
Subtotal	120
In file	3
Total	123

Table 5.3 Number of copies of the press release about the Jackie Robinson VOA broadcast sent to the Near East, Africa and South Asia

Source: 'Jackie Robinson, Leading American Baseball Star, Broadcast over the Voice of America', Box 5, 'Near East—Jackie Robinson' Folder.

file, the program date for South America is specified as February 10, 1952.[38] The press release and photograph were sent to South America on January 31, 1952.[39] Below is the text of the press release sent to South America:

JACKIE ROBINSON, LEADING NORTH AMERICAN BASEBALL STAR, TO BE INTERVIEWED OVER THE VOICE OF AMERICA, FEBRUARY 10

NEW YORK—Jackie Robinson, leading North American baseball player, demonstrates batting techniques to Bob Allison, Voice of America sports editor, while preparing for a special English-language interview to be heard on VOA's 'In the Spotlight', Sunday, February 10 at 8 PM, New York Time.

Mr. Robinson, second baseman for the famous Brooklyn 'Dodgers' and recipient of many major sports awards, will broadcast from a Boy's Recreational Club in New York's 'Harlem' district. During his seasonal vacation from professional baseball, Mr. Robinson gives sports instruction to youngsters who belong to this club.

On the VOA broadcast Mr. Robinson will discuss baseball interest in North and South America, reminisce about the season he spent playing baseball in Venezuela (1945), and give 'Big League' advice to young athletes.

Asked to state his personal code of sportsmanship, Mr. Robinson said, in a pre-broadcast interview, 'Sportsmanship is the most important characteristic in athletics. When a young boy is able to lose gracefully as well as win, he's almost sure to become a leader in his field, in later life!'

Voted the 'most valuable player in the National League in 1949', Mr. Robinson also received twice the George Washington Carver medal for 'contributions to betterment of race relations'.

B-222[40]

The press release for South America and that for the Near East both indicate that the interview took place in a 'boys' recreational club' in Harlem, leading one to conclude that both recordings come from the same interview. Though the documents state that both the Near East and South American versions of

---

38 'Jackie Robinson, Leading North American Baseball Star, to be Interviewed over the Voice of America, February 10', Box 8, 'LATAM—Jackie Robinson' Folder.

39 Ibid.

40 Ibid.

the broadcast aired on February 10, 1952, it is possible that the Near East program aired in 1951, at around the time when the program for Japan aired, and the year of broadcast of the Near East program may have just been a typographical error.

Possible evidence for this theory is based on an error in the press release sent to Japan that was repeated on that sent to the Near East but corrected on the press release sent to South America. The press release sent to Japan and the one sent to the Near East are wrong about the year Robinson won the National League's Most Valuable Player (NL MVP) award. Both releases indicate he won the MVP in 1948, when, in fact, St. Louis Cardinals player Stan Musial won the award that year. The press release sent to South America correctly reports that Robinson won the NL MVP in 1949. In addition, while the press release sent to Japan states that Robinson was awarded the George Washington Carver Award only once, that sent to the Near East and South America states he won it twice. There is no evidence that Jackie Robinson was awarded the George Washington Carver Award twice, but it is clear that he won the NL MVP award only once, in 1949. Another possibility is that both the Near East and South American versions of the broadcast aired on February 10, 1952, and the information about him receiving the George Washington Carver Award on the press release for Japan was amended to 'received twice' on that for the Near East and South America. If the handwritten notes in the margins are correct, the program should have been sent to South America on January 31, 1952 and to the Near East four days later on February 4, 1952.[41]

Minor factual errors on the press releases are not important. What is important is that, by touting Jackie Robinson as a symbol of improved race relations, VOA had discovered an effective method to communicate with the people of these regions. Robinson represented someone familiar to the audience in these regions. For the listeners in South America, VOA emphasized the fact that Robinson played a season in Venezuela before his debut in the Major League. For Japanese listeners, the program stressed that Robinson was familiar with Korakuen Stadium and that he found the Japanese fans to be enthusiastic. Table 5.4 presents a list, broken down by country and city, of the number of copies of the VOA press packages sent to South America (including Mexico, Central America and the Caribbean).

---

41 As far as the date is concerned, the only clue to the broadcasting date and date the photos were sent to the cities and countries is the handwritten memo in the margin of the press release.

Again, the numbers in parenthesis indicate that the original number was crossed-out and a new number was handwritten next to it.

The reason VOA did not send any packages to Brazil was probably because Portuguese, not Spanish, was spoken in that country. Proof that the State Department considered South American nations politically significant can be found in the fact that 200 photographs of Robinson with Bob Allison (see Photo 5.5) were sent to the region, more than were sent to the Near East

Latin America	Copies Sent
Argentina: Buenos Aires	12
Bolivia: La Paz	10
Brazil: Porto Alegre Rio de Janeiro Recife San Paulo	0 0 0 0
Chile: Santiago	10
Colombia: Bogota	10
Costa Rica: San Jose	10
Cuba: Havana	11
Dominican Republic: Ciudad Trujillo	12
Ecuador: Quito	15
El Salvador: San Salvador	9
Guatemala: Guatemala City	2
Haiti: Port au Prince	10
Honduras: Tegucigalpa	8
Mexico: Mexico City Monterrey	12 8
Nicaragua: Managua	10
Panama: Panama City	10
Paraguay: Asuncion	8
Peru: Lima	12
Uruguay: Montevideo	8 (9)
Venezuela: Caracas Maracaibo	7 0
Subtotal	194
In file	6
Total	200

Table 5.4 Number of copies of the press release about the Jackie Robinson VOA broadcast sent to South America

or Far East. Because of its proximately to the U.S., the American government believed that it was crucial to have friendly nations in South America.

During World War II, Hollywood reinforced the positive image of the U.S. in South America and helped promote Franklin D. Roosevelt's 'Good Neighbor Policy' in that region. The film industry worked closely with the Coordinator of Inter-American Affairs (CIAA)—a wartime agency established by the government. Financial considerations also influenced the movie industry's involvement in the Latin American market. The war closed most of the European market to Hollywood filmmakers, and, even before Pearl Harbor, growing tension between the U.S. and Japan meant that practically no American movies were being shown in the Far East. The same was true for the sports industry, especially baseball. South America not only offered a potential market for American-made sporting goods, it also had the potential to become a significant source of future professional baseball players. Consequently, after the war, many saw South America's importance as a region interested in baseball as second to only that of Japan.

In addition to Japan, VOA also sent a broadcast to the Philippines and other nations in the Far East. The broadcast to the Far East, excluding Japan, was aired on March 2, 1952. Not only did VOA send packages to fewer places in the Far East than it did to South America or the Near East, Africa

Photo 5.5
Jackie Robinson with Bob Allison (publicity photo for Special Program for South America)

Source:
National Archives and Records Administration (VOA publicity photos).

or South Asia, VOA also generally sent fewer press releases to each Far East location. The press packages sent to the Far East, however, contained additional material not sent to other locations, including three sets of a three-page document entitled 'Story', which explained the background of the broadcast, as well as two manuscripts for recordings of promotional announcements, one thirty seconds long and the other fifteen seconds long. The file also contains a memo dated February 7, 1952, written by the program's English-speaking host, Hank Miller, which was sent to Jean Baer in the Philippines congratulating her for a 'very nice job on the sports special of America Calling the Philippines'.[42] The press release for the Philippines apparently refers to a boys track meet in Legaspi (Legazpi), the capital city of the Philippine province of Albay.[43] Below is the text of the press release sent to the Philippines:

BASEBALL STAR JACKIE ROBINSON SALUTES LEGASPI MEET ATHLETES ON VOICE OF AMERICA'S 'AMERICA CALLING THE PHILIPPINES', MARCH 2

NEW YORK—Jackie Robinson (left), leading American baseball star, will offer an 'opening day salute' to the young athletes participating in the Interscholastic Athletic Meet in Legaspi, on The Voice of America's 'America Calling the Philippines', Sunday, March 2. Here the crack second baseman for the Brooklyn 'Dodgers' is shown discussing the forthcoming broadcast with VOA's Hank Miller, program host.

'America Calling the Philippines' is broadcast over VOA medium wave at 7:30 PM; at 9:30 PM over DZFM and at 8:00 PM in Cebu. (All times local Manila Time.)

B-223[44]

'Story', the three-page document containing background material on the broadcast, featured additional information not aired on the program. The VOA probably included it with the package in the hope that local members of

---

42 Letter from Hank Miller to Jean Baer, 2/7/1952, Box 15, 'Far East—Jackie Robinson' Folder.

43 'Baseball Star Jackie Robinson Salutes Legaspi Meet Athletes on Voice of America's "America Calling the Philippines", March 2', Box 15, 'Far East—Jackie Robinson' Folder.

44 Ibid.

the Philippine media would write articles promoting the program. According to the materials, in addition to Jackie Robinson, other individuals associated with sports in the U.S. sent comments, including Dr. Randolph Manning, the chairman of the Foreign Relations Committee of the United States Football Association, Dr. Bernard Landuyt, the former assistant track and field coach of the Philippines delegation to the Far Eastern Games held in Manila in 1934, Dr. W.W. Marquardt, who served as the Director of Education of the Philippines in 1916, and Joe Lapchick, the head coach of the New York Knickerbockers professional basketball team. The press material shows that the broadcast also featured Francisco Salvacion, a Filipino folk singer, performing 'Take Me Out to the Ball Game'. It was Salvacion's third appearance on VOA.[45]

Dr. Landuyt's statement echoed U.S. sports policy, as applied to the occupation of Japan:

> We Filipinos and Americans who have worked and fought together for great causes, must never forget our common understanding of athletic competition. Sports contributes to the Philippine tradition of fair play, and hence to the national strength of character.[46]

Prior to gaining independence in 1946, and excluding World War II when it fell under Japanese control, the Philippines had been occupied by the United States. Gen. Douglas MacArthur, who served as Chief of Staff of the United States Army, was also the Military Advisor to the Commonwealth Government of the Philippines, before he reigned in occupied Japan. As a result, like Japan, the Philippines became a stronghold for U.S. policy in the Far East. In addition, because English was the official language of the Philippines, the VOA's decision to establish a special program for the island nation made sense. Table 5.5 presents a list, broken down by country and city, of the numbers of copies of the VOA photographs of Robinson with Hank Miller (see Photo 5.6), 'Story' and promotional announcements that were sent to the Far East. [47]

45 'Story', Box 15, 'Far East—Jackie Robinson' Folder.
46 'Baseball Star Jackie Robinson Headlines Guest List for Voice of America Tribute to Legaspi Meet', Box 15, 'Far East—Jackie Robinson' Folder.
47 Box 15, 'Far East—Jackie Robinson' Folder.

The Far East	Photos	Stories	Promos
Australia: Melbourne	0	0	0
Sydney	0	0	0
Burma: Rangoon	0	0	0
Mandalay	0	0	0
China: Hong Kong	0	0	0
Formosa: Taipei	0	0	0
Indonesia: Djakarta	7	2	3
Medan	0	0	0
Surabaya	0	0	0
Japan: Tokyo	0	0	0
Ido	0	0	0
Korea: Pusan	10	3	3
Malaya: Kuala Lumpur	5	2	2
Penang	0	0	0
Singapore	7	3	3
New Zealand: Wellington	0	0	0
Philippines: Cebu	8	3	3
Davao	8	2	2
Manila	12	4	4
Thailand: Bangkok	0	0	0
Vietnam (Indochina): Saigon	0	0	0
Subtotal	57	19	20
In file	3	0	0
Total	60	19	20

Table 5.5 Number of copies of photographs, 'Story' and promotional spots about the Jackie Robinson VOA broadcast sent to the Far East

Photo 5.6
Jackie Robinson
with Hank Miller
(publicity photo for
Special Program for the
Far East—except Japan)
Source:
National Archives and
Records Administration
(VOA publicity photos).

Apparently, none of these packages were sent to Japan, although, as discussed above, the VOA had previously broadcast a program about Jackie Robinson perhaps as early as 1951. There are two destinations listed under Japan: one is 'Tokyo' and the other is 'Ido'. 'Ido' is not the name of a major Japanese city. This destination appears to be a mystery, but one of the meanings of '*ido*' in Japanese is 'moving'. Movie showings of CIE films, which I discussed in Chapter Four, were called '*ido eisha*' in Japanese, which literally means 'traveling movie showings'. So, it is possible that 'Ido' as one of the destinations indicates that the VOA office in Japan was handling 'radio-listening gatherings of Japanese people' in rural areas.

The nations and regions in which Robinson's program was broadcast were very important strongholds for U.S. international cultural diplomacy. These places included Japan, where, as an occupied nation, interest in baseball was exceptionally high; the Near East and Africa, where many people had black skin like Robinson; South America, where potential Major League talent resided; and the Philippines, an English-speaking former American colony.

U.S. authorities believed that baseball, especially with Jackie Robinson serving as a symbol of racial harmony, was an effective method to spread a positive image of America. The U.S., engaged in a Cultural Cold War with the Soviet Union, resolved to send its propaganda message to the rest of the world.

The special VOA broadcast featuring Jackie Robinson was an example of the politically motivated use of sports by the U.S. government to showcase the assault on racial discrimination and other progressive social changes reputed to be taking place in America. The message was clear: regardless of one's racial background, if one put in the effort, one could succeed in the U.S. This message seemed to prove that America's democratic society was superior to the socialist society of the Soviet Union. Robinson's special program was strategic, and it served its purpose well.

Robinson was not the only vehicle used by the U.S. government to spread this message. The government reinforced its racial progressivism by including a program about Frederick D. 'Fritz' Pollard, a talented African American football player, in the VOA broadcasts to Japan. The press release promoting the show on Pollard carried the following quote from President-Elect (presidential candidate) Dwight D. Eisenhower:

As you perhaps know, I have always been interested in the problems of minority groups and have been particularly impressed by the tremendous progress of the Negro race. I am convinced that much of this growth and development has been directly due to the inspiration and example of outstanding Negro athletes.[48]

Pollard was one of two African American men who played in the National Football League (NFL; then called the American Professional Football Association) in 1920, the league's inaugural season. A running back, Pollard helped his team, the Akron Pros, win the first NFL championship with a record of eight wins, zero losses and three ties. Pollard, however, did more than play football—he also coached it. In 1921, while still a running back on the team, he was named co-head coach. Pollard became a member of the Professional Football Hall of Fame in 2005.[49] It is, however, almost certain that Pollard did not have the same impact as Jackie Robinson in Japan. While baseball was very popular in Japan, Japanese sports fans had almost no knowledge about American football, despite the fact that both sports were immensely popular in the U.S.

In this chapter, I examined how Robinson, as a positive image of the U.S., was used in VOA radio programs in the nations and regions including Japan that the U.S. regarded as key strongholds for its international cultural diplomacy.

At least especially in Japan, the favorable image of Jackie Robinson was stressed in the context of the Cultural Cold War, not only in VOA radio programs, but also in the print media including baseball fan magazines and comic books for the younger generation. I will focus on these printed media in the next chapter.

---

48 'Chairman of Negro Athlete Hall of Fame Reports on Negroes' Contribution to U.S. Community Life', Box 1, 'Japan—Negro Hall of Fame: Frederick D. Pollard (C-424)' Folder.

49 http://www.profootballhof.com/hof/member.aspx?PLAYER_ID=242 (last date of access: July 28, 2020).

The Use of the Image of Jackie Robinson in the Print Media

▌ Biographical film, *The Jackie Robinson Story*

Before examining the use of the favorable image of Jackie Robinson in the print media, including baseball fan magazines and comic books, I consider the motion picture version of Robinson's story to compare its contents and depiction with the print media version.

Jackie Robinson was so popular in the U.S. that, in 1950, Hollywood turned his life into a movie. In an unusual move, Robinson portrayed himself in *The Jackie Robinson Story* (see Fig. 6.1). At the time, it was not uncommon for a celebrity who was not an actor/actress to play him/herself in a cameo role in a film. For instance, former New York Yankee slugger George Herman 'Babe' Ruth portrayed himself in *The Pride of the Yankees*, a 1942 biopic about Ruth's deceased teammate, Lou Gehrig. In Ruth's case, it was just a cameo appearance and the sequences in which he appeared were limited. Robinson's case was different — he, a non-actor, starred in the film.

Unlike Ruth, who had been retired for seven years when he appeared in *The Pride of the Yankees*, Robinson was in the prime of his career during the filming of *The Jackie Robinson Story*, having just won the National League's Most Valuable Player award. Except for scenes depicting his childhood, Robinson portrayed himself throughout the film. African American journalist Wendell Smith wrote the narrative upon which the film was based,[1] and film producer Mort Briskin offered to transform Smith's story into a film. Regarding the pre-production process, it is said that Dodgers co-owner Branch Rickey gave permission for the film to go ahead on one condition — that Robinson and other members of the Brooklyn Dodgers played themselves in the film. Screenwriter Louis Pollock, who would later work on the television series, *Alfred Hitchcock Presents*, turned Smith's

---

1 As a reporter for the *Pittsburgh Courier*, a leading African American newspaper with a nationwide audience, and the *Chicago Herald American* in Chicago, Illinois, Smith published the book as a verbatim record of Robinson's own words, just after the end of his Major League debut in the 1947 season.

narrative into a screenplay, which was further polished-up by Lawrence Taylor and Arthur Mann. Veteran director Alfred E. Green, who had already established a name for himself with the 1946 biopic *The Jolson Story*, oversaw the filming.[2]

The Jackie Robinson Story opens with a narrator saying, 'This is the story of a boy and his dream. But more than that, it is the story of an American boy'. The movie begins by depicting Robinson's childhood, before moving on to his college career at the University of California, Los Angeles, where he lettered in four varsity sports: baseball, football, basketball and track and field. The film then turns to Robinson's baseball career, including his stint

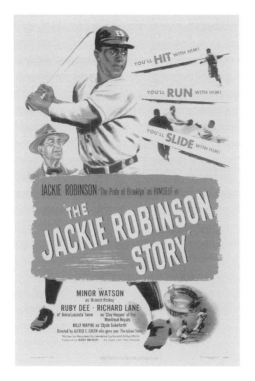

Figure 6.1 The Jackie Robinson Story original movie poster (1950)
Source: © *Eagle Lion Films (Takeshi Tanikawa Collection).*

2 Jonathan Eig, *Opening Day: The Story of Jackie Robinson's First Season* (Simon & Schuster, 2007), p. 263; *American Film Institute Catalog of Motion Pictures Produced in the United States: Feature Films, 1941–1950, Film Entries A–L* (AFI Volume F4) (University of California Press, 1999), p. 1201; Jackie Robinson (As told to Wendell Smith), *Jackie Robinson: My Own Story* (Greenberg, 1948).

with the Kansas City Monarchs of the Negro American League where he attracted the attention of Branch Rickey, then looks at his year with the Minor League Montreal Royals of the International League and finally depicts his promotion to the Brooklyn Dodgers. Although the film does not identify the committee, it ends with Robinson giving his pro-America address before the House Committee on Un-American Activities in July 1949.[3]

The Jackie Robinson Story appeared in theaters in the U.S. in May 1950, but, despite the fact that Japanese audiences had proved fond of American-made baseball movies offered by the CIE and baseball programs aired by VOA, the film was not released in Japan. This is surprising, considering that not only was Robinson a popular figure in Japan, but the release of the film would have also offered an excellent opportunity to positively display improving race relations in the U.S.

The reason *The Jackie Robinson Story* did not show in Japan is very simple. During the occupation, the Central Motion Picture Exchange, the Japanese branch of the Motion Picture Export Association, which distributed American films overseas, only had access to American films produced by the eight major studios—Columbia, MGM, Paramount, RKO, 20th Century Fox, Warner Bros., United Artists and Universal. Although the Central Motion Picture Exchange later came to deal with Republic Pictures, and Daiei, one of the major Japanese studios, started to deal with another medium-sized studio, Walt Disney, GHQ/SCAP established a 'one nation, one distributor' rule when the occupation started. *The Jackie Robinson Story*, however, was produced by a small, relatively unknown production company called Jewell Pictures, and was distributed in the U.S. by Eagle-Lion Films, a B-class-film producer specializing in small productions located on Hollywood's 'Poverty Row'. Although after a long period of time it became easier to see *The Jackie Robinson Story* in Japan on television or DVD, the film has never been distributed to theatres in that country.[4]

According to a public opinion survey, after Bing Crosby, Jackie Robinson was the next most admired man in the U.S. in 1947.[5] Why was his biographical film—a high profile film in which Robinson played

---

3 DVD Movie (Region Free), *The Jackie Robinson Story*, MMIII Miracle Pictures, a Division of PMC Corp. De., 2004.

4 Akio Hata, ed., *Nijusseiki America Eiga Jiten* (The encyclopedia of 20th century American Movies) (Cataloghouse, 2002).

5 LeRoy Ashby, *With Amusement for All: A History of American Popular Culture Since 1830* (University Press of Kentucky, 2006), p. 287.

himself—produced by a small-scale, shabby film company located on Poverty Row? One theory suggests that when the film's producer contacted the two major studios, the studios requested that the script be changed to indicate that Robinson's baseball skills developed from the instruction he received from white coaches. The producer refused this request and instead looked for another studio to make the picture.[6] Regarding his experience making the film, Robinson stated in his autobiography, 'It was exciting to participate in it. However, I later realized it had been made too quickly, that it was budgeted too low, and that, if it had been made later in my career, it could have been done much better'.[7]

Even if the film had been produced by a major studio without plot alterations, *The Jackie Robinson Story* would probably not have been available in Japan. During the occupation, U.S. policy prohibited the Japanese release of any film that contained negative depictions of American society, even if such depictions constituted a small part of the movie. For example, Frank Capra's 1939 film *Mr. Smith Goes to Washington* was released in Japan in 1940 with the approval of Japan's Ministry of Home Affairs, despite the fact that the U.S.-Japan relationship was deteriorating in the lead-up to the Pacific War. After the war ended, however, GHQ/SCAP banned the reissue of the film in Japan because it illustrated U.S. political corruption.[8]

Without depicting the hardships Robinson faced, including racial hatred, verbal abuse and explicit threats directed at the African American community, *The Jackie Robinson Story* would not have been as compelling. Censorship, of course, was not limited to Japan. From 1934, the 'Breen Office' (the Production Code Administration), set the rules for what Hollywood could and could not portray in its motion pictures.[9] The Breen Office, however, implemented a form of self-censorship rather than government-imposed restrictions. Despite complaints about the film's depiction of racial tensions,

---

6 Donald Bogle, *Toms, Coons, Mulattoes, Mammies, and Bucks: An Interpretive History of Blacks in American Films*, 4th edition (Continuum International Publishing Group Ltd., 2001), p. 184.

7 Jackie Robinson (As told to Alfred Duckett), *I Never Had It Made* (G. P. Putnam's Sons, 1972), p. 101.

8 Kyoko Hirano, *Mr. Smith Goes to Tokyo: Japanese Cinema Under the American Occupation, 1945–1952* (Smithsonian Institution Press, 1992), p. 246.

9 Richard Maltby, 'The Production Code and the Hays Office', in Tino Balio, ed., *Grand Design: Hollywood as a Modern Business Enterprise, 1930–1939* (University of California Press, 1995), pp. 37–72.

the problems it portrayed were mild compared to their representation in Robinson's autobiography.

In many ways, *The Jackie Robinson Story* presented a sanitized version of the racial challenges Robinson faced. For instance, one commentator noted that the film 'could not really use the language that was thrown at Robinson on the field because that would never have passed the censor'.[10] Adding to the controversy, however, was the film's inclusion of a scene in which an Italian American ballplayer objects to Robinson playing on the team. As a result of that scene, an Italian American organization in Jersey City, New Jersey, complained to both of New Jersey's U.S. senators, which prompted Senator H. Alexander Smith to bring the scene to the attention of Senator Edwin C. Johnson, the chairman of the Senate's Interstate and Foreign Policy Committee. Johnson contacted Eric Johnston, the president of the Motion Picture Association of America (MPAA). The MPAA investigated *The Jackie Robinson Story*, and other films, to determine whether Italian Americans were misrepresented in movies. Joseph I. Breen, the director of the 'Breen Office' as noted above, dismissed the complaints by pointing out that, in a later scene in the film, Robinson's Italian American teammates come to his defense when he is threatened by an opposing player. According to Breen, these two scenes balanced each other out when considered from the standpoint of fairness sought by the Production Code.[11]

Although *The Jackie Robinson Story* included depictions of less than ideal race relations in the U.S., this was not the reason the movie was not exported to Japan. The film had no chance of being distributed in Japan simply because it was not produced by one of the eight major studios. Instead, the State Department and Central Motion Picture Exchange eagerly issued other baseball-related films in Japan. Among the movies available to the Japanese public after the war were *The Pride of the Yankees*, the 1942 biopic about the late-Yankees first baseman Lou Gehrig; *The Stratton Story*, a 1949 film about a baseball player who successfully struggles to resume his career after losing his leg in a hunting accident; and 1948's *The Babe Ruth Story*, a biography about baseball's all-time home run king.[12]

---

10 Jay Robert Nash and Stanley Ralph Ross, *The Motion Picture Guide H-K 1927-1983* (Cinebooks, Inc., 1986), p. 1441.

11 *American Film Institute Catalog of Motion Pictures Produced in the United States: Feature Films, 1941–1950, Film Entries A–L*, p. 1202; Alan Gevinson, ed., *Within Our Gates: Ethnicity in American Films, 1911–1960* (AFI, 1977), p. 515.

12 Akio Hata, ed., *Nijusseiki America Eiga Jiten*, pp. 858, 864, 894.

In 1953, President Eisenhower established the United States Information Agency (USIA), which took over control of VOA. The CIE films discussed in Chapter Four were distributed by the USIA after the organization was established as part of its cultural diplomacy mission. Though it was impossible in occupied Japan to distribute *The Jackie Robinson Story*, produced by a Hollywood film company, it seems to me that the USIA may have found it desirable to create an informational film about Robinson for screenings for foreign audiences.

Although there is no evidence that such a film was ever produced, the USIA did prepare a film script about Jesse Owens, the African American track and field athlete who, in the face of white supremacist rhetoric from German Chancellor Adolph Hitler, excelled at the 1936 Summer Olympics in Berlin.[13] In 1955, as a cultural ambassador of the United States Information Service (USIS), the overseas name for the USIA, Owens toured India, Singapore, Malaya and the Philippines. According to the script, titled *The USIA Activities Overseas*, Owens gave athletic tips to Malayans, who enthusiastically welcomed him to their country. Owens' visit to India was widely covered in the local press.[14] The USIA sent other athletes, both black and white, on 'goodwill tours'. Dave Albritton, an African American track star who was Owens' teammate at the 1936 Berlin Olympics, visited Tehran, Iran, while future U.S. Congressman Bob Mathias, a white athlete who won the decathlon at both the 1948 Summer Olympics in London and the 1952 Summer Olympics in Helsinki, visited Cairo. The script contains the note, 'Through exchange of students and leaders, like these outstanding athletes, the United States is making real progress in increasing mutual understanding with people of other nations'.[15]

---

13 There is a short film clip about USIS programs overseas, including Jesse Owens giving track tips to a Malayan audience, but it does not mean that the film was actually produced based on the script. http://www.criticalpast.com/video/65675024538_international-programs_King-Paul_Queen-Frederika_William-Portner (last date of access: July 30, 2020).

14 'USIS Activities Overseas', July 18, 1956, Movie Scripts, 1942–1965, RG 306, NARA, Records of the U.S. Information Agency, Box 47, Entry 1098, p. 11.

15 Ibid.

Distribution of *The Jackie Robinson Story* via the print media and comics

Although *The Jackie Robinson Story* was not released in Japan, people in Japan came to know Robinson well through other media, such as magazines and comic books. As a result, the Japanese audience became exposed to the racial struggle then taking place in the U.S.

When Jackie Robinson made his Major League debut in 1947, breaking the racial barrier in American baseball, Japanese sports magazines quickly picked up the story. Many of these magazines had only recently resumed publication following the war. For instance, *Baseball Magazine* published its first post-war issue in April 1946. The magazine's June 1, 1947 issue carried an article titled 'Jackie Robinson',[16] which appeared only six weeks after Robinson's first bat with the Dodgers. Considering the speed of information at the time, the fact that this article was published so soon after Robinson's debut can only be attributed to the cultural impact of the event. In August 1949, while Robinson was enjoying the most successful season of his career, *Baseball Fan* published an article about him and Cleveland Indians pitcher Bob Feller.[17] Two months later, *Baseball News* contained an article titled 'Amazing black player: Jackie Robinson from the Dodgers: Will he be chosen as the first Negro MVP?: A brief note on the recent American baseball world'.[18]

In October 1950, the year *The Jackie Robinson Story* was released in theaters in the U.S., *Baseball Magazine* carried a USIS-authored article called 'The Robinson Story' (see Fig. 6.2). The article focused on Robinson's life story, pointing out that 'four years ago, Robinson was an unknown athlete; no one even knew his name. Today, he is, however, one of the most well-known sports athletes'. The article not only reported on Robinson's success

---

16 Masamichi Ohashi, 'Jackie Robinson', *Baseball Magazine*, Vol. 2, No. 5, June 1947, pp. 20–21.

17 Seikichi Nakamura, 'Bei Dai-Rīgu Wadai: Bob Feller to Jackie Robinson' (Topics of the Major League: Bob Feller and Jackie Robinson), *Yakyu-Fan*, Vol. 3, No. 7, August 1949, pp. 46–49.

18 Hiroshi Okamoto, 'Kyoui no Mato Kokujin-Senshu: Dodgers no Jackie Robinson: Hatsu no Saiyuushuu-Senshu to Naruka: Saikin no America Kyuukai Tanshin' (Amazing black player: Jackie Robinson from the Dodgers: Will he be chosen as the first Negro MVP?: A brief note on the recent American baseball world), *Baseball News*, No. 637, pp. 40–41.

with the Dodgers, it also discussed his entire life and how he overcame the challenges he faced through extraordinary focus and dedication.

The article emphasized Robinson's patriotism, and gave special attention to his testimony before the House Committee on Un-American Activities (HUAC). Of the 223 lines in the story, forty-nine of them, nearly one quarter, focused on Robinson's patriotism.

Figure 6.2 Translation of 'The Robinson Story' in *Baseball Magazine*, October 1950, supported by the USIS
Source: ©Baseball Magazine Sha (Takeshi Tanikawa Collection).

Three photographs of Robinson accompanied the article: one in his Dodgers uniform, one with his family and one of suit-clad Robinson testifying before the HUAC.[19] Taken together, the three photos portray a well-balanced individual pursuing an extraordinary baseball career while, at the same time, being a happy family man and a patriotic American.

The article contained Robinson's quote from the HUAC, in which he gave an exemplary testimony as an American who was a devout Christian and a patriot.[20] The article also included Robinson's assurance to the HUAC that African Americans could achieve equality in the U.S. without turning to communism:

> I understand that there are some few Negroes who are members of the Communist Party, and in the event of war with Russia they'd probably act just as any other communist would. So would members of other minority and majority groups […]. And most Negroes—and Italians and Irish and Jews and Swedes and Slavs and other Americans—would act just as all these groups did in the last war. They'd do their best to help their country win the war—against Russia or any other enemy that threatened us. This isn't said as any defense of the Negro's loyalty, because any loyalty that needs defense can't amount to much in the long run. And no one has ever questioned my race's loyalty except a few people who don't amount to very much […]. I am a religious man. Therefore I cherish America where I am free to worship as I please, a privilege which some countries do not give. And I suspect that 999 out of almost any thousand colored Americans you meet will tell you the same thing. But that doesn't mean that we're going to stop fighting race discrimination in this country until we've got it licked. It means that we're going to fight it all the harder because our stake in the future is so big. We can win our fight without the communists and we don't want their help.[21]

Robinson's statement seemed to indicate that he believed American society was superior to that of the Soviet Union. That was exactly the type of thinking that the U.S. government was promoting in its diplomatic policy. Not only did Japanese sports magazines publish stories on

---

19 'USIS Teikyou: Robinson Monogatari' (USIS presents: Robinson story), *Baseball Magazine*, Vol. 5, No. 110, October 1950, pp. 86–87.

20 Ibid.

21 Ibid; https://archive.org/stream/JackieRobinson/robsn3_djvu.txt (last date of access: July 30, 2020).

Jackie Robinson, but his life also became fodder for children's books and magazines. In May 1950, the *Chugakusei no Tomo* (Junior high school students' companion) series distributed by Japanese publisher Shogakukan issued a comic book called *Jackie Robinson* (see Fig. 6.3), as the *furoku* (supplement) to its June issue.[22] *Jackie Robinson* was a Japanese-language comic book that was identical to one issued in the U.S. by Fawcett Publications called *Jackie Robinson: Baseball Hero*.[23] The comic book did not carry a publication date, but information from the University of Michigan, which maintains a comic book archive, indicates that *Jackie Robinson: Baseball Hero* was issued in May 1950 (see Fig. 6.4).[24]

Jackie Robinson: Baseball Hero, which closely followed the plot of the film, *The Jackie Robinson Story*, contained a sanitized version of Robinson's biography. The comic book omitted the harsher events, including the racial slurs, insults and heckling he received from opposing players and fans.

Fawcett Publications, which had been in business since 1919, published numerous serial comic books that focused on heroic characters, including *Captain Marvel*, *Bulletman* and *Spy Smasher*. Fawcett went on to publish at least five more editions of *Jackie Robinson* comic books called the 'Jackie Robinson Series', possibly because of the enormous popularity of the first comic.

At first, Fawcett published a new edition of the 'Jackie Robinson Series' every two months, with a second edition appearing in July 1950, a third in September that year and a fourth in November. After that, new books in the series came out once per year, with the fifth edition appearing in 1951 and the sixth in 1952.[25] The success of the 'Jackie Robinson Series' may have inspired Fawcett to issue more comic books featuring other baseball players, including *Roy Campanella: Baseball Hero*, a biography of another African American Major Leaguer who was the catcher on Robinson's team; *Don*

22 *Jackie Robinson*, a supplement of *Chugakusei no Tomo* (Junior high school students' companion), Vol. 27, No. 3, Shogakukan, June 1950.

23 *Jackie Robinson: Baseball Hero* (Fawcett Publications, May 1950); and *Jackie Robinson*, a supplement of *Chugakusei no Tomo* (Junior high school students' companion), Vol. 27, No. 3, Shogakukan, June 1950.

24 Michigan State University Libraries, Special Collections Division, Reading Room Index to the Comic Art Collection 'Fawcett Publications' (A–Z titles), http://comics.lib.msu.edu/rri/frri/fawc_p.htm (last date of access: July 31, 2020).

25 http://comicbookrealm.com/series/23181/218194/Jackie%20Robinson (last date of access: July 31, 2020).

Figure 6.3 Cover of comic book, *Jackie Robinson*, a supplement of *Chugakusei no Tomo* (Junior high school students' companion), Vol. 27, No. 3, June 1950

Source: © Shougagukan (Takeshi Tanikawa Collection).

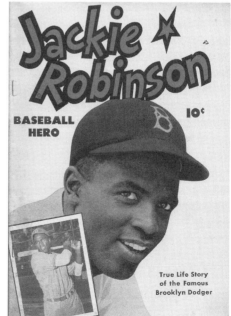

Figure 6.4 Cover of comic book, *Jackie Robinson: Baseball Hero*, published by Fawcett Publications

Source: © Fawcett Publications (Takeshi Tanikawa Collection).

Newcombe: Baseball Hero, a biography of another of Robinson's teammates; and *Larry Doby: Baseball Hero*, a biography of another African American Major Leaguer who made his debut next to Robinson at the Cleveland Indians. Both Newcombe and Doby would later play with the Chunichi Dragons of the Central League of Japanese professional baseball in 1962. Comic books on white ballplayers also appeared, including *Yogi Berra*, a biography of the New York Yankees' catcher, and *Phil Rizzuto* on the Yankees' shortstop, etc. In 1952, Fawcett released *Baseball Heroes*, which is supposedly an anthology of its previously released baseball comic books.[26]

Fawcett's *Jackie Robinson: Baseball Hero*, the original volume in the series, and Shogakukan's *Jackie Robinson* were published almost simultaneously in the U.S. and Japan. Despite the paper shortage then affecting Japan, GHQ/SCAP allowed the comic book to be copyrighted and approved its publication in Japan. It is likely that GHQ/SCAP approved the publication of *Jackie Robinson* because it wanted to promote the story of Jackie Robinson in Japan in order to demonstrate improving race relations in the U.S.

Another possibility is that, although there is no evidence to support my theory, perhaps the U.S. Department of State negotiated with Fawcett to give the copyright to Shogakukan, one of Japan's most reliable and representative publishers, via the CIE (USIS) to publish it in Japan simultaneously. It seems rather natural to think that GHQ/SCAP simply assisted Shogakukan in its purpose.

According to *Honyakuken no Sengoshi* (A postwar history of translation rights), written by Noboru Miyata, the CIE issued intermediate copyrights to the George Thomas Folster Agency and three other parties from France, England and Italy on March 18, 1949.[27] It is possible that Shogakukan obtained its copyright to *Jackie Robinson* from the Folster Agency. In any event, it is significant that *Jackie Robinson* was among the first foreign copyrighted material published in post-war Japan.

There are significant differences between the American *Jackie Robinson: Baseball Hero* and the Japanese version. Generally, American comic books open to the left—they are stapled on the left edge, and the pages are turned from right to left. Japanese comic books, however, open the other way—

---

26 http://www.comicvine.com/fawcetts-baseball-heroes/4050-26321/ (last date of access: July 31, 2020).

27 Noboru Miyata, *Honyakuken no Sengoshi* (Post-war history of translation rights) (Misuzu-Shobou, 1999), pp. 112, 162–175.

stapled on the right edge, the pages are turned from left to right. Therefore, the arrangement of the Japanese book produced a mirror image of *Jackie Robinson: Baseball Hero*. In order to prevent confusion that might be caused by depicting left-handed batters as righties, and right-handed pitchers as southpaws, the individual players were not reversed. The Japanese version of the comic book did, however, reverse the photograph of Robinson that appeared on the cover. The photo was altered so that the letter 'B' on his cap (which stood for 'Brooklyn') was facing in the proper direction.

Both editions were of identical length—thirty-six pages, including sixteen leaves and the inside and outside of both the front and back covers. The American edition was printed in full color, while only the front and back covers of the Japanese version were printed in full color. One side of the sixteen leaves of the Japanese version was printed in two colors, while the other side was printed in only one color.[28]

The symbolic discrimination experienced by Robinson

In addition to the fact that the production process created different versions of the comic book in the U.S. and Japan, the editions also handled sensitive material differently. Of particular interest are the similarities and differences in how the two versions depicted negative events, such as the discrimination experienced by Robinson.

Although Wendell Smith's original narrative explicitly depicted the racial discrimination faced by African Americans, the Production Code enforced by the Breen Office prohibited the makers of *The Jackie Robinson Story* from portraying such incidents in the film. The Breen Office, however, had no control over the print media, and when the movie was turned into a comic book, ten scenes from the thirty-two inner pages displayed either discrimination against African Americans or personal insults directed at Robinson.

The first of these scenes appears on page three of both the American and Japanese version of the comic book in a scene depicting Robinson's college experience. The frame indicates that Robinson was an all-around athlete but showed him applying much more attention to playing football than baseball. In the graphics, Robinson says, 'There's no future for a colored boy in

---

28 *Jackie Robinson*, a supplement of *Chugakusei no Tomo* (Junior high school students' companion), Vol. 27, No. 3, Shogakukan, June 1950.

baseball, sir! They'd never let me in the big league! But, I can make money playing pro football!'[29] These words give the impression that Robinson had given up on the idea of becoming a baseball player due to racial prejudice.

The second scene showing racial tension is found on page seven of both editions. In the frame, Robinson, who had just been discharged from the army and was now a member of the Kansas City Monarchs of the Negro leagues, and Clyde Sukeforth, a scout for the Brooklyn Dodgers, were at a train station attempting to buy tickets to travel to New York. The drawing depicts the clerk in the ticket booth looking at Robinson with disdain.[30]

The third example of racial tension appears on page nine in the American edition and page eight in the Japanese version. The scene takes place shortly after Robinson signed a Minor League contract to play for the Montreal Royals, the top farm club of the Brooklyn Dodgers. In the scene, not only do top MLB officials state their opposition to signing a black player, Robinson also receives a threatening letter from the Ku Klux Klan.[31]

The fourth example is depicted on the following page in both editions. In the scene, an angry fan warns, 'Tell him to get outta town or there'll be trouble at the ball field tomorrow'. The frame also shows Robinson staying at the home of an African American family because he was not allowed to lodge at the hotel with his teammates.[32]

The fifth scene showing racial tension is on page eleven of the American edition and page ten of the Japanese version. The scene depicts Clay Hopper, the manager of the Montreal Royals, standing with Robinson after the club boycotted a spring training game with the Jersey City Giants in Jacksonville, Florida, after a local police officer announced that it was illegal for a black man to play baseball with white players in that city.[33]

The sixth example appears on page eleven of both versions. In this scene, Robinson voluntarily withdraws from the Royals' exhibition game with the Dodgers and keeps his temper in check after the local sheriff ordered

29 Ibid., p. 3; *Jackie Robinson: Baseball Hero* (Fawcett Publications, May 1950), p. 3.

30 *Jackie Robinson*, a supplement of *Chugakusei no Tomo* (Junior high school students' companion), p. 7; *Jackie Robinson: Baseball Hero*, p. 7.

31 *Jackie Robinson*, a supplement of *Chugakusei no Tomo* (Junior high school students' companion), p. 8; *Jackie Robinson: Baseball Hero*, p. 9.

32 *Jackie Robinson*, a supplement of *Chugakusei no Tomo* (Junior high school students' companion), p. 9; *Jackie Robinson: Baseball Hero*, p. 10.

33 *Jackie Robinson*, a supplement of *Chugakusei no Tomo* (Junior high school students' companion), p. 10; *Jackie Robinson: Baseball Hero*, p. 11.

him to leave the field. The frame makes it clear that it was against the law in Daytona Beach, Florida, the location of the game, for white and black players to play baseball together.[34]

Page thirteen features the comic's seventh example of racial tension. In this scene, as Robinson is taking the field for the Montreal Royals, a member of the opposing team yells an insult at Robinson as a black cat appears on the field. The scene also indicates that Robinson led the International League in hitting in 1946.[35] This frame is significant as the symbol of the black cat suggests that, to the opposing team, Robinson was considered an animal.

All of the abovementioned scenes depicted discriminatory treatment that Robinson experienced in his rise to the Major League. The comic books show that, for Robinson, this type of hardship was a test of his ability to tolerate abuse and control his temper. The eighth through tenth scenes continue to show Robinson receiving racial abuse, even after being promoted to the Brooklyn Dodgers of the National League.

The eighth scene of racial abuse, which appears on page nineteen in both the American and Japanese versions of the comic book, shows a racial incident that is treated in a slightly different matter in each edition. The scene, which depicts a game against the Philadelphia Phillies, shows a beanball being thrown at Robinson's head while the Phillies bench jeers at the Dodgers player. In the American version, a Phillies player shouts 'Put the @ξ#%#* in the hospital!' In the Japanese version, the player shouts 'Take the Black player to the hospital'.[36] The first difference can be found in the choice of verbs. 'Put the player in the hospital' conveys a malicious message, while 'Take the player to the hospital' sounds a lot more benevolent. More important is the use of symbols in place of a word in the American edition, representing the traditional form of comic book self-censorship. In all comic books, such symbols indicate that something unpleasant has been said without actually printing the word. Therefore, at first glance, it might appear that the American edition was taking a more sensitive approach than the Japanese edition. A closer examination, however, reveals that it was the Japanese edition that offered the sanitized version of the story. The symbols

---

34 *Jackie Robinson*, a supplement of *Chugakusei no Tomo* (Junior high school students' companion), p. 11; *Jackie Robinson: Baseball Hero*, p. 11.

35 *Jackie Robinson*, a supplement of *Chugakusei no Tomo* (Junior high school students' companion), p. 13; *Jackie Robinson: Baseball Hero*, p. 13.

36 *Jackie Robinson*, a supplement of *Chugakusei no Tomo* (Junior high school students' companion), p. 19; *Jackie Robinson: Baseball Hero*, p. 19.

used in the American version did not replace the term 'Black player'. There is no question that the American edition used the symbols to replace the word '*nigger*', a highly offensive contemptuous term for an African American. Any comic book reader in post-war America would have understood the symbols' intended meaning. By instead using the term 'Black player', the Japanese edition is actually toning down the rhetoric, which makes the scene less offensive.

The ninth scene appears on page twenty-nine of both versions. The scene, which is almost certainly exaggerated and devoid of reality, takes place during a game in Atlanta, Georgia, a city in the Deep South. In the scene, members of the Ku Klux Klan, wearing white hoods, are discussing a plan to lynch Robinson. Later, during the game, one of the Klan members is sitting in the outfield bleachers watching the game. When Robinson comes to bat, he hits a line-drive home run that smacks the Klan member in the chest, knocking him out and putting an end to his scheme. The scene is obviously fictitious, but the author of the comic book saw the need to make it clear that the Ku Klux Klan did not represent all the citizens of Atlanta.

In the next frame, baseball fans are patiently awaiting the arrival of Robinson and the Dodgers. One fan says, 'The Klan is a disgrace to our city!' A second continues, 'There is no law against Negroes and white players meeting in a baseball game! The Dodgers are welcome here!' A third fan adds, 'And I want to see Robinson play!'[37] These statements express the author's desire to display a positive view of Atlanta.

The tenth scene depicting racial tension appears on page thirty-one of both versions. Like the eighth scene found on page nineteen, this one depicts a pitcher throwing a baseball intentionally at Robinson's body.[38] The message is, as Robinson became a superstar, he would continue to face abusive behavior, and the challenges he would face because of his race were incessant.

Despite all the abuse, Robinson kept his cool and never panicked or retaliated. In this manner, he kept the promise he made to Branch Rickey when the Dodgers first signed him to a baseball contract. Because Robinson withstood this abuse, he eventually became a hero, not only supported and admired by the black community, but also by white fans. Within the context of a comic book, however, it was not appropriate to present catharsis to the readers.

37 *Jackie Robinson*, a supplement of *Chugakusei no Tomo* (Junior high school students' companion), p. 29; *Jackie Robinson: Baseball Hero*, p. 29.

38 *Jackie Robinson*, a supplement of *Chugakusei no Tomo* (Junior high school students' companion), p. 31; *Jackie Robinson: Baseball Hero*, p. 31.

The expression of catharsis in the ninth scene proved acceptable, however, because Robinson had no intention of injuring his enemy. The home run hit the Klansman by chance, providing the perfect resolution to the threat he posed.

The comic book depictions of the hardships Robinson faced may have reminded Japanese readers of Chushingura, the Japanese national legend about the hardships faced by the Ako-roshi, a band of forty-seven masterless samurai in the early eighteenth century who avenged the death of their late lord.[39] Like the Ako-roshi, to achieve his dream, Robinson needed to bear the hardship without any form of retaliation. If he became angry, even once, his career and the goodwill that he had amassed would be destroyed. During the occupation, GHQ/SCAP not only prohibited *chanbara* (sword-fighting) films, it also banned films about the national legend of Chushingura. Japanese filmmakers, however, found a way around the ban by placing the legend in a modern context. For instance, *Aoi Sanmyaku* (blue mountain range) (1949) ostensibly depicted two Japanese high school students who fell in love despite adults' opposition. In reality, however, the story reflected the context of the themes found in the national legend. The film, which was widely recognized by Japanese movie-goers as a retelling of the national legend, became very popular during the U.S. occupation.[40]

The ultimate goal of the members of Ako-roshi in Chushingura is to reveal the injustice of the Shogunate by exacting revenge on Kira Kouzukenosuke, who bullied their late lord Asano Takuminokami until he lost his temper in Edo Castle, which resulted in Asano's death by *seppuku* suicide ordered by the Shogun. Conversely, the ultimate goal of *The Jackie Robinson Story* was to transform American society into one in which African Americans would no longer face discrimination. Robinson wanted to eliminate deep-rooted prejudice by proving that African Americans were equal to whites.

---

39 To understand the detail and meaning of Chushingura, see Takeshi Tanikawa, *Sengo Chushingura-Eiga no Zenbou* (All about post-World War II Chushingura films) (Shueisha Creative, 2013).

40 Tadao Sato, *Chushingura: Iji no Keifu* (Chushingura: Genealogy of stubbornness) (Asahi Sensho, 1976), pp. 153–158.

Moral/ethical model behaviors and symbolism in Robinson and others

Of interest is also the manner in which both editions of the comic treated positive subjects, such as moral and ethical behavior. The first such scene appears on page two of both editions. As a child from a poor family, Robinson is depicted as someone who helped his family by working part-time while still managing to maintain high grades at school. As a result of all his hard work, Robinson is rewarded with the opportunity to meet a Minor League baseball player.[41] This frame displays Robinson as a role model proving to young people that it is possible to work hard and pursue happiness at the same time.

Three other scenes focus on Robinson's responsibilities as a role model. One scene, found on page seven in the American edition and page six in the Japanese version, shows Robinson promising himself he will become a great example for the poor, black children hanging around in the street when he arrives in New York with Dodgers scout Clyde Sukeforth.[42] Another example can be found on page twenty-six of both editions. This scene depicts Robinson, who had just received the Rookie of the Year award, on a nationwide speaking tour of boys' clubs, schools and colleges, giving a speech expressing his desire to help boys in both sports and in life.[43] Finally, on page twenty-eight of both editions, the comic book shows Robinson promising to help prevent juvenile delinquency by providing opportunities for children to play sports.[44]

Two other frames in the comic suggest that, as a black man, Robinson could not have made it to the Major League without the help of whites. Page seven of the Japanese version and page eight of the American version contain a scene in which Robinson signs a Minor League contract with the Montreal Royals. In this scene, Brooklyn Dodgers President Branch Rickey

---

41 *Jackie Robinson*, a supplement of *Chugakusei no Tomo* (Junior high school students' companion), p. 2; *Jackie Robinson: Baseball Hero*, p. 2.

42 *Jackie Robinson*, a supplement of *Chugakusei no Tomo* (Junior high school students' companion), p. 6; *Jackie Robinson: Baseball Hero*, p. 7.

43 *Jackie Robinson*, a supplement of *Chugakusei no Tomo* (Junior high school students' companion), p. 26; *Jackie Robinson: Baseball Hero*, p. 26.

44 *Jackie Robinson*, a supplement of *Chugakusei no Tomo* (Junior high school students' companion), p. 28; *Jackie Robinson: Baseball Hero*, p. 28.

is depicted as a moral person who wanted to defeat prejudice.[45] The message here is that Robinson's hard work and determination brought him to the attention of a white man, who was able to help Robinson achieve his dream. This is the message that the major studios wanted to convey in *The Jackie Robinson Story*.

Another such scene can be found on page twenty of both the American and Japanese versions of the book. In this scene, Ford Frick, the president of the National League, responds to a threat by members of the St. Louis Cardinals to boycott a game against the Dodgers if Robinson plays. In the scene, Frick issues a statement saying 'If the Cards strike, they'll be barred from the League... This is the United States of America and one citizen has as much right to play baseball as another!'[46] Again, it is clear that, without a white ally with power and status, Robinson would not have been able to play in the Major League.

Changes in the translation from the American to Japanese version

The Japanese version of the comic book generally copied each page of the American version and translated the graphics into Japanese. The two editions, however, contain some key differences. Most notable is the Japanese version's exclusion of Robinson's relationship with his wife, Rachel, including their college romance, marriage and establishment of a happy family.

The Japanese version did not simply omit entire pages. Rather, various frames were eliminated while others were enlarged to fill the space. For example, one of the missing frames depicts Branch Rickey giving advice to Robinson as the young ballplayer is signing his contract. 'Have you got a steady girl?' the president of the Dodgers asks. 'Why...Yes, sir', Robinson responds. 'Then marry her. I like my ballplayers to be steady married men!' (see Fig. 6.5).[47] This scene includes a precautionary message to Robinson, perhaps emphasizing the dangers a star athlete could face if he developed a

---

45 *Jackie Robinson*, a supplement of *Chugakusei no Tomo* (Junior high school students' companion), p. 8; *Jackie Robinson: Baseball Hero*, p. 7.

46 *Jackie Robinson*, a supplement of *Chugakusei no Tomo* (Junior high school students' companion), p. 20; *Jackie Robinson: Baseball Hero*, p. 20.

47 *Jackie Robinson: Baseball Hero*, p. 8.

reputation as a womanizer. A married athlete in a stable marriage was less likely to have his career ruined by bad publicity. The frame might even have been written to suggest that an exemplary athlete like Robinson naturally enjoys a stable romantic life.

The people of Japan were busy rebuilding their lives during the occupation. Consequently, few in Japan viewed romantic love as a high priority. As a result, the U.S. authorities, who promoted Jackie Robinson as an American model for the new Japanese society that they were trying to construct, probably did not want him to be depicted as someone who was focused on romance. Many people in Japan may have found it difficult to accept the reality of Robinson's personal life if it included romance, especially at a time when the U.S. occupation force was trying to teach Japanese people how to kiss (public displays of affection were not the norm in Japan at the time, which may have led the Americans to think that kissing was not part of Japanese intimate relationships). Furthermore, as the readers of the Japanese version of the comic book were middle school students, the decision to eliminate Robinson's love life does not seem too unusual.

Rachel, however, represented more than Robinson's fiancée and eventual wife. She was an independent woman who held strong opinions and believed that women were equal to men. After graduating from UCLA with a bachelor's

Figure 6.5 Removed frames from original English version (Branch Ricky giving advice to Robinson)

Source: © Fawcett Publications (Takeshi Tanikawa Collection).

Figure 6.6 Removed frames from original English version (Rachel had her own opinions)

Source: © *Fawcett Publications (Takeshi Tanikawa Collection).*

Figure 6.7 Removed frames from original English version (Jackie and Rachel's first home)

Source: © *Fawcett Publications (Takeshi Tanikawa Collection).*

Figure 6.8 Removed frames from original English version (Rachel was replaced by Jackie's mother)

Source: © *Fawcett Publications (Takeshi Tanikawa Collection).*

degree in nursing, Rachel worked as a nurse and was an independent career woman. Before Jackie and Rachel got married and settled in Montreal, she had turned down Jackie's marriage proposal, insisting 'What's the use Jack? We can never have a home because you're always traveling with the ball club!' (see Figs. 6.6 and 6.7). The independence and forthrightness displayed by Rachel was the exact image of women that GHQ/SCAP encouraged the Japanese film industry to promote to the women of Japan's new generation.[48]

Robinson's relationship with Rachel was also eliminated in the alteration of the frame showing him going off to war. Instead of depicting him saying goodbye to his girlfriend, the Japanese edition shows him saying goodbye to his mother. In the Japanese version, the graphics are changed so that Robinson is comforting his mother with the words 'Mother, I'll be back soon. Take care of yourself' (see Fig. 6.8).[49] This scene between worried mother and concerned son was clearly written in the context of pre-war Japanese textbooks, thus aligning with the traditional moral and cultural values of the Japanese people.

Other alterations place the comic book into a context familiar to Japanese fans. For example, on page thirty-one of the Japanese edition, the graphics read 'In Japan, Kawanishi, Kizuka and Hagiwara, etc. are the players who are good at stealing bases. However, Jackie is better because he is the king of stealing bases, and a power hitter beyond Fujimura, Kawakami or Nakatani'.[50] The comic book refers to another Japanese player on the next page, noting that Robinson is 'the best second base player, like Chiba in the Giants'.[51]

For Japanese fans unfamiliar with the organization of American baseball, the following comment was added as background information:

> The teams—appearing in the major leagues or Minor League—indicate the class of the league. The two major leagues are the American League and the National League, while there are tens of small leagues. The Seals just visited Japan belonging to the [Pacific] Coast League, which is a second-class league.[52]

---

48 Kyoko Hirano, pp. 165–170.

49 *Jackie Robinson*, a supplement of *Chugakusei no Tomo* (Junior high school students' companion), p. 5.

50 Ibid., p. 31.

51 Ibid., p. 32.

52 Ibid.

From this statement, it is clear that the translation and production of the Japanese edition of the comic book happened immediately after the San Francisco Seals' visit to Japan in the autumn of 1949. As will be discussed in Chapter Seven, by visiting Japan, the Seals intended to revive Japanese-American baseball games. According to the design of Maj. Gen. William F. Marquat, the head of the Economic and Scientific Section of GHQ/SCAP, during the 1949 off-season, the Japanese Baseball Association established the two-league system — the Central League and the Taiheiyo Baseball Association (later known as the Pacific League). With the goal of simultaneously publishing the comic book in the U.S. and Japan in the spring of 1950, work on translating and printing the manuscript had started before the reorganization of Japanese baseball and the creation of other Japanese leagues.

Key messages in the American and Japanese versions of the comic book

Jackie Robinson's life, as presented in the comic book, was the story of an iconic leader of society who could lead and support marginalized people because he had accomplished his goal through tremendous effort despite experiencing extreme hardship. His position reminded the Japanese that they were living under the U.S. occupation and that they had to rebuild their lives in desperate circumstances during the aftermath of World War II.

Through his own talents, in an American society that discriminated against African Americans, Jackie Robinson achieved his goal of playing in the Major League. The comic book implicitly argues that Robinson succeeded with the strong support of white leaders who wished to make a difference.

The relationship between Robinson, an ideal black athlete personifying a high standard of morality, and the white leaders who had the power to help Robinson achieve his Major League goal, could be perceived as analogous to that between the people of Japan and their U.S. occupiers. To the Japanese people, the comic book sent the message that, if they worked hard and had the strong will to rebuild Japan under the tough conditions they were facing, with the support of the U.S. they would have a bright future.

The Japanese version of the book was modified so that Robinson, already a perfect model for Japanese people to imitate, became even more acceptable to the Japanese. By replacing his girlfriend with a mother who adored her caring son, the comic book showed the traditional Japanese mother-son relationship. In addition, in order to demonstrate his talent using a yardstick understood by Japanese baseball fans, the Japanese edition of the comic book included references to Japanese baseball players. Furthermore, the story of Robinson's life reflected well-known Japanese stories, such as Chushingura, which promised that enduring hardship would be followed by great success. Such modifications made the life of Jackie Robinson more relatable to Japanese readers and helped increase Robinson's impact on Japanese society.

As discussed earlier, Hollywood placed limits on depictions of racial discrimination in the film *The Jackie Robinson Story*. It seems that the comic book met with less censorship and a greater tolerance of free expression. As a result, the comic book better captured Robinson's victory over racial oppression and conveyed a more positive message.

On the whole, the contents of both editions of the comic book are similar to the film, *The Jackie Robinson Story*. The film, as noted at the beginning of the chapter, was not released in Japan for various reasons. Furthermore, GHQ/SCAP strictly banned *chanbara* films even if the sword was only used as a stick, because the CIE regarded swords as instruments that kill people.[53] The comic book arena in Japan seemed to escape the careful scrutiny that GHQ/SCAP applied to the film media. Early in his career, popular Japanese animator Osamu Tezuka created a six-frame comic strip called 'Tameshi-giri', in which he depicted a *tonosama* (a lord), who had just acquired a fine sword, testing the sharpness of his weapon by trying to kill a subordinate and failing due to a quick-thinking vassal. Despite the violent nature of the strip, it met with no objection from the Civil Censorship Detachment.[54]

When Americans argued that their democratic system was superior to the socialist system of the Soviet Union, Jackie Robinson's embodiment of improving race relations in the U.S. seem to prove the point. The U.S. used Robinson as an example to the world that it had the capacity and freedom to build a better society by resolving problems like racial discrimination.

Comic books were used not only to entertain Japanese citizens, but also to provide an easy-to-understand media to help people in Japan understand the image of Jackie Robinson that the U.S. government wanted to convey.

---

53 Memorandum for Record: Motion Picture Section of CI&E policy on sword fighting scenes in pictures (Memo by WYM), 2 March 1948, Box 8579, Folder 26 'Movie Films (Censorship) 1948' File, Civil Intelligence Section, GHQ/SCAP Records, RG 331.

54 Takeshi Tanikawa, 'Senryouki no Tezuka Osamu' (Osamu Tezuka in occupied Japan), in Taketoshi Yamamoto, ed., *Senryouki Bunka wo Hiraku: Zasshi no Shosou* (Open the culture in occupied Japan: Various images of magazines) (Waseda University Press, 2006), pp. 44–46.

Following the 1949 visit of the Minor League San Francisco Seals, which will be examined in more detail in the next chapter, other American baseball teams would visit Japan. In the fall of 1951, an American all-star baseball team featuring Joe DiMaggio and Lefty O'Doul toured Japan. In 1952, the Pacific Coast College All-Stars, a team of college ballplayers from California that featured future Hiroshima Carp all-star outfielder Kenshi Zenimura, also toured Japan. In 1953, after the U.S. occupation of Japan ended, another selected Major League All-Star team led by Eddie Lopat toured Japan, and a single Major League team, the New York Giants, visited Japan later in the same year. Two years later, in 1955, another Major League team, the New York Yankees, visited Japan. On October 17, 1956, the Brooklyn Dodgers, with Jackie Robinson, became the third American Major League baseball team to visit Japan (see Fig. 6.9).[55] Robinson had just completed his tenth Major League season.

Although it is reported that several Dodgers were reluctant to go to Japan, Robinson did not hesitate. This was a relief to the State Department which regarded Robinson's presence in Japan as a diplomatic contribution of inestimable value. For this Japan tour, the Dodgers travelled to many cities throughout Japan, and played nineteen games against All Japan, All Central League, All Pacific League, All East, All West, Giants-Tigers-Dragons United and the Tokyo Yomiuri Giants.

Robinson batted forty-nine times getting sixteen hits, a .327 average, and hit two homers in the first game on October 19 and the eighteenth game on November 12, both at Korakuen Stadium. He also showed his fighting spirit, unsuccessfully attempting a home steal and becoming the first Dodger to be ejected by an umpire (an American, Jocko Conlan) while playing baseball in Japan.

In comparison with his teammates, Robinson's average was eclipsed by Jim Gentile (.471 / eight homers), Don Demeter (.329 / five homers) and Gil Hodges (.333 / six homers), and was better than James Gilliam (.317 / two homers), Duke Snider (.305 / six homers), Roy Campanella (.268 / four homers) and Pee Wee Reese (.260 / two homers).

In addition to his average, on the top of the ninth inning in the nineteenth and final game, Robinson hit a game-winning single. This became the very last opportunity at the bat for Robinson as a professional ballplayer.

---

55 Hatano, *Nichibei Yakyu Shi*, pp. 240–242; *1934-2004 Pro-Yakyu 70 Nenshi* (1934–2004, 70 years of professional baseball) (Baseball Magazine-Sha, 2004), p. 153.

The Dodgers played well in Japan, winning fourteen games, losing four and tying one against Japan.

Before returning to the U.S., Robinson received a special message from John M. Allison, the U.S. ambassador, praising Robinson's magnificent sportsmanship and his contribution while in Japan.[56]

The club returned to the U.S. on November 16. Branch Rickey no longer owned the Dodgers, having been forced out of its financial management by Walter O'Malley, the team's chief legal counsel, in 1950. After the Dodgers returned to the U.S., rumors started circulating that O'Malley was negotiating a deal to secretly trade Robinson to the New York Giants. Unwilling to play for Brooklyn's chief rival, Robinson called a quickly arranged press conference and announced his retirement.[57] Like Joe DiMaggio five years earlier, Jackie Robinson played in his final game as an active Major Leaguer in Japan, before announcing he was leaving the game.

Figure 6.9 1956 U.S.-Japan baseball games pamphlet (Brooklyn Dodgers)
Source: Takeshi Tanikawa Collection.

---

56 Arnold Rampersad, *Jackie Robinson: A Biography* (Alfred A. Knopf, 1997), pp. 300–301.

57 Robinson and Duckett, *I Never Had It Made*, pp. 181–184.

The San Francisco Seals and Coca-Cola

Japan-U.S. baseball revival and Japan's baseball revitalization

Led by manager Frank 'Lefty' O'Doul, the San Francisco Seals of the Pacific Coast League arrived in occupied Japan in October 1949. This was more than four years after Japan's defeat in World War II, when the end of the occupation was in sight and Japan was preparing to rejoin the international community.[1] One of the strongest clubs in Minor League baseball, the Seals was an established team whose history dated back to the formation of the Pacific Coast League in 1903. Their reputation as 'one of the strongest teams in the Minor League' was established after around 1918, when former Major Leaguer Charlie Graham, who had formed a battery with Cy Young at the Boston Red Sox, began participating in the team's management. Although the club was not affiliated with any Major League teams, many San Francisco players had been promoted to such teams. O'Doul and National Baseball

---

1 I analyze these events based on information from GHQ/SCAP documents, baseball periodicals from the Gordon W. Prange Collection and the '20th Century Media Information Database'. For my research, I selected periodicals based on their titles according to periodical codes from the Prange Collection (microfiche version) at the National Diet Library Constitutional Material Room in Tokyo, Japan. In addition, I included the periodicals from my database search of 'The Database of Newspapers and Magazines Published during the Post-war Occupation Period from 1945 to 1949' (it has now changed its name to '20th Century Media Information Database') based on keywords (e.g. 'the Seals', 'cola') from relevant themes or subjects. I then chose seventy-five titles (650 microfiches) as the result. I prioritized these titles in the order of the database search results, and examined the contents of microfiches in the Constitutional Material Room. Furthermore, I made an effort to obtain actual copies of periodicals from second-hand bookstores if they seemed to be particularly important. Among these were *Baseball Magazine*, which still exists today, followed by *Baseball News*, *Baseball*, *Ball Friends*, *Home Run*, *Kindai Yakyu* and *All Yakyu*, all of which covered the Seals' visit.

Hall of Fame members Joe DiMaggio, Earl Averill and Vernon Louis 'Lefty' Gomez were all former Seals players.[2]

Frank O'Doul was well-known as a benefactor of Japanese baseball long before his San Francisco Seals visited Japan in 1949. He first visited with a Major League all-star team in 1931 when still an active player. O'Doul returned to Japan often, including in 1934 when he convinced Babe Ruth to join a team of Major Leaguers traveling to that country. Because of his experience in Japan and because of his contacts in Major League Baseball (MLB), O'Doul worked as an advisor to the Dainippon Tokyo Yakyu Kurabu (Great Japan Tokyo Baseball Club), the pioneer of Japan's professional baseball, when that club was first established. When a Japanese baseball club traveled to the U.S. in 1935 and 1936, O'Doul, who was then the Seals' manager, exerted every effort to arrange a game with the Japanese team. During the 1935 visit, he helped promote the Dainippon Tokyo Yakyu Kurabu in the U.S. media by giving it a nickname, the 'Tokyo Giants'.[3]

As noted in Chapter One, baseball quickly returned to Japan after the war, with the East-West baseball game played only 100 days after Japan's 'unconditional surrender'. Shortly after that, the Tokyo Big Six Baseball League, the Selected Middle-School Baseball Games and the Inter-City Match Amateur Baseball Tournament resumed play, one after another. In his address at the opening ceremony of the revived Selected Middle-School Baseball tournament held on March 30, 1947, Maj. Gen. William F. Marquat, the head of the Economic and Scientific Section (ESS), said, 'Japan's baseball enthusiasm is unprecedented. It is expedient that this tournament will lead and encourage sports at schools'.[4] GHQ/SCAP supported all levels of Japan's baseball revival during the post-war era. In this context, the Seals' visit coincided with the revival of baseball in Japan. With the San Francisco Seals' 1949 tour of Japan, U.S.-Japanese baseball relations resumed for the first time in the fifteen years since 1934, when Major League players like Babe Ruth, Lou Gehrig and Lefty O'Doul last visited the country.

---

2 http://www.joedimaggio.com/the-ballplayer/pre-yankees/ (last date of access: August 1, 2020); http://www.kidsneedbaseball.com/index.php?option=com_content&view=article&id=212:college-feature-1&catid=50:foundation&Itemid=477 (last date of access: August 1, 2020).

3 Yoichi Nagata, *Tokyo Giants Hokubei-Tairiku Ensei-Ki* (The Tokyo Giants North American tour of 1935) (Toho Shuppan, 2007), pp. 36–38.

4 Masaru Hatano, *Nichibei Yakyu Shi:Major wo Oikaketa 70 Nen* (The history of U.S.-Japan baseball: 70 years chasing the Major League) (PHP, 2001), p. 196.

Insistence on friendship and Japan-U.S. baseball business

The people of Japan saw the Seals' visit as something that was not only special for Japan's baseball community, but also as special for the country at large. It confirmed the friendship between Japan and the U.S. in the post-war framework established during the occupation. At the ballpark, Japan's national flag flew side by side with the Stars and Stripes. This may have left a strong impression on the Japanese, because GHQ/SCAP had completely prohibited the flying of Japan's national flag until March 4, 1948, and had given restricted permission to the flying of the flag only on national holidays until the end of that year, just ten months before the Seals' visit to Japan.[5] The tour set a precedent for Japanese citizens — Japan was, once again, a member of the international community, but under specific conditions set by the U.S. However, GHQ/SCAP did not act alone in organizing the baseball tour. The Seals' visit was also arranged by key members of Japan's baseball groups, including Ryuji Suzuki, Sotaro Suzuki and Matsutaro Shoriki. Furthermore, without the support of William F. Marquat and his aide-de-camp Tsuneo 'Cappy' Harada, the tour would not have taken place.

Marquat was widely known to be a baseball fan, a fact that Prime Minister Shigeru Yoshida often exploited. Before meeting with Marquat, Yoshida would have his assistant, Jiro Shirasu, contact Marquat's assistant, Cappy Harada, who once played ball for the semi-pro Santa Maria Indians[6] and was scouted by the St. Louis Cardinals before the war, to inquire about Marquat's mood. If Marquat was unhappy, Shirasu would feed Harada baseball stories to tell Marquat. Discussing baseball always seemed to cheer up Marquat. Yoshida would wait until Marquat's mood improved before arriving at the ESS head's office.[7] Marquat also served as the chairman of the United States Amateur Baseball Association's Japan branch.

The branch held the Inter-Hemisphere Non-Pro Baseball Championship Series at Korakuen Stadium, Koshien Stadium and Nishinomiya Ball Field in Japan from September 10 to 17, 1950. The All-Kanebo team, which had won the summer Inter-City Match Amateur Baseball Tournament, represented

---

5 Kazuhiko Kawamura, *Sengoshi GHQ no Kensho* (Post-World War II history: Verifying the GHQ) (Hon-no Fuukei-sha, 2014), pp. 90, 102.

6 Sayuri Guthrie-Shimizu, *Transpacific Field of Dreams: How Baseball Linked the United States and Japan in Peace and War* (University of North Carolina Press, 2012), p. 205.

7 Hatano, p. 194.

Japan in the Championship Series. The Capehearts, an integrated amateur team sponsored by an electric appliance store in Fort Wayne, Indiana, won the series four games to one.[8] In 1952, the second Inter-Hemisphere Non-Pro Baseball Championship Series (also known as the Inter-Hemisphere Semi-Pro Baseball World Series) took place in Tokyo and Osaka. The Fort Myer Colonials, a U.S. Army team, won four games to none against the All-Kanebo team.[9]

Silent 35mm film footage of the first game of the Inter-Hemisphere Non-Pro Baseball Championship Series, including the opening ceremony, is preserved at the U.S. National Archives and Records Administration (NARA). The film clearly shows the excitement felt by Japanese fans, even a year after the San Francisco Seal's visit. Prior to the ceremony, the people of Japan welcomed the ballplayers with a parade through Tokyo's Ginza District. The players moved along the parade route in convertibles, as if they were members of a high-profile American Major League team. Jean MacArthur, the wife of Gen. Douglas MacArthur, threw out the ceremonial first pitch. Marquat, who eagerly promoted baseball in Japan and made the remark at the welcome ceremony, watched the game from a seat next to her.[10]

Marquat was not only a baseball fan, he also loved to play the sport. According to Theodore Cohen who served under Marquat at the ESS, Marquat was the president of the unit's softball team and played second base on a team mostly composed of younger men. One day, while Marquat, who was fifty-four years old at the time, and the young driver of his car were practicing, a young military police officer (M.P.) attempted to issue a citation to Marquat because, in violation of military regulations, he had not locked the parked car he was using. At first, the M.P. could not believe that the middle-aged man in sportswear was Marquat.

According to Cohen, the car Marquat's driver had parked was in temporary use, and the license plate did not sport the star used by general officers of government. Although Marquat insisted that the lock was broken, the M.P. did not accept his claim. The officer started writing a ticket, but was then perplexed and started to tear the ticket up when he was informed that

---

8 *Nihon no Yakyu Hattatsushi* (A pictorial history of baseball in Japan) (Tosei Godo Tsushin-Sha, 1959), p. 202.

9 Sayuri Guthrie-Shimizu, p. 223.

10 'Five Years After baseball', Tokyo, Japan, 09/11/1950 ARC Identifier 22422 / Local Identifier 111-ADC-8657, Motion Picture, Sound, and Video Records Section, Special Media Archives Services Division, NARA.

this middle-aged lieutenant in casual attire of T-shirt and pants was in fact a major general. However, Marquat prevented the M.P. from destroying the ticket, and made him issue the ticket as was usually issued to military men. A few days later, this regulation was revised.[11]

Not only was he well-respected by both the young GHQ/SCAP staff members and the Japanese citizens who interacted with him, Marquat also valued fairness and belittled anyone who showed a haughty attitude.[12] Some observers perceived Marquat as someone who wanted, first, to establish an organization for both amateur and professional baseball in Japan and, second, to become the commissioner to 'rule Japan's baseball management'.[13] Even if this were true, there is no evidence that Marquat sought to do this for personal or financial gain. Rather, he seems to have been motivated solely by his love for baseball.

As the head of the ESS, Marquat was responsible for supervising three Japanese ministries—the Ministry of Finance, the Ministry of Commerce and the Ministry of Health and Welfare. He also oversaw the headquarters of the Economic Bureau and the Bank of Japan. It is clear that Marquat was keen to revive Japan's baseball establishment during the U.S. occupation, and he set about doing so with the same powerful leadership and enthusiasm that he devoted to managing Japan's economic ministries. Without Marquat's dedication and the assistance of Cappy Harada, the U.S.-Japan baseball friendship would not have been restored during the U.S. occupation.

Marquat's duties as head of the ESS included approving applications from private American corporations seeking to conduct business in Japan. As a result, Marquat proved especially useful when the Seals sought to schedule a tour of Japan. Documents extant in files of the Legal Section of GHQ/SCAP indicate the challenges faced by the Seals in getting their visit to Japan approved by the American authorities. How could GHQ approve the visit of an American professional baseball team, which would essentially be providing for-profit entertainment, when foreign commerce in Japan was

---

11 Theodore Cohen, *Nihon-Senryou-Kakumei: GHQ karano Shougen* (The third turn: MacArthur, the Americans and the rebirth of Japan), Vol.1, translated by Masaomi Omae (TBS Britannica, 1983), pp. 149–150.

12 Ibid.

13 Hatano, p. 199.

strictly regulated? Likewise, would the San Francisco Seals be willing to accept U.S. control in occupied Japan?[14]

Under the occupation, GHQ/SCAP rarely allowed American corporations to do business in Japan. The few exceptions were highly extraordinary cases. For instance, GHQ/SCAP did grant an exception to the American motion picture distribution business because it reinforced the U.S. objective by distributing high quality films of American life that the U.S. government wanted the Japanese people to see. These films, however, were distributed by the Central Motion Picture Exchange (CMPE), which was established by the CIE as both an extra-governmental agency and as an outpost of the Motion Picture Export Association. After deduction of CMPE expenses, the profits earned by these films did not flow back to the eight major film studios which constituted the CMPE. Rather, the eight major studios of the U.S. motion picture industry were forced to freeze the assets and only use the money to defray other expenses, such as film developing costs.[15]

GHQ/SCAP adopted a superficial reason for the Seals' visit to Japan—to provide comfort to U.S. military personnel serving in the Far East. As a result, the Seals would play four games with baseball teams from the U.S. Armed Forces, including the Far East Air Force team and the U.S. Army-Navy team. Moreover, a total of six games were scheduled against professional Japanese teams—the Yomiuri (Tokyo) Giants, the All-Japan team, the All-East team and the All-West team. The purpose of the tour was to promote friendly relations between Japan and the U.S.[16]

To prepare for the Seals' visit, Marquat, along with eminent Japanese citizens, organized the San Francisco Seals Goodwill Tour Committee. As head of the ESS, Marquat supervised the committee. Marquat appointed Takizo Matsumoto, a member of the National Diet, Japan's bicameral legislature, to act as the committee's executive chairman. Matsutaro Shoriki, the president of the Yomiuri media group, suggested that Sotaro

---

14 San Francisco Seals Goodwill Tour Committee, Tokyo, Japan, to Foreign Investment Board, General Headquarters, Supreme Commander for the Allied Powers, Tokyo, Japan, October 1, 1949, #300 San Francisco Seals Folder, 1948–1950, Box 1031, ARC Identifier 322831, Legal Section, GHQ/SCAP Records, RG 331, NARA.

15 Takeshi Tanikawa, *America-Eiga to Senryou Seisaku* (American films and occupation policy) (Kyoto University Press, 2002), pp. 356–362.

16 *Shinzen Nichibei-Yakyu: San Francisco Seals—Zen Nihon Gun, Zen Kaisai Gun, Zen Kanto Gun, Kyojin Gun, showa 24 Nen 10 Gatsu* (Souvenir program: San Francisco Seals Goodwill Baseball Tour of Japan, October 1949), p. 2 (English page) and p. 1 (Japanese page).

Suzuki, the vice president of the Japanese Baseball Association, become the committee's executive vice chairman.[17] Although Shoriki was accused of war crimes, American authorities deemed the charges against him were mostly 'ideological and political in nature' and released him from custody in 1947. In February 1949, Shoriki became the first commissioner and honorary president of the Japanese Baseball Association (Nihon Yakyu Renmei). GHQ/SCAP, however, objected to anyone tainted with war crime accusations serving in public office, and Shoriki resigned as commissioner but remained president of the Japanese Baseball Association.[18]

In the official tour program commemorating the Seals' visit, Marquat and nine other ESS staff members, including Lt. Cappy Harada, were listed as members of the San Francisco Seals Goodwill Tour Committee of Japan. Separately, the program listed Takizo Matsumoto, Sotaro Suzuki, Masaichi Nagata (the owner of Daiei, a major Japanese film company) and eleven other people as members of the Japanese Committee on Arrangements for the San Francisco Seals Goodwill Tour.[19] Marquat, as a representative of the committee, signed the required paperwork with the foreign investment board.[20] Presumably, Matsumoto and Suzuki handled the logistics of the Japanese tour, while Marquat and other ESS staff members acted as mediators between the Seals and the internal affairs division of GHQ/SCAP.

According to Marquat's estimate, the total cost of the Seals' tour was $36,000, in addition to $6,000 in accommodation costs. Estimates indicated that the tour was projected to raise $20,000 in admission fees.[21] As a result, promoters realized from the beginning that the tour would operate at a loss. As for the Seals' expenses while in Japan, it was expected they would be covered by income earned in yen. Still, as ticket sales would not raise enough money to pay for the costs associated with the tour, other sources of income were considered, including selling billboard space in the stadiums where the games

---

17 Hatano, p. 201.

18 Ibid., pp. 197–199.

19 *Shinzen Nichibei-Yakyu: San Francisco Seals—Zen Nihon Gun, Zen Kaisai Gun, Zen Kanto Gun, Kyojin Gun, showa 24 Nen 10 Gatsu* (Souvenir program: San Francisco Seals Goodwill Baseball Tour of Japan, October 1949), pp. 6, 81 (English pages).

20 San Francisco Seals Goodwill Tour Committee, Tokyo, Japan to Foreign Investment Board, General Headquarters, Supreme Commander for the Allied Powers, Tokyo, Japan, 1 October 1949.

21 Memorandum, #300 San Francisco Seals Folder, 1948–1950, UD 1200, Box 1031, ARC Identifier 322831, Legal Section, GHQ/SCAP Records, RG 331, NARA.

were played and selling space for corporate advertisements in the official programs. Both U.S. and Japanese corporations were sought as advertisers.[22]

On July 12, the committee met with the Foreign Investment Board of GHQ/SCAP to discuss the cost of the trip. A memorandum from the meeting indicated that the San Francisco Seals Goodwill Tour Committee was a non-profit organization, and that the committee proposed to import, exhibit and sell professional baseball services in Japan. The memorandum also indicated that the board found that the proposed business activities of the committee met the required minimum standards set by GHQ/SCAP and that the trip would further the objectives of the American occupation.[23]

Marquat's influence on Japanese baseball was substantial. He 'Americanized' the game in Japan by imposing a U.S.-style commissioner system to govern it and by establishing a two-league scheme that allowed for a championship series modeled on the American World Series.[24] Furthermore, the San Francisco Seals' visit to Japan would likely not have happened without Marquat's leadership. Still, it is clear that Marquat was working within the frame of the U.S. occupational sports policy adopted by GHQ/SCAP.

▌ The capriccio of the Seals' visit

The first U.S.-Japan goodwill baseball games played after World War II were a monumental event not only for baseball fans, but for citizens throughout the country. The games became the major topic of discussion while the Seals were in Japan. Japanese baseball magazines included special articles about the Seals' visit, and, as a result, their sales increased dramatically. General magazines also published special issues for the Seals' visit. For example, *Shounen Shoujo Tankai* added a special news extra titled 'Seals-gun Tokuhou' (Seals special report) as the supplement for its December 1949 issue (see Fig. 7.1).

---

22 Ibid.

23 Minutes, Meeting 12 July, 0830, 12 July 1949, #300 San Francisco Seals Folder, 1948 –1950, UD1200, Box 1031, ARC Identifier 322831, Legal Section, GHQ/SCAP Records, RG 331, NARA; Memo for Record, Foreign Investment Board, 5 October 1949, #300 San Francisco Seals Folder, 1948 –1950, UD1200, Box 1031, ARC Identifier 322831, Legal Section, GHQ/SCAP Records, RG 331, NARA.

24 *Nippon Series no Kiseki* (Nippon series history since 1950) (Baseball-Magazine-Sha, 2001), p. 36. The championship series started in 1950 and was called the 'Nippon World Series' for the first four years, then changed its name to 'Nippon Series' in 1954.

The Japanese film industry also seemed to be caught up in the excitement. The Press, Pictorial, and Broadcast Division (PPB) of GHQ/SCAP permitted ZM Productions (Zenier-Mutsu Productions) to show a Japanese-edited version of *The San Francisco Seals*, a two-reel documentary film based on U.S. newsreel footage, to Japanese audiences on September 30, 1949.[25]

On October 12, 1949, Col. R.M. Levy signed the final document granting the Seals permission to visit Japan, and the team arrived at Haneda International Airport on the same day. Upon their arrival, the ballplayers were greeted by thirty of Japan's most popular actresses, including Kinuyo Tanaka, as well journalists, Japanese baseball officials, and, of course, fans.[26]

Film companies arranged for actresses to be waiting at the airport in order to reinforce the perception that the Japanese movie and baseball industries had been working together. Four of the six major Japanese film studios, or their parent company, owned professional baseball teams. The Hankyu Braves was owned by the Toho Group, and the Tokyu Group, of which Toei studio was a subsidiary, owned the Kyuei Flyers. In fact, Kyuei was the temporary name designated under the partnership between the Tokyu Group and Daiei Studios, headed by Masaichi Nagata, and the team was on the verge of splitting into two teams—the Toei Flyers and the Daiei Stars. Later, the Shochiku Group took over the Taiyo Robbins, and joined the league as the Shochiku Robbins from 1950.[27] The Seals' visit to Japan presented the Japanese film industry with an excellent opportunity to advertise their connection to baseball by participating in the event.

On October 13, the Shiba Sports Center hosted a welcome party for the American ballplayers. Suisei Matsui, a *benshi*,[28] had been scheduled to host the party, but he became ill at the last minute. Instead, Tony Tani, an unknown vaudevillian at the time who later became one of Japan's top celebrities, filled in as his replacement, his first big job.[29]

---

25 ZM Productions, 'The San Francisco Seals' (Memorandum for record), 1 October 1949, 'Relation with CI&E' File, PPB Division Central File, Box 8579, RG 331, NARA.

26 Tatsuichi Morooka, 'San Francisco Seals to Fumin-sho: Showa 24 nen niokeru Yakyu Ninshiki no Shougeki—Mutodoke-teki Score sheet kara Zen 6 Shiai wo Shousai ni Kenshou'(San Francisco Seals and insomnia: Impact of the recognition of baseball in 1949—Verifying all six games from unofficial score sheets), *Baseballogy*, No. 2, 2001, p. 294.

27 Ritomo Tsunashima, *Pro Yakyu Uniform Monogatari* (The history of the uniform) (Baseball Magazine-Sha, 2005), pp. 102, 125, 136, 194–195, 199, 224–225.

28 *Benshi*, also called *katsudou-benshi* or *katsu-ben*, were Japanese performers who provided live narration for silent films (both for Japanese and Western films).

29 Hatano, p. 202.

The visit of the San Francisco Seals was the biggest news not only among baseball fans but also among all Japanese citizens. Due to the visit's broad popularity, a confectionary company decided to offer a prize in the publicity campaign. Though the specifics of the campaign are not clear, one of the prizes was called the 'Sports Gum Prize', and a team photograph of the Seals, which was probably taken after they came to Japan, was prepared for the winner (see Photo 7.1). If you look at the photograph carefully, you will notice several

Figure 7.1 'Seals-gun Tokuhou' (Seals special report), supplement for the December 1949 issue of *Shounen Shoujo Tankai*

Source: ©Bunkyou Shuppan (Takeshi Tanikawa Collection).

Photo 7.1 San Francisco Seals Goodwill Baseball Tour of Japan, team photo ('Sports Gum Prize' for the campaign)

Source: Takeshi Tanikawa Collection.

couples consisting of a U.S. soldier and a young Japanese woman sitting behind the dugout seats in the background of the team photo. During the occupation period, CCD censorship strictly prohibited showing any images, photographs or comic strips of Japanese women flirting with U.S. soldiers/officers on any form of the print media. This photograph appears to have avoided this ban and was printed and given to the winner of the campaign. The reason why the CCD missed this case is not clear—probably because it was not submitted to the CCD for some reason—but it reveals something of the true nature of spectators in Japan at the time.

The tour opened at Korakuen Stadium in Tokyo on October 15, with the Yomiuri Giants as the opposition. Tickets for a reserved seat in the grandstand cost 300 yen, while a seat in the outfield bleachers was 100 yen. All tickets sold out quickly, and, as a result, no same-day tickets were available. Scalpers rushed to meet the demand, re-selling reserved seats for as much as 2,000 yen, while netting 500 yen for bleacher seats. At the game, Japanese audiences tasted Coca-Cola, Pepsi-Cola, popcorn and hot dogs for the first time. In the game, the Seals crushed the Giants by a score of thirteen

Figure 7.2 'Kyujou no Ninkimono' (Popular shop in the ballpark), *Baseball News*, No. 640, November 1949

Source: © *Baseball News (Takeshi Tanikawa Collection).*

to four.[30] The article in the November 1949 issue of *Baseball News* tells us how Coca-Cola was sold in the stadium (see Fig. 7.2).

Tatsuichi Morooka, at the age of thirteen, enjoyed the opening game in the grandstand, with the ticket given to him by his father who worked for the *Mainichi Shimbun*, part of the mass media that had received an allotment of tickets. Morooka recalls that he arrived at Korakuen Stadium at the practice time before the game started and found the behind-the-plate seats filled with foreigners—staff, he guessed, of GHQ/SCAP and their families—and he was unable to get into that section. Other grandstand seats were available because the reserved tickets for that area were general admission, and he changed seats several times until he found a better seat with a good view of the game.[31]

Before the game, a newspaper photographer took a picture of Eigoro Maedayama, the *yokozuna* (grand champion) of sumo, shaking hands with Seals' manager O'Doul. The *yokozuna* was a big baseball fan who even had his own amateur baseball team and played the game with other sumo wrestlers as a player-manager. He was able to attend the game because an injury had forced him out of the Osaka Sumo Tournament, which was then underway 300 miles to the west.

When published in the newspaper, the photograph created a problem for Maedayama. As a member of the East Group, he had won his match on the opening day of the Osaka tournament, but then lost his next five matches. On October 15, the seventh day of the contest, Maedayama officially defaulted, and also lost that day's match to Mitsuneyama by default, when he left the tournament to be examined at a hospital in Tokyo. After the hospital visit, Maedayama attended the ballgame. Believing it would generate positive publicity for the ballgame, someone at GHQ/SCAP probably requested that Maedayama shake hands with O'Doul and pose for the photo.

Outraged that he had attended the game rather than behaving himself while the sumo tournament was still in progress,[32] the Japan Sumo Association ordered Maedayama to return to Osaka. Maedayama expressed

---

30 Morooka, pp. 301–302, 306–311.

31 Interview with Tatsuichi Morooka, December 22, 2015, Tokyo.

32 From the standpoint of the Japan Sumo Association, Maedayama was required to either stay at home or in hospital to concentrate on his treatment quietly. The secession of the Yokozuna Grand Champion from the tournament affected the tournament's income, and seeing him participate in other sports events put into question his decision to withdraw from the tournament.

his remorse and asked the association if he could return to the tournament in order to make a ceremonial entrance into the ring. The association rejected his request and, instead, suspended him from the tournament. Disheartened by the blow to his pride and honor, Maedayama announced his retirement to the Japan Sumo Association on October 23, the last day of the tournament.[33] The November 18 issue of *Nikkan Sports* newspaper reports the details of what happened to Maedayama (see Fig. 7.3).

Despite the negative publicity, the Maedayama incident did have a long-term positive impact on sumo. Feeling responsible for the problems encountered by Maedayama, GHQ/SCAP offered him the opportunity to put on sumo demonstrations in the United States. Maedayama, who was in the process of becoming an instructor for the sumo wrestlers in his stable as Takasago-Oyakata (Stable Master Takasago), accepted the invitation and arrived in the U.S. with three other sumo wrestlers in

Figure 7.3 'Maedayama Intai no Shinso' (The truth about Maedayama's retirement), *Nikkan Sports*, No. 1343, November 18, 1949

Source: © *Nikkan Sports (Takeshi Tanikawa Collection).*

33 Juzen Imada, *Dokankai: Harite Ichidai Maedayama Eigoro: Kokusaika wo Kakenuketa Otoko* (Get out of my sight: Eigoro Maedayama, 'Harite' sumo wrestler) (BAB Japan, 1995), pp. 199–209.

June 1951. The trip itself was significant because GHQ/SCAP rarely permitted Japanese citizens to leave the country during the occupation. Maedayama's trip was successful, especially in Hawaii, where Japanese Americans enthusiastically welcomed the wrestlers. Many in Hawaii still remembered the tour fondly more than a decade later. Consequently, in 1962 the Japan Sumo Association conducted an overseas tour in that state. While on tour, Takasago-Oyakata, who was appointed as the head of the Hawaii tour group by the Japan Sumo Association, found a Hawaiian-born American named Jesse James Wailani Kuhaulua and recruited him into the sport. In 1972, Kuhaulua, by then known as Daigoro Takamiyama, won the sumo championship at the July 1972 tournament, becoming the first ever foreign-born sumo champion.[34] Therefore, the controversy caused by Maedayama's attendance at the Seals' game may have created inroads toward the globalization of the Japan Sumo Association.

Figure 7.4 'Shinzen' (Goodwill), *Asahigraph*, Vol. 52, No. 20, November 11, 1949

Source: © *Asahigraph (Takeshi Tanikawa Collection).*

---

34 Taketoshi Takanaga, *Sumo Showa-Shi: Gekidou no Kiseki* (History of sumo in the Showa Era: The track in convulsions) (Koubunsha, 1982), pp. 259–266.

The Seals played a busy schedule in Japan, competing in eleven games between October 15 and October 30. After playing against the Yomiuri Giants at Korakuen Stadium, the Seals played three games at Jingu Stadium in Tokyo, facing the Far East Air Force team on October 16, the All-East Japan team on October 17—the day the Crown Prince watched the game and shook hands with O'Doul (see Fig. 7.4)—and the Army-Navy joint team on October 19. GHQ/SCAP referred to Jingu Stadium, which had been commandeered by the U.S. Eighth Army in 1945, as Stateside Park. Following four games in Tokyo, the Seals moved on to the Kansai region in the south-central area of Japan's main island of Honshu for three more games. The team played the All-West Japan team at Nishinomiya Stadium in the city of the same name on October 21, before moving on to two games at Koshien Stadium in the same city—an October 22 rematch against the Army-Navy joint team and a game against the All-Japan team on October 23. This was the first time in the history of Japanese professional baseball that an 'All-Japan' team had been formed. On October 26, the Seals played against the Army-Navy team for a third time, this time at Chunichi Field in Nagoya. The next day, San Francisco played another game at Chunichi Field, a rematch against the All-Japan team. The Seals played their last scheduled game, a final match against the All-Japan team, on October 29 at Jingu Stadium in Tokyo. The Seals lost to the Far East Air Force team on October 16 by a score of two to four,[35] but they swept to victory in the six games played against their Japanese opponents.[36]

Figure 7.5 San Francisco Seals Goodwill Baseball Tour of Japan, game 7 (O'Doul Day) ticket stub
Source: Takeshi Tanikawa Collection.

35 Hiroshige Ichioka and Ami Fukunaga, *Pro Yakyu wo Sukutta Otoko Cappy Harada* (Cappy Harada: The man who saved professional baseball) (Soft Bank Creative, 2009), p. 197.

36 Morooka, pp. 306–346.

At the last minute, an eleventh game was scheduled for October 30 (the seventh game against a Japanese team), this one against players selected from the Tokyo Big Six Baseball League. Prior to the Seals' arrival, executives from the Japanese Baseball Association, Japanese ballplayers themselves and Japanese fans optimistically expected the local teams to hold their own against the Americans. After all, as a member of the U.S. Minor League system, the San Francisco club did not even represent the highest caliber of baseball in the U.S. All four of the Seals' Japanese opponents — the Yomiuri Giants, the All-East Japan team, the All-West Japan team and the All-Japan team — wilted in the face of the Seals' opposition. Everyone affiliated with Japanese baseball felt an overwhelming sense of defeat and disappointment. For example, Tetsuharu Kawakami, Japan's 'God of Batting', expressed the following:

> Although the fast ball of [Con] Dempsey, the starting pitcher […] was faster than [Takehiko] Bessho [the Yomiuri Giants' ace pitcher], he was not pitching fast balls very often. At the [bottom of the] fifth inning, I was trying to aim slow curve balls by Dempsey. However, the pitcher was replaced by [Bill] Werle, thus there was nothing I was able to do.
>
> The most impressive fact about the U.S. players was that under no circumstances do they swing at balls thrown out of the strike zone, nor do they take their eyes off the ball. As far as batting is concerned, the U.S. players seemed not to focus on small details of form, like the Japanese players did […].
>
> Overall, the Japanese players realized that they would need to learn more baseball and work harder on their technique.[37]

Promoters of the tour invited orphans in Tokyo to attend, free of charge, the Seals' game against the Far East Air Force team on October 16. The game was designated as 'A Comfort Day for War Orphans'. The same idea was applied to the last game of the tour, when 40,000 boys and girls aged fifteen or younger were invited to 'Lefty O'Doul Day'.[38]

It is commonly believed in Japan that it was O'Doul's idea to add the final game to the schedule after the Seals' manager saw thousands of children along the roadside waving at the ballplayers as their motorcade snaked

---

37 Tetsuharu Kawakami, 'Seals to Tatakatte' (After fighting with the Seals), *Yakyu-kai*, December 1949, p. 42.

38 Morooka, pp. 336–340.

through Tokyo. The fact that tickets for the final game were not printed and instead remaining tickets for other games were reused (see Fig. 7.5), and the fact that the final game was not listed in the official Seals' program, seems to confirm this theory.

The September 1, 1950 issue of *Kindai Yakyu* magazine reported that the 'All Japan College Baseball Association released on the 14th an announcement of a game with the Seals. This decision is controversial because the Seals are a professional team'.[39] Although the popular belief in Japan is that O'Doul suggested the game (and conceivably that he made the suggestion with the waving children in mind), the magazine's publication date indicates that this game was announced before the Seals arrived in Japan. It is possible that the game was omitted from the program because the details had not been finalized before the Seals arrived, or perhaps before the program was printed.

The controversy surrounded the fact that the San Francisco Seals were a professional club, while the college players were amateurs. After reviewing documentation submitted for the tour, including an English-language translation of the rules and regulations of the Japan Amateur Athletic Association and its organizational chart, GHQ/SCAP approved the game. Perhaps because of the controversial nature of the game, it was officially considered an 'instructional college baseball game'.[40]

From the standpoint of Japanese baseball fans, the fact that the game would be held on this 'Lefty O'Doul Day' between a U.S. professional team and an All-College team was nothing less than a dream within a dream, because, at that time, college baseball was far more popular than professional baseball in Japan.[41]

Junzo Sekine, a senior and ace pitcher for the Hosei University team, started the game for the college all-stars. Perhaps to make the game more competitive, O'Doul pitched for the Seals, even though he had retired from baseball fifteen years earlier and despite the fact that he had not pitched in

---

39 'Rokudaigaku Seals to Tatakauka' (Will Six-University fight the Seals?), *Kindai Yakyu*, September 1949, p. 27.

40 Tadashi Arima, 'Seals Sen wo Mite: Roku-Daigaku no Shourai' (Watching the game with the Seals: The future of the Six-University League), *Yakyu News*, No. 40, Yakyu News-Sha, December 1949, pp. 40–41.

41 Interview with Tatsuichi Morooka.

a Major League game since 1923, and professionally since 1940.[42] Sekine pitched magnificently. Both teams scored two runs early on, but the game remained tied at two runs apiece at the end of the ninth inning and through the twelfth. San Francisco added two more runs in the thirteenth inning, winning the game for the Americans.[43] Sekine pitched unrelieved for the entire thirteen-inning game. He would go on to have an impressive career with Kintetsu (1950–1964) and Yomiuri (1965) and was inducted into the Japanese Baseball Hall of Fame in 2003.

Hosei University team was in a good position in the pennant race of the Tokyo Big Six Baseball League that year. At the very last phase, they needed just one more win to capture the pennant when 'O'Doul Day' was scheduled. On November 6, 7 and 8, the last three games against Meiji University were held, and Hosei University couldn't win a game (lost two games and tied one). They missed victory in the pennant race, mainly because Junzo Sekine, their ace pitcher, had pitched too much and thus lost his edge. After having pitched on 'O'Doul Day' for thirteen innings, Sekine pitched all three games against Meiji University as starter, pitching a total of thirty-four innings unrelieved.[44]

It is easy to say that the college all-stars should have replaced their pitcher, but Tatsuichi Morooka has a different view. He guesses that the college all-stars thought it could be disrespectful toward the Seals if they did not let Sekine, their ace pitcher, finish the game.[45] Sekine himself later reflected on 'O'Doul Day', revealing the fact that he asked Shozo Fujita, the manager for Hosei University who managed the college all-stars team, why he didn't send in a reliever despite the fact that many other pitchers were on the bench. Fujita had replied, 'I was also thinking about sending [in a] reliever, but couldn't because other college team's managers came to me one after another, saying never change Sekine during this game because we have to win the game!'.[46]

Morooka also claims that he did not feel the game was an unusual or trivial exhibition game even if O'Doul himself was the Seals' starter, because in Japanese professional baseball at the time there had been a situation

---

42 O'Doul made his debut as a Major Leaguer when he was promoted to the New York Yankees in 1919, at that time as a pitcher. He pitched for the Yankees and the Boston Red Sox until the 1923 season, and then was converted to outfielder.

43 Morooka, pp. 338–340.

44 Interview with Tatsuichi Morooka.

45 Ibid.

46 Junzo Sekine, *Sekine Junzo Yakyu Houdan: Yakyu ga dekite Arigatou* (Sekine Junzo's essay on baseball: Thanks for letting me play baseball) (Shougakukan, 1998).

in which the manager of a team, who used to be a player and had retired many years ago, had pitched the game. In fact, the record shows that at the game between the Mainichi Orions and the Hankyu Braves on November 5, 1950, Yoshio Yuasa, a forty-eight-year-old manager for Mainichi and Shinji Hamazaki, another forty-eight-year-old player-manager for the Braves, both pitched as starters.[47]

Despite the early projections of a financial loss, the tour eventually turned a profit. As discussed in a small article in *Home Run* magazine of February 1950, it would have been awkward if GHQ/SCAP had kept the profit. Thus, the surplus was donated to a fund to train more umpires for Japanese baseball.[48] In addition to using the money to train umpires, the profit was used to finance the tours of semi-pro teams from Hawaii to Japan, and to send Japanese semi-pro teams to the U.S.[49]

The Coca-Cola and Pepsi-Cola companies

In order to ensure that the tour did not operate at a loss, Marquat arranged for the sale of advertising to help fund the trip. Two separate programs were published for the tour: a 200-yen, 122-page deluxe booklet (with ninety-two pages in English plus thirty in Japanese) issued by the Seals Goodwill Baseball Association (see Fig. 7.6), and a twenty-yen, eight-page simple pamphlet with scorecard (see Fig. 7.7). Small advertisements and announcements from twenty-nine different Japanese companies filled the latter program.

The ESS expected that sales of the deluxe program, along with the sale of advertising space within the program, would defray the cost overruns projected to plague the tour. In addition to ads for U.S. military clubs, the deluxe program contained more than forty ads, most of which were full-page, from U.S. corporations.[50]

---

47 Ibid.

48 'Seals Shikin Hyakuman-en Shinpan-bu e' (A million yen of Seals' fund goes to Umpire Division)', *Home Run*, February 1950, p. 45.

49 Sayuri Guthrie-Shimizu, p. 235.

50 *Shinzen Nichibei-Yakyu: San Francisco Seals — Zen Nihon Gun, Zen Kaisai Gun, Zen Kanto Gun, Kyojin Gun, showa 24 Nen 10 Gatsu* (Souvenir program: San Francisco Seals Goodwill Baseball Tour of Japan, October 1949), pp. 1, 3, 7–11, 13, 15, 17, 19, 21, 23, 25, 27, 29–31, 33, 35, 37–41, 66–71, 73, 75–77, 79–80, 83, 87–88, 90–92.

Figure 7.6 'San Francisco Seals Japan Tour' pamphlet issued by the Seals Goodwill Baseball Association (122-page deluxe booklet)
Source: Takeshi Tanikawa Collection.

Figure 7.7 'San Francisco Seals Japan Tour' pamphlet issued by Japanese Baseball Association (eight-page simple pamphlet)
Source: Takeshi Tanikawa Collection.

Among the full-page ads in the deluxe program were advertisements for two popular beverages in the U.S. — Coca-Cola (see Fig. 7.8) and Pepsi-Cola (see Fig. 7.9). Both soft drink companies ran full-page color ads on the inside covers of the pamphlet, Coca-Cola on the right-hand side and Pepsi on the left-hand side (English pages are designed to open to the left, and Japanese pages vice versa). Furthermore, Coca-Cola inserted a twenty-four-page scorecard, along with a half-page ad in the deluxe program.[51]

In addition to the company's ads, other documents suggest a close relationship between Coca-Cola and GHQ/SCAP. The summer before the Seals visited Japan, GHQ/SCAP issued a program for two ballgames, actually, both played on July 4, 1949, an American holiday marking U.S. Independence, three months before the Seals' arrival in Japan (see Fig 1.1). One game was the GHQ/SCAP internal baseball game played at Stateside Park (Jingu Stadium); the other was a GHQ/SCAP softball game played at Doolittle Field (Hibiya Park). A four-page program was created for each game which contained a full-page scorecard that carried the ad, 'Between innings…have a Coke'.[52]

There is no information available on how much Coca-Cola or Pepsi-Cola paid for their ads in the Seals' tour material. The amount, however, must have been considerable, given the fact that they not only placed prominent ads in the programs, but also were allowed a trial run selling their colas at the ballgames. At most games, both companies sold their beverage for fifty yen. At the extra game against a team made up of players from the Tokyo Big Six Baseball League, to which 40,000 young people were invited, the beverages were sold for just twenty-five yen. The Japanese baseball periodical *Baseballogy* notably described what can only be called an all-American scene: '[In] the evening, a number of boys were strolling toward the Suido-bashi Station holding blue scorecards, white balls and red Coca-Cola'.[53]

In order to sell its product in foreign markets, the Coca-Cola Company created the Coca-Cola Export Corporation in New York in 1930. Its Japanese branch was founded in Yokohama in October 1945 after GHQ/SCAP invited the Coca-Cola Company to send representatives to Japan. From 1946 to 1952, mostly during the occupation, Coca-Cola established the foundations for its business in Japan by building six plants in the country, stretching

---

51 Ibid., rear covers, pp. 42–65.

52 'HQ & SV.GP. Special Services Presents 4th of July Sports Program, Tokyo Japan 1949'.

53 Morooka, p. 340.

Figure 7.8 Coca-Cola ad in deluxe program (inside back cover of Figure 7.6)
Source: Takeshi Tanikawa Collection.

Figure 7.9 Pepsi-Cola ad in deluxe program (inside back cover of Figure 7.6)
Source: Takeshi Tanikawa Collection.

from Sapporo in the north to Kokura in the south. During this era, Coke's only business partner in the country was GHQ/SCAP, as the beverage was marketed to Americans in Japan. Nonetheless, it is fair to assume that the company was preparing to make its product available to Japanese consumers once the occupation ended. In 1947, two years after Coca-Cola's arrival in Japan, Pepsi went on sale to members of the occupational forces.[54]

ESS-related GHQ/SCAP documents reveal that Coca-Cola and Pepsi-Cola were establishing concrete plans for new business opportunities in Japan during the occupation. From July 1947 to August 1948, both Coke and Pepsi submitted a written estimate to the Lumber Department of the Bureau of Food and Trade. The report shows inquiries made to multiple corporations in Japan about production capacities and unit prices for wooden cases to hold soda bottles.[55] Moreover, the documents suggest that Ray D. Spencer, the manager of Coca-Cola Japan, met with Marquat as early as the beginning of 1949 to discuss plans to launch its new business in Japan.[56]

According to the previously mentioned study by Sayuri Guthrie-Shimizu, the office of the Nippon Shakaijin Yakyu Kyokai (the Japanese Industrial Baseball Association) was established within the ESS in February 1949, and Ray D. Spencer was selected as a member of the committee involved in preparing the binational semipro championship. Also on the committee were Marquat, Harada and J.J. McSweeney—the head of Chase Manhattan Bank's new Japan Branch—as well as Japanese members including Takizo Matsumoto and representatives from Korakuen Stadium and Mainichi Shimbun Corporation. These facts suggest that Coca-Cola Japan was deeply involved in the baseball business in that country.[57]

According to an official company-sponsored history of Coca-Cola Japan, Marquat advised company officials that it would not be a 'good time to sell

---

54 *Aisarete 30 Nen* (30 years of being loved), Coca-Cola (Japan) Company, Limited, 1987, pp. 26–32. Until at least the end of 2016, it used to be claimed on Pepsi's official home page that they started to sell their product to members of the occupational forces in Japan in 1947 (http://www.pepsi.co.jp/history/japan), but now their home page has changed and states that their worldwide business expanded in 1954 when their international division was launched (https://www.pepsi.co.jp/history/) (last date of access: August 2, 2020).

55 'Pepsi Cola & Coca Cola Bottle Cases' Folder, June 1947—August 1948, Box 6477, Economic and Scientific Section, GHQ/SCAP Records, RG 331, NARA.

56 'Coca-Cola Export Corporation' Folder, January 1949, Box 1040, Legal Section, GHQ/SCAP Records, RG 331, NARA.

57 Sayuri Guthrie-Shimizu, p. 207.

luxury items in Japan, like Coca-Cola, while the country is experiencing supply shortages'.[58] Marquat also warned that importing the undiluted syrup to produce cola would consume precious foreign currency, and, therefore, would not be permitted until the end of the occupation.[59] Marquat's reversal of this decision in 1949 was based on his knowledge of American corporations and his need to raise funds to cover the cost of the Seals' visit. No documentation exists, however, in either the GHQ/SCAP papers or the Coca-Cola Company's public relations material, that indicates a quid-pro-quo agreement between the company and GHQ/SCAP in which Coke agreed to help fund the Seals' trip to Japan in exchange for the right to trial the sale of its product there.

The September 1, 1949 issue of *Eiga Stars* (Movie stars) magazine, which appeared shortly before the Seals' arrival in Japan, contained an article about Coca-Cola's Yokohama factory entitled 'Coca-Cola Sweet Girl'. The article begins with the statement, 'Do you know about the Coca-Cola beverage from America?' Later, the article states, 'Sooner or later, we will be seeing it', and, later still, 'although this beverage is not currently available, we believe that the day that it will be available will arrive soon'.[60] Here, the article seems to indicate that a trial sale of the beverage to the Japanese people had been scheduled.

The article followed three actresses on a tour of the Yokohama Coca-Cola factory—Michiko Ikuno, who worked for Shochiku Studios, Akiko Sawamura, a new actress who had appeared in multiple Daiei films, and Kumiko Mizuhara from the Shintoho Motion Picture Company. It is likely that actresses from these three companies took the tour because of the close connection between baseball and the Japanese motion picture industry. As noted above, Daiei Studios owned a baseball team called the Daiei Stars. Shochiku was also attempting to enter the baseball industry.[61] If the Coca-Cola Company had informed the studios that it had plans to sell its product to the Japanese people during the Seals' tour, the studios might have seen an advantage in participating in the publicity tour. The arrangement would have been equally beneficial to the Coca-Cola Company, as baseball and the movie business were already affiliated with each other.

---

58 *Aisarete 30 Nen* (30 years of being loved), p. 30.

59 Ibid.

60 'Coca Cola Sweet Girl', *Eiga Star* (Movie stars), Romance-Sha, Vol. 1, No. 7, September 1949, pp. 26–27.

61 Tsunashima, pp. 125, 136.

The government of Japan, however, did not issue a permit to Coca-Cola or Pepsi-Cola for the importation of the undiluted syrup necessary to produce cola until 1956, four years after the end of the occupation. As a result, Japanese customers were unable to purchase cola until 1957.[62]

The American soda companies had a close relationship with Japanese baseball, but they never became involved in the ownership of Japanese teams. Pepsi, however, almost became a team owner in the 1970s. With the outbreak of the 'Black Mist Scandal', in which a number of Japanese ballplayers were accused of accepting money from gamblers to intentionally lose games, the owners of the financially struggling Nishitetsu Lions put their team up for sale. According to Nagayoshi Nakamura, the owner of the Lotte Orions, in 1972 Pepsi expressed a strong interest in buying the team. In February 1973, however, Toei Co. Ltd. decided to sell the Toei Flyers, another team from the same Pacific League. Toei's exit from baseball raised questions about the stability of the Pacific League, and Pepsi withdrew its offer.[63] On the other hand, Coca-Cola became interested in the movie business, and purchased Columbia Pictures in 1982. Today, Columbia is owned by Sony, a Japanese corporation.[64]

The Seals' visit and its spin-offs

In Japan, the visit by the San Francisco Seals ranked as one of the biggest events of the year. This was clear among the country's baseball community, as important Japanese sports periodicals, including *Baseball Magazine*, which still exists today, as well as *Baseball News*, *Baseball*, *Ball Friends*, *Home Run*, *Kindai Yakyu* and *All Yakyu* (The all ball), covered the Seals' visit.[65] The tour, however, was significant as more than just a sporting event—*The 1949 Almanac of Advertising & Economic Activity* placed it number four on

62 https://www.cocacola.co.jp/history_ (last date of access: August 2, 2020).

63 Yasuyuki Sakai, *Haran Koubou no Kyufu: Ushunawareta Lions-Shi wo Motomete* (A record of baseball in storms and rise and fall: Seeking the lost history of the Lions), Baseball Magazine-Sha, 1995, pp. 36–40.

64 http://www.sonypictures.jp/corp/history/28386 (last date of access: August 2, 2020).

65 Special issues on the Seals of each periodical are: *Baseball Magazine*, September & November 1949; *Baseball News*, No. 638, October 1949; *Baseball*, No. 27, October 1949; *Ball Friends*, September & November 1949; *Home Run*, August to October 1949; *Kindai Yakyu*, September & October 1949; *All Yakyu* (The all ball), October 1949.

its list of 'The Top Ten Domestic News Items in 1949', right up there with Hironoshin Furuhashi setting a new world record in freestyle swimming, Dr. Hideki Yukawa winning the Nobel Prize in Physics and the Shimoyama, Mitaka and Matsukawa incidents, a series of unsolved crimes of sabotage against the Japanese National Railways.[66]

Free tickets given to children to attend 'A Comfort Day for War Orphans' and 'Lefty O'Doul Day' may have simply been a scheme cooked up by GHQ/SCAP to win support for the occupation from the people of Japan. The gesture, however, genuinely touched the Japanese people, giving them the impression that baseball was a great cultural tool of the United States. Not only did children have the opportunity to observe heroic American baseball players, but adults were given their first chance to experience the taste, color, aroma, and bottle designs of American colas, which, even more than baseball, represented the culture of the United States of America.[67]

Because free trade with Japan was restricted during the occupation, the Seals' visit was designated as an event to give comfort to American occupational forces. For U.S. soldiers who had been away from home for a long period of time, the Seal's arrival meant they could watch a baseball game, and watch the stars of the Pacific Coast League, even while still in Japan. As administered and executed by the leadership of GHQ/SCAP, the Seals' visit catered to the Japanese people. The U.S. was proud of its aim to further international understanding through sports, a policy that it thought demonstrated the 'American Way'. On the other hand, in addition to its acknowledged intention, the tour had a 'hidden agenda' of gaining a foothold for American corporations to start businesses in Japan. This double-edged sword is also evident in the film policy the U.S. adopted for Japan, which, rather than concentrating on indoctrinating American values, seemed to be more interested in rebuilding the Far East film market for the American movie industry.

The Seals' visit should also be examined in the context of the revival of baseball in Japan. On September 14, about a month before the Seals' arrival, the existing world of Japan's eight major professional baseball teams changed when the Kinki Nihon Tetsudo Corporation (Kintetsu) submitted an application for a new baseball team. Five days later, the Nishi-Nihon Shimbun

---

66 *Visual Ban DENTSU Koukoku-Keiki-Nenhyou 1945-2003* (Visual version of DENTSU chronological table of advertisement and economy 1945–2003) (DENTSU, 2004), p. 36.

67 Strictly speaking, imported Coca-Cola was sold at the cafés in Ginza from the pre-war Taisho Era, but these were only for a small number of intellectuals.

Corporation, the Mainichi Shimbun Corporation, the Taiyo Gyogyou Corporation and the Hoshino-Gumi Corporation submitted applications for teams. The growth in the number of professional teams created the need for a two-league system in Japan, which had been Marquat's intention all along. On April 15, 1949, Matsutaro Shoriki, Japan's first baseball commissioner, issued the 'Shoriki Proclamation', which included an agreement to build a new stadium in Tokyo and an announcement of the transition to a two-league system.[68]

The Seals returned to California on November 7. On November 26, twenty days after their departure, the Japanese Baseball Association was dissolved, and four of the association's teams—the Daiei Stars, the Hankyu Braves, the Nankai Hawks and the Tokyu Flyers—established the Taiheiyo Baseball Association (now known as the Pacific League). Joining the four former Japanese Baseball Association teams were the following new teams: the Kintetsu Pearls, the Nishitetsu Lions and the Mainichi Orions. Three weeks later, on December 15, the remaining four teams from the Japanese Baseball Association—the Chunichi Dragons, the Hanshin Tigers, the Shochiku Robins and the Yomiuri Giants—established the Central League with three other new clubs: the Maruha Team (Taiyo Gyogyou; later the Taiyo Whales), Hiroshima Carp and Nishi Nippon Pirates.[69] Although the merits of Japan's two-league system are still debated in Japan today, it is without doubt that in 1950 Marquat's vision for Japanese baseball finally became a reality.

From the above, it is clear the San Francisco Seals' visit was important for three reasons. First, baseball represented American-Japanese friendship before World War II and, despite the post-war conqueror-occupied relationship between the U.S. and Japan, the visit revived the friendship. Second, the San Francisco Seals' visit to Japan was one of the most significant events to happen in that country in the post-war period. The Seals' visit also set the groundwork for American corporations like Coca-Cola to do business in Japan.

---

68 *1934-2004 Pro Yakyu 70 Nen-Shi* (1934–2004: 70 years of professional baseball), History Edition (Baseball Magazine-Sha, 2004), pp. 88–91. Hiroyuki Yamamuro, *Pro Yakyu Fukko-Shi: MacArthur kara Nagashima 4 Sanshin made* (History of the revival of professional baseball: From MacArthur to Nagashima four struck out) (Chuko Shinsho, 2012), pp. 72–73.

69 Ibid., pp. 94–96.

Finally, the Seals' visit and the connections to Lefty O'Doul opened the door of opportunity for a player who would later be recognized as 'the Jackie Robinson of Japanese baseball'. Wally Yonamine was the first American to play professional baseball in Japan after World War II. Born in Hawaii, the two-sport athlete played professional football for the San Francisco 49ers in 1949 and baseball for the San Francisco Seals in 1950. Realizing that post-war America was not quite ready to embrace a ballplayer of Japanese ancestry, O'Doul encouraged Yonamine to pursue a professional baseball career in Japan. The bespectacled outfielder made his debut for the Yomiuri Giants in 1951 and over the course of a twelve-year career he was a member of four Japan Series Championship teams, was named the Central League MVP in 1957 and was a consecutive seven-time Best Nine Award winner (1952–58), an eleven-time All-Star, a three-time batting champion and the first foreigner to manage a professional Japanese ballclub (Chunichi Dragons, 1972–77). Yonamine not only changed the pace of Japanese baseball with his aggressive American style of play, he also inspired future generations of stars in Japan. Home run king Sadaharu Oh often tells the story of how Yonamine forever touched his heart as an aspiring ballplayer. As an eleven-year-old fan, Oh attended a Yomiuri Giants game and meekly asked for players' autographs. One by one the ballplayers passed him, except for Yonamine. 'He took my board, asked for my name—which I could barely get from my lips—and signed his autograph', said Oh. When he became a professional ballplayer many years later, Oh confessed that he readily signed autographs because 'of the joy Wally Yonamine brought into my life one afternoon in my boyhood'.

Regarding U.S.-Japan baseball games, the San Francisco Seal's visit also triggered the revival of constant tours of Major League teams to Japan. In 1951, Joe DiMaggio brought selected players as player-manager and his team played a total of sixteen games. DiMaggio was called back to New York before the tour ended, despite the fact that several games were yet to be played, where he announced his retirement after refusing to be traded. In 1953, the *Mainichi Shimbun* invited selected MLB teams to visit Japan, and the *Yomiuri Shimbun* invited the New York Giants. Since then, many Major League teams have been invited to Japan, including:

1955	New York Yankees
1956	Brooklyn Dodgers
1958	St. Louis Cardinals
1960	San Francisco Giants
1962	Detroit Tigers
1966	Los Angeles Dodgers
1968	St. Louis Cardinals
1970	San Francisco Giants
1971	Baltimore Orioles
1974	New York Mets
1978	Cincinnati Reds
1981	Kansas City Royals
1984	Baltimore Orioles
1993	Los Angeles Dodgers

In addition to individual teams, in 1986, MLB assembled all-star teams to visit Japan every two years, a tradition that lasted twenty years, with the exception of the strike-eliminated season of 1994. After an eight-year break from 2006, the MLB All-Star-Japan series resumed in 2014. The series was eventually discontinued and replaced by the World Baseball Classic (WBC), an international baseball tournament supported by the International Baseball Federation, MLB, the Major League Baseball Players Association and the World Baseball Softball Confederation. As of the date of this publication, Team Japan has won the WBC championship twice, first in the inaugural series in 2006 and again in 2009.

Conclusion

The United States adopted occupation policies for virtually every field imaginable in Japan, including politics, economics, agriculture, education, labor unions and media. Japan's post-war societal model developed during the occupation, and it influenced every aspect of Japanese life, culture, art and sports. During the war, a group of intellectuals within the State Department drafted a 're-education' or 'reorientation' policy to implement in Japan when the war was over. These policies were meant to reorient the Japanese people, whom the U.S. government believed to be temporarily misguided by Japan's previous militaristic, autocratic government. The U.S.'s ultimate goal with the occupation was to instill democracy in the Japanese people.

Some American occupation officers, however, acted as if their charge included disciplining the 'uncivilized' Japanese. Japanese officials who worked closely with GHQ/SCAP staff members were highly educated and fluent in English. Notwithstanding this fact, they were seldom able to bring to attention the mistreatment of Japanese civilians by U.S. occupational officers or ill-mannered GHQ/SCAP staff. Because the U.S. officials dictated the terms of the surrender and controlled the country during the occupation, it is unlikely that Japanese officials, as people of a defeated country, reported many cases of oppression. Therefore, it is almost certain that some members of the occupational force were responsible for inflicting some measure of excessive, extreme or unnecessary cultural abuse towards the Japanese people.

For example, GHQ/SCAP prohibited *kabuki*, a form of classical Japanese theater. The ban not only included revenge plays like *Kana Dehon Chushingura* but extended to almost all classic *kabuki* performances on the false assumption that these plays reflected the underlying theme of feudalism. Faubion Bowers, Gen. MacArthur's aide-de-camp and a noted scholar of Japanese theater, attempted to abolish the ban on *kabuki*. Bowers is on record as saying, 'I believe the occupation destroyed Japanese culture. The Americans tend to think that the U.S. saved Japan, but I disagree'.[1]

In fact, on the question of whether GHQ staff and occupation policymakers tried to extend new values — like democracy, gender equality, teamwork and sportsmanship — while respecting and protecting Japanese

---

1 Bowers, Faubion. Interview: 'Senryou ha Nihon no Bunka wo Hakai shita (kikite: Takeshi Tanikawa)' (The occupation destroyed Japanese culture), *Senryouki-Zasshi-Shiryou-Taikei: Taishui-Bunka-Hen* (The occupation period periodical materials compendium: Popular culture series), Geppou 1 (Monthly Newsletter 1) (Iwanami-Shoten, 2008), p. 9.

culture, the answer is a firm 'No'. The reason why *kabuki* was able to survive was only because there was a person like Bowers who enthusiastically worked to protect the tradition of *kabuki* culture. The reason why traditional judo changed into a completely different sport is because mainstream judo participants tried to survive and be accepted by GHQ by stressing judo's nature as a sport, abandoning traditional aspects in the process. Given these facts, I can say that the occupation force was nothing more than a destroyer of the Japanese culture.

Some Japanese claim that the Japanese people were persecuted by GHQ/ SCAP and that the new Japanese constitution should be amended because it was written under strong GHQ/SCAP supervision and therefore does not reflect the common will of the Japanese people. On the other hand, some argue that the U.S. occupation of Japan was successful when compared to the outcome of the Iraq war and occupation.[2] For example, John W. Dower insists that the reason for the success of the U.S. occupation of Japan is because, rather than imposing an entirely totalitarian government, the Americans administered Japan with the cooperation of the Japanese. As a result, the type of democracy found in Japan is a unique hybrid created via the collaboration of U.S. and Japanese leaders.[3]

My standpoint on the U.S. occupation of Japan is close to Dower's view, and I formed this position through my long-term research on U.S. film policy in occupied Japan. It is true that GHQ/SCAP film policy does display a marked lack of knowledge of Japanese culture, as many Japanese films produced before or during the World War II period were abandoned or destroyed by GHQ/SCAP officials who did not understand their importance. This is further supported by the fact that *seppun-eiga* (exploitation films), which feature kissing scenes, were encouraged by the CIE and eroded Japanese ideals of modesty and traditional expressions of love. Looking at the overall intent of the American policy, however, it is clear that the Japanese people did learn from American films, whether it was lessons in American democracy, gender equality, materialistic wealth or accepting GHQ/SCAP policies. From the standpoint of U.S. cultural diplomacy

---

2 Nina Serafino, Curt Tarnoff and Dick K. Nanto, *U.S. Occupation Assistance: Iraq, Germany and Japan Compared*, CRS Report for Congress (Received through the CRS Web / Order Code RL33331), March 23, 2006, Accession number: ADA458270.

3 John W. Dower, *Embracing the Defeat: Japan in the Wake of World War II* (W. W. Norton and Co., 2000); comments from Prof. Dower were recorded when I visited his office at MIT on November 24, 1999.

policy, the U.S. military occupation of Japan succeeded in Americanizing post-war Japan by using Hollywood movies to indoctrinate America's social values. Once Japan's filmmakers accepted CIE censorship—the CIE didn't think of it as 'censorship' and called their function 'supervision'—and the film review process conducted by the Civilian Censorship Detachment, the U.S. occupation policy also helped revive the Japanese film industry.[4] As a result, the 'Golden Age' of Japan's film industry grew from the policies of the post-war period.

Some of Japan's film experts who ingratiated themselves with the imperial military during the war were upset that young Japanese Americans who lacked knowledge of Japanese culture criticized the scripts of Japanese films during the occupation. Others claimed that, during the occupation, the CIE was open to ideas from experts from the Japanese film industry, while pointing out that Japan's domestic censorship was one-sided during the war. Some filmmakers expressed appreciation for CIE censorship, indicating that a new era had come in which they could discuss films openly and freely.[5]

During the post-war era, Japan's film industry became recognized internationally when *Rashomon*, directed by Akira Kurosawa, won the Golden Lion Prize at the 1951 Venice Film Festival.[6] During the post-war period, Japan was able to rejoin the international community through such cultural exchanges because of the positive relationship between the Japanese film industry and the U.S. authorities during the occupation. As a filmmaker, Kurosawa represented a hybrid between American and Japanese culture, and he became successful with the support of the CIE.[7]

If the occupation had a positive impact on Japan's film industry, is it possible that it had a similar impact on Japan's sports world? In other

---

4 Kyoko Hirano, *Mr. Smith Goes to Tokyo: Japanese Cinema under the American Occupation, 1945-1952* (Smithsonian Institution Press, 1992).

5 Kajiro Yamamoto, a leading director of TOHO, represents the former view, while Akira Kurosawa, his pupil, represents the latter.

6 Akira Iwasaki, *Gendai Nihon no Eiga: Sono Shisou to Fuzoku* (Modern Japanese films: Their ideology and customs) (Chuo-Koron-Sha, 1958), pp. 218–225.

7 It is a well-known fact that Kurosawa had learned how to cut a number of frames in order to increase the speed of running horses from John Ford directly, and his dynamic way of directing was always evaluated as 'Westernized' or 'far from the ordinary Japanese style of directing' by the critics. Besides, he was regarded as a favorite director amongst CIE staff, who wished to make Japanese studios produce films to democratize and educate the Japanese audience. The CIE willingly held a party to celebrate the completion of Kurosawa's *No Regrets for Our Youth* (1946, TOHO).

words, was the U.S. occupation successful in Americanizing post-war Japan by using popular sports, such as baseball, to indoctrinate America's social values?

During the occupation, the Japanese people welcomed GHQ/SCAP policies that promoted sports—both participant sports and spectator sports. Furthermore, some historians argue that the people of Japan were receptive to the '3-S Policy' adopted by GHQ/SCAP, one that offered 'Screen, Sports and Sex' as a means to ease the complaints and frustration of the Japanese people during the occupation.[8] Not only did authorities from Japan's amateur and professional sporting world, including people associated with baseball like Matsutaro Shoriki, Sotaro Suzuki and Ryuji Suzuki, applaud GHQ/SCAP sports policy, the policy was also supported by many of Japan's intellectuals, including writer Ango Sakaguchi, lyricist Hachiro Sato and poet Shuuoushi Mizuhara.[9] The GHQ/SCAP's sports policy even had the support of Emperor Hirohito. The Emperor's love of sports was perhaps a little greater than both GHQ/SCAP and the Imperial Household Agency desired, as it helped to create a new imperial identity for Hirohito.

Baseball (*yakyu*) was already very popular with the average Japanese sports fan before World War II. As a result, the Japanese were already baseball hungry when Maj. Gen. William F. Marquat, addressing the opening ceremony of the revived Select Middle-School Baseball tournament held on March 30, 1947, announced that 'Japan's baseball enthusiasm is unprecedented'.[10] As I explored in Chapter Five, the U.S. did not use baseball as a tool for their worldwide cultural diplomacy policy in places where the sport was not very popular. In Japan, the U.S. was certain that baseball, as a tool of the occupation, could successfully be used to transform Japanese society. Had U.S. authorities felt otherwise, it is unlikely that they would have promoted the sport.

---

8 Masahiro Yasuoka, *Unmei wo Tsukuru: Ningen-Gaku Kouwa* (Creating destiny: Anthropology lecture) (President-Sha, 1985), p. 39.

9 Ango Sakaguchi, 'Nihon Yakyu ha Pro ni Arazu' (Japan's baseball is not professional), *Baseball Magazine*, Vol. 3, No. 89, August 1948, Koubun-Sha, pp. 16–17; Hachiro Sato, 'Seals Gun wo Mukaeru Waga besuto nain wo utau' (Lyricize our best nine who will meet the Seals), Vol. 4, No. 14, November 1949, Koubun-sha, pp. 50–51; Shuuoushi Mizuhara, 'Korakuen Kyujou Nite' (At Korakuen Stadium), *Home Run*, Vol. 3, No. 10, October 1948, Homurun-Sha, p. 13.

10 Masaru Hatano, *Nichibei Yakyu Shi:Major wo Oikaketa 70 Nen* (History of U.S.-Japan baseball: 70 years chasing the Major League) (PHP, 2001), p. 196.

During the American occupation of Japan, the Cold War between the U.S. and the Soviet Union broke out. With tensions growing between the two countries, the U.S. began to look at the Soviet Union as a hypothetical enemy. As a result, American policy in Japan became a frontline for the cultural diplomacy pursued by the U.S. in the East-West conflict. This made Japan different from Germany, which was divided into Eastern and Western sectors.

Occupied Japan, which was controlled solely by the U.S., experienced a substantial economic and cultural revival. Many in Japan concluded that rebuilding the country in the image of American democracy would create a more pleasant and more prosperous society than one modeled on the Soviet socialist system. When one considers that the American policies in Japan were part of a worldwide cultural and diplomatic strategy, the U.S. attempt to use sports to influence culture in Japan was significant.

Many Americans were exposed to the propaganda images of the Japanese during World War II, and to most Americans, the Japanese were of low intelligence and were regarded as 'Yellow Monkeys'.[11] Thinking of them as something less than human, many in America viewed the Japanese as fanatical and illogical. Most Americans could not understand why Japanese soldiers were willing to die for their Emperor. With the occupation, however, American authorities realized that the Japanese loved baseball and recalled that prior to World War II they had enthusiastically welcomed Babe Ruth, Lou Gehrig and Jimmie Foxx to their country in 1934. Thus, GHQ/SCAP began to communicate to the Japanese in the common language of baseball.

The occupation policies in the fields of media, culture and sports did not originate by chance within GHQ/SCAP. Instead, the Office of War Information (OWI) and other wartime agencies devised them before the war was over. With the end of the war, those responsible for these policies were transferred to the State Department. Some of them were sent to Japan and became GHQ/SCAP officers.[12] Thus, continuity existed between policies devised in Washington before the end of the war and those implemented

---

11 Yumiko Murakami, *Yellow Face: Hollywood Eiga ni miru Asia-jin no Shouzo* (Yellow face: Portraits of Asians through Hollywood films) (Asahi Sensho, 1993), p. 114.

12 Takeshi Tanikawa, *America-Eiga to Senryou Seisaku* (American films and occupation policy) (Kyoto University Press, 2002), p. 265.

in Japan during the occupation.[13] The State Department's Office of International Information and Cultural Affairs (OIC) was the division that designated sports as a tool of foreign policy. This division became the United States Information Agency (USIA) in August 1953. The staff who worked at these agencies shared information with GHQ/SCAP and other American embassies all over the world. It is likely that they sought the most effective way to communicate with the local population in each country. One of the most effective means to communicate with the people in Japan was through baseball. Baseball provided American authorities with a positive sanction or reward that could be used in Japan. In other words, baseball was an active tool used during the occupation to symbolize how Japan should progress in the future.

The San Francisco Seals' visit in 1949, which was enthusiastically organized by Maj. Gen. Marquat and important figures from Japan's baseball world, helped heal the rift with the United States. Even though the Seals won every game against their Japanese opponents, the fact that players from Japan and the U.S. gathered on the same field and intently played the game provided proof of the deepening of the Japan-America friendship. When both nations' flags — the Rising Sun and the Stars and Stripes — were displayed side by side at the ballpark, many Japanese fans must have thought, 'We will work together with America as a partner and a model that is stronger than us, but willing to work hard with us'.

If baseball represented a positive aspect of the American occupation policy, the banning of traditional *budo* (Japanese martial arts) sports such as kendo, which was regarded as being rooted in feudalistic values and in the nationally designated religion of Shinto, represented a negative aspect. During the occupation, U.S. authorities directed those participating in Japanese sports into scientifically-based activities rather than spiritual disciplines and practices. In other words, American policy shifted the way people thought about sports, moving from an attitude in which athletes wept at their losses to one, like that stressed by Jackie Robinson in his Voice of America (VOA) broadcasts, in which athletes embraced their losses. The Americans also forced the traditional Japanese sports that were not banned,

---

13 Concrete examples of former OWI staff who were transferred to the Department of State and then sent to occupied Japan are Don Brown, the chief of the Information Division of the CIE, and Michael Bergher, the first representative of the CMPE. For detailed information, see Takeshi Tanikawa, *America-Eiga to Senryou Seisaku* (American films and occupation policy).

such as sumo and *kento* (boxing), and that were banned temporarily but later permitted, such as judo and *kyudo*, to reform and adopt a Western system of promotion.

The reason kendo retained its traditional pre-war and wartime form was paradoxically due to the fact that GHQ/SCAP prohibited the teaching of kendo at school throughout the occupation period and banned the practice of kendo at police stations after 1949. In other words, the purity of kendo was able to survive only because the Japanese people associated with kendo bided their time until the day when the ban was cancelled by GHQ/SCAP. In this context, the negative aspects of the occupation sports policy had a greater impact than its positive aspects, and the American staff of GHQ/SCAP displayed an arrogance in their lack of concern for the destruction of another nation's culture.

The American authorities actively sought to revive certain Japanese sports, especially baseball. GHQ/SCAP encouraged Japanese people associated with baseball to organize the East-West Game only one hundred days after the war ended. The professional pennant race, the Tokyo Big Six Baseball League Tournament and the Inter-City Match Amateur Baseball Tournament returned the following year. In the spring of 1947, the Select Middle School Baseball Tournament (currently the High School Baseball Tournament) resumed. Baseball steadily recovered during the post-war period, and the visit of the San Francisco Seals represented the completion of that process.

GHQ/SCAP's sports policies not only shifted how Japanese people thought about sports and which sports they watched and played, their influence also extended beyond the stadium and arena. Occupational authorities used sports to introduce CIE films into Japan, such as *Let's Play Baseball* and *Baseball Swing King*. VOA thoughtfully executed sports policies through the efforts of Jackie Robinson and other Major League athletes.

This book has examined the role that sports played in democratizing Japan. As discussed above, American authorities executed U.S. cultural diplomacy policies in a variety of ways, including in the domain of sports. Proving the effectiveness of the U.S. policy is not easy. Proof of such a theory would necessitate providing evidence that democracy actually took root in post-war Japan. Perhaps more useful is the question, 'Were the sports policies of GHQ/SCAP effective in carrying out the goals of the occupation?' According to information released by the Information

Dissemination Section (IDS), the Initial Post-Surrender Policy Relating to Japan had three goals:

1. Militarism and militant nationalism will be removed;

2. To develop a desire for individual liberties and respect for fundamental human rights, particularly the freedoms of religion, assembly, speech, and the press;

3. To ensure that Japan will not again become a menace to the U.S. or to the peace and security of the world.[14]

While the above goals seem to serve a purpose, and were undoubtedly accomplished during the occupation, in reality, the U.S. had a more pressing goal. Under occupied Japan, the General Headquarters / U.S. Army Forces Pacific (GHQ/AFPAC)—another GHQ—and GHQ/SCAP were both led by Gen. Douglas MacArthur. The purpose of the occupational policies was to redirect Japan to serve U.S. national interests. Written evidence indicating this is difficult to find. According to scripts from VOA broadcasts, the goal of the occupation was to 'enable Japan to achieve an economic environment in which democracy can take root and survive'.[15]

Ultimately, this goal would be achieved by firming Japan's economy as a capitalist system, which would advance the adoption of democracy; but the American policy had another goal—to foster Japan as an American ally in its struggle against the communism of the Soviet Union. In other words, the occupation not only attempted to re-educate the Japanese people in order to convert them into citizens who were pro-American, it also attempted to recruit Japan to become a member of the U.S. Far East alliance and establish it as a breakwater against communism.

There is just one more pressing question—have Japanese citizens become truly pro-American? In other words, was the U.S. successful in converting Japan into an American ally?

---

14 Akira Shimizu, '20•9•22 Kara 23•8•19 made — Senryou-ka no Eiga-Kai no Kiroku' (From September 22, 1945 to August 19, 1948 — A record of the motion picture industry under the occupation), *Film Center*, No. 7, 1973, p. 9. Original Source: SWNCC 150/4/A (U.S. Initial Post-Surrender Policy for Japan), September 21, 1945.

15 VOA Transcript, October 19, 1948, Radio Branch Bureau, OIE—IBD, Department of State, RG 306, NARA, New York Branch.

GHQ/SCAP and the State Department's Office of International Information and Cultural Affairs and its successor agency, the USIA, nourished the discipline of sportsmanship in Japan through baseball. As Gen. Douglas MacArthur observed, 'Baseball helps nourish one's endurance and a great sense of teamwork. Moreover, it also helps promote a sense of emulation that is necessary for our society to expand its socio-economic-political liberty'.[16]

Most people in Japan supported the U.S. occupation's goals because those welcoming the post-war, high-growth economy likely possessed the motivation to build a society with abundant materials by sharing American values. In this sense, sports, and especially baseball, succeeded in promoting Japan's democratization. Furthermore, the U.S. military occupation achieved the Americanization of post-war Japan by vulgarizing sports, especially baseball, in order to indoctrinate its social values.

---

16 'Ma-Gensui So-Kei-Sen ni Shukuji' (Gen. MacArthur gives a remark at the So-Kei game), *Baseball Magazine*, Koubun-Sha, Vol. 4, No. 10, August 1949, p. 48. The quotation is translated from the Japanese version which appeared in the above magazine.

Appendix 1

Number of Film Showings and Viewers of Eight Baseball-Related CIE Films

(Prefectural monthly report from Jan. to Dec. 1950)

		Jan.	Feb.	Mar.	Apr.	May
#12 **Baseball Instructions**	Tokyo (Showings)	0	7	8	0	0
	(Viewers)	0	2,140	1,600	0	0
	Ibaraki (Showings)	0	0	0	0	0
	(Viewers)	0	0	0	0	0
	Niigata (Showings)	0	0	0	0	0
	(Viewers)	0	0	0	0	0
	Fukushima (Showings)	0	0	N/A	0	0
	(Viewers)	0	0	N/A	0	0
	Subtotal (Showings)	0	7	8	0	0
	(Viewers)	0	2,140	1,600	0	0
#14 **Let's Play Baseball**	Tokyo (Showings)	29	21	45	24	36
	(Viewers)	7,270	9,040	14,414	7,245	22,123
	Ibaraki (Showings)	3	1	21	32	80
	(Viewers)	1,400	700	18,100	9,450	20,364
	Niigata (Showings)	22	15	19	28	20
	(Viewers)	12,885	2,894	6,253	9,601	7,230
	Fukushima (Showings)	15	5	N/A	3	7
	(Viewers)	3,304	1,617	N/A	550	766
	Subtotal (Showings)	69	42	85	87	143
	(Viewers)	24,859	14,251	38,767	26,846	50,483
#113 **Baseball Swing King**	Tokyo (Showings)	0	0	0	44	31
	(Viewers)	0	0	0	19,652	9,930
	Ibaraki (Showings)	6	4	0	30	40
	(Viewers)	3,000	1,200	0	24,000	21,800
	Niigata (Showings)	38	3	3	0	19
	(Viewers)	16,810	3,830	780	0	9,537
	Fukushima (Showings)	17	6	N/A	0	0
	(Viewers)	7,668	1,670	N/A	0	0
	Subtotal (Showings)	61	13	3	74	90
	(Viewers)	27,478	6,700	780	43,652	41,267

June	July	Aug.	Sept.	Oct.	Nov.	Dec.	Total
0	0	0	0	0	0	0	15
0	0	0	0	0	0	0	3,740
0	0	0	0	0	0	N/A	0
0	0	0	0	0	0	N/A	0
0	0	0	0	0	0	0	0
0	0	0	0	0	0	0	0
0	0	0	0	0	0	N/A	0
0	0	0	0	0	0	N/A	0
0	0	0	0	0	0	0	15
0	0	0	0	0	0	0	3,740
0	0	40	19	18	35	13	280
0	0	42,587	19,225	10,083	21,100	3,040	156,127
1	0	6	0	27	25	N/A	196
500	0	3,100	0	12,500	12,000	N/A	78,114
0	0	22	6	16	3	34	185
0	0	7,310	2,350	4,320	2,230	16,530	71,603
0	0	0	6	0	2	N/A	38
0	0	0	2,850	0	4,870	N/A	13,957
1	0	68	31	61	65	47	699
500	0	52,997	24,425	26,903	40,200	19,570	319,801
27	17	36	23	6	16	16	216
27,705	4,035	28,815	29,314	1,310	5,780	5,460	132,001
9	20	5	0	23	20	N/A	157
2,952	6,260	1,600	0	13,140	11,000	N/A	84,952
22	15	23	1	5	20	12	161
6,780	4,221	15,390	260	2,350	6,595	3,660	70,213
12	4	9	38	0	8	N/A	94
5,945	1,830	3,322	15,430	0	2,840	N/A	38,705
70	56	73	62	34	64	28	628
43,382	16,346	49,127	45,004	16,800	26,215	9,120	325,871

(Table continues)

		Jan.	Feb.	Mar.	Apr.	May
#125 *Topics of America*	Tokyo (Showings)	0	0	0	0	0
	(Viewers)	0	0	0	0	0
	Ibaraki (Showings)	0	0	0	0	0
	(Viewers)	0	0	0	0	0
	Niigata (Showings)	0	0	0	0	0
	(Viewers)	0	0	0	0	0
	Fukushima (Showings)	0	5	N/A	28	0
	(Viewers)	0	1,770	N/A	7,921	0
	Subtotal (Showings)	0	5	0	28	0
	(Viewers)	0	1,770	0	7,921	0
#129 *Sports Revue*	Tokyo (Showings)	42	28	0	49	29
	(Viewers)	13,031	9,965	0	20,290	17,990
	Ibaraki (Showings)	17	0	0	0	24
	(Viewers)	2,200	0	0	0	8,480
	Niigata (Showings)	49	9	1	8	21
	(Viewers)	17,852	2,070	600	1,857	6,324
	Fukushima (Showings)	49	36	N/A	0	5
	(Viewers)	16,787	17,690	N/A	0	2,545
	Subtotal (Showings)	157	73	1	57	79
	(Viewers)	49,870	29,725	600	22,147	35,339
#140 *Sports' Golden Age*	Tokyo (Showings)	N/A	0	34	78	81
	(Viewers)	N/A	0	10,238	26,013	35,266
	Ibaraki (Showings)	N/A	N/A	21	23	20
	(Viewers)	N/A	N/A	11,100	15,350	12,620
	Niigata (Showings)	N/A	N/A	14	47	62
	(Viewers)	N/A	N/A	3,405	14,710	24,292
	Fukushima (Showings)	N/A	N/A	N/A	29	13
	(Viewers)	N/A	N/A	N/A	7,689	2,465
	Subtotal (Showings)	N/A	0	69	177	176
	(Viewers)	N/A	0	24,743	63,762	74,643

June	July	Aug.	Sept.	Oct.	Nov.	Dec.	Total
0	0	2	17	1	0	0	20
0	0	1,600	13,460	70	0	0	15,130
0	0	0	19	25	5	N/A	49
0	0	0	9,365	6,626	2,100	N/A	18,091
0	0	8	26	1	12	20	67
0	0	7,080	7,482	674	4,650	4,315	24,201
0	4	0	20	0	0	N/A	57
0	950	0	7,680	0	0	N/A	18,321
0	4	10	82	27	17	20	193
0	950	8,680	37,987	7,370	6,750	4,315	75,743
28	15	45	12	18	21	25	312
27,932	15,000	49,590	4,490	3,995	10,300	8,300	180,883
32	16	0	0	20	5	N/A	114
8,710	8,300	0	0	8,240	3,700	N/A	39,630
21	2	0	1	3	18	3	136
14,280	550	0	450	1,290	4,270	1,250	50,793
0	8	12	6	0	7	N/A	123
0	4,950	1,810	5,400	0	1,452	N/A	50,634
81	41	57	19	41	51	28	685
50,922	28,800	51,400	10,340	13,525	19,722	9,550	321,940
51	18	23	9	22	24	15	355
16,295	11,344	29,665	6,730	6,185	11,360	3,585	156,681
12	39	8	0	48	57	N/A	228
7,600	13,600	5,100	0	24,330	12,231	N/A	101,931
39	54	0	6	51	43	20	336
13,940	18,175	0	1,923	16,071	15,345	3,570	111,431
13	16	8	0	0	0	N/A	79
3,610	5,450	1,364	0	0	0	N/A	20,578
115	127	39	15	121	124	35	998
41,445	48,569	36,129	8,653	46,586	38,936	7,155	390,621

(Table continues)

		Jan.	Feb.	Mar.	Apr.	May
#182 *The* *Television* *Workshop*	Tokyo (Showings)	N/A	N/A	N/A	N/A	0
	(Viewers)	N/A	N/A	N/A	N/A	0
	Ibaraki (Showings)	N/A	N/A	N/A	N/A	N/A
	(Viewers)	N/A	N/A	N/A	N/A	N/A
	Niigata (Showings)	N/A	N/A	N/A	N/A	N/A
	(Viewers)	N/A	N/A	N/A	N/A	N/A
	Fukushima (Showings)	N/A	N/A	N/A	N/A	N/A
	(Viewers)	N/A	N/A	N/A	N/A	N/A
	Subtotal (Showings)	N/A	N/A	N/A	N/A	0
	(Viewers)	N/A	N/A	N/A	N/A	0
#206 *Boys'* *Baseball* *League*	Tokyo (Showings)	N/A	N/A	N/A	N/A	N/A
	(Viewers)	N/A	N/A	N/A	N/A	N/A
	Ibaraki (Showings)	N/A	N/A	N/A	N/A	N/A
	(Viewers)	N/A	N/A	N/A	N/A	N/A
	Niigata (Showings)	N/A	N/A	N/A	N/A	N/A
	(Viewers)	N/A	N/A	N/A	N/A	N/A
	Fukushima (Showings)	N/A	N/A	N/A	N/A	N/A
	(Viewers)	N/A	N/A	N/A	N/A	N/A
	Subtotal (Showings)	N/A	N/A	N/A	N/A	N/A
	(Viewers)	N/A	N/A	N/A	N/A	N/A
	Grand total (Showings)	287	140	166	423	488
	(Viewers)	102,207	54,586	66,490	164,328	201,732

June	July	Aug.	Sept.	Oct.	Nov.	Dec.	Total
13	11	46	54	56	28	0	208
5,150	10,660	51,085	39,630	30,970	14,820	0	152,315
6	39	27	25	38	0	N/A	135
1,650	17,230	7,450	12,000	15,381	0	N/A	53,711
0	14	38	37	29	3	4	125
0	8,077	13,590	10,163	8,147	780	760	41,517
2	2	9	5	3	0	N/A	21
1,275	1,800	1,183	847	1,500	0	N/A	6,605
21	66	120	121	126	31	4	489
8,075	37,767	73,308	62,640	55,998	15,600	760	254,148
N/A	0	48	34	25	60	43	210
N/A	0	40,585	17,735	9,350	34,600	11,985	114,255
N/A	N/A	35	60	0	11	N/A	106
N/A	N/A	14,800	19,700	0	5,670	N/A	40,170
N/A	N/A	21	49	44	25	23	162
N/A	N/A	11,365	15,765	9,560	7,016	5,831	49,537
N/A	N/A	14	23	0	24	N/A	61
N/A	N/A	8,366	11,173	0	12,757	N/A	32,296
N/A	0	118	166	69	120	66	539
N/A	0	75,116	64,373	18,910	60,043	17,816	236,258
288	294	485	496	479	472	228	4,246
144,324	132,432	346,757	253,422	186,092	207,466	68,286	1,928,122

Appendix 2

Number of Film Showings and Viewers of Five Sports-Related CIE Films

(Prefectural monthly report from Jan. to Dec. 1950)

		Jan.	Feb.	Mar.	Apr.	May
#16 ***White*** ***Carnival***	Tokyo (Showings)	25	44	8	5	20
	(Viewers)	5,836	13,982	2,900	3,000	10,025
	Ibaraki (Showings)	24	2	4	0	19
	(Viewers)	16,950	??48	2,000	0	6,200
	Niigata (Showings)	1	0	0	0	0
	(Viewers)	280	0	0	0	0
	Fukushima (Showings)	12	9	N/A	0	2
	(Viewers)	2,789	2,041	N/A	0	580
	Subtotal (Showings)	62	55	12	5	41
	(Viewers)	25,855	16,071+α	4,900	3,000	16,805
#132 ***Vacation*** ***Sports***	Tokyo (Showings)	33	51	45	0	21
	(Viewers)	11,398	12,465	17,696	0	25,640
	Ibaraki (Showings)	16	13	15	0	0
	(Viewers)	10,000	10,400	9,100	0	0
	Niigata (Showings)	25	57	41	12	0
	(Viewers)	8,224	22,490	12,275	2,680	0
	Fukushima (Showings)	26	14	N/A	0	4
	(Viewers)	8,889	3,610	N/A	0	2,020
	Subtotal (Showings)	100	135	101	12	25
	(Viewers)	38,511	48,965	39,071	2,680	27,660
#154 ***Glimpses*** ***of America***	Tokyo (Showings)	22	55	43	48	36
	(Viewers)	8,072	21,002	13,285	15,670	15,630
	Ibaraki (Showings)	23	22	25	2	0
	(Viewers)	14,700	10,370	10,980	650	0
	Niigata (Showings)	19	44	19	32	33
	(Viewers)	8,660	19,690	4,140	15,775	8,506
	Fukushima (Showings)	8	43	N/A	24	8
	(Viewers)	1,963	8,943	N/A	10,590	1,772
	Subtotal (Showings)	72	164	87	106	77
	(Viewers)	33,395	60,005	28,405	42,685	25,908

June	July	Aug.	Sept.	Oct.	Nov.	Dec.	Total
16	2	16	26	12	26	8	208
13,910	950	15,750	7,187	3,750	8,970	1,310	87,570
3	6	20	20	39	28	N/A	165
1,577	2,100	5,803	10,150	12,300	12,560	N/A	69,688+α
0	0	0	0	0	0	0	1
0	0	0	0	0	0	0	280
0	0	0	1	0	0	N/A	24
0	0	0	130	0	0	N/A	5,540
19	8	36	47	51	54	8	398
15,487	3,050	21,553	17,467	16,050	21,530	1,310	163,078+α
42	11	33	29	23	23	21	332
46,038	4,550	35,550	31,570	11,480	13,465	7,690	217,542
6	24	20	21	75	75	N/A	265
3,100	8,650	7,700	9,600	28,335	29,440	N/A	116,325
0	26	29	19	7	16	0	232
0	4,552	15,985	8,600	2,298	4,070	0	81,174
0	1	26	11	0	12	N/A	94
0	50	7,542	10,600	0	12,970	N/A	45,681
48	62	108	70	105	126	21	913
49,138	17,802	66,777	60,370	42,113	59,945	7,690	460,722
0	0	11	1	0	7	0	223
0	0	11,050	700	0	2,480	0	87,889
0	0	3	5	23	20	N/A	123
0	0	1,100	2,100	13,140	11,000	N/A	64,040
0	1	4	1	0	17	6	176
0	60	900	90	0	3,055	2,300	63,176
0	0	4	10	3	0	N/A	100
0	0	1,524	3,165	700	0	N/A	28,657
0	1	22	17	26	44	6	622
0	60	14,574	6,055	13,840	16,535	2,300	243,762

(Table continues)

		Jan.	Feb.	Mar.	Apr.	May
#174 *Views of America*	Tokyo (Showings)	N/A	N/A	N/A	0	22
	(Viewers)	N/A	N/A	N/A	0	7,084
	Ibaraki (Showings)	N/A	N/A	N/A	N/A	5
	(Viewers)	N/A	N/A	N/A	N/A	1,860
	Niigata (Showings)	N/A	N/A	N/A	N/A	5
	(Viewers)	N/A	N/A	N/A	N/A	805
	Fukushima (Showings)	N/A	N/A	N/A	N/A	0
	(Viewers)	N/A	N/A	N/A	N/A	0
	Subtotal (Showings)	N/A	N/A	N/A	0	32
	(Viewers)	N/A	N/A	N/A	0	9,749
#213 *Let's Square Dance*	Tokyo (Showings)	N/A	N/A	N/A	N/A	N/A
	(Viewers)	N/A	N/A	N/A	N/A	N/A
	Ibaraki (Showings)	N/A	N/A	N/A	N/A	N/A
	(Viewers)	N/A	N/A	N/A	N/A	N/A
	Niigata (Showings)	N/A	N/A	N/A	N/A	N/A
	(Viewers)	N/A	N/A	N/A	N/A	N/A
	Fukushima (Showings)	N/A	N/A	N/A	N/A	N/A
	(Viewers)	N/A	N/A	N/A	N/A	N/A
	Subtotal (Showings)	N/A	N/A	N/A	N/A	N/A
	(Viewers)	N/A	N/A	N/A	N/A	N/A
Grand Total (Showings)		234	354	200	123	175
(Viewers)		97,761	125,041+α	72,376	48,365	80,122

June	July	Aug.	Sept.	Oct.	Nov.	Dec.	Total
47	25	20	29	0	0	11	154
20,345	19,955	13,340	19,850	0	0	4,130	84,704
35	32	21	40	0	7	N/A	140
9,556	13,790	8,975	22,208	0	2,630	N/A	59,019
0	35	55	27	19	11	22	174
0	12,285	13,760	9,728	5,147	2,532	5,231	49,488
2	38	12	18	10	1	N/A	133
70	8,391	1,670	10,010	2,603	600	N/A	23,344
84	130	108	114	29	19	33	549
29,971	100,451	37,745	61,796	7,750	5,762	9,361	262,585
N/A	0	45	20	34	63	43	205
N/A	0	46,520	7,719	18,970	22,861	15,259	111,329
N/A	N/A	54	27	0	30	N/A	111
N/A	N/A	22,250	12,970	0	14,750	N/A	49,970
N/A	N/A	22	34	0	49	40	145
N/A	N/A	11,638	13,674	0	13,313	10,747	49,372
N/A	N/A	35	23	16	17	N/A	91
N/A	N/A	14,884	11,365	4,222	11,574	N/A	42,045
N/A	0	156	104	50	159	83	552
N/A	0	95,292	45,728	23,192	62,498	26,006	252,716
151	201	430	352	261	402	151	3,034
94,596	121,363	235,941	191,416	102,945	166,270	46,667	1,382,863+α

Appendix 3

Educational Film Attendance Report, Fukushima Prefecture

(June to Nov. 1950)

Date	Venue	Town
6/19/50	A square in Manpuku-ji	Oomachi, Wakamatsu-Shi
6/20/50	Yumoto Primary & Middle School, PTA	Higashiyama-Mura, Kita-Aizu-Gun
6/21/50	Ikki-Mura Primary & Middle School	Ikki-Mura, Kita-Aizu-Gun
6/22/50	A square in Amida-Cho	Amida-Cho, Wakamatsu-Shi
6/23/50	Playground at Nagano Primary School	Nagano, Tajima-Cho, Minami-Aizu-Gun
6/24/50	A private garden in Ojio-Mura	Ojio, Arakai-Mura, Minami-Aizu-Gun
6/25/50	Takinohara Primary School	Takinohara, Arakai-Mura, Minami-Aizu-Gun
6/26/50	Egawa-Mura Primary & Middle School	Egawa-Mura, Minami-Aizu-Gun
6/27/50	Asahida Primary & Middle School	Aza Asahida, Narahara-Cho, Minami-Aizu-Gun
6/28/50	Kawara-Cho Primary & Middle School	Kawara-Machi, Wakamatsu-Shi
6/29/50	Monden-Mura Primary & Middle School	Kadota-Mura, Kita-Aizu-Gun
6/30/50	A square at the Kitakata-Cho Board of Education	Kitakata-Cho, Yama-Gum
7/3/50	Gyonin Primary School	Kojin-Cho, Wakamatsu-Shi
7/4/50	Arakai-Mura Primary & Middle School	Arakai-Mura, Minami-Aizu-Gun
7/5/50	Senri-Mura Primary & Middle School	Senri-Mura, Yama-Gun
7/6/50	Higashiyama-Mura Oosugo Primary & Middle School	Oosugo, Higashiyama-Mura, Kita-Aizu-Gun
7/7/50	Precinct of Higashiyama-Shrine, Higashiyama-Mura	Higashiyama-Mura, Kita-Aizu-Gun
7/9/50	Takeda Hospital	Sakae-Cho, Wakamatsu-Shi
7/10/50	A square at the automobile company	Nishi-Sakai-Cho 1 Cho-me, Wakamatsu-Shi
7/11/50	Narahara Primary & Middle School	Narahara-Cho, Minami-Aizu-Gun
7/13/50	Ooto Primary & Middle School, Ooto-Mura	Ooto-Mura, Kata-Aizu-Gun
7/15/50	Narahara-Cho Oouchi-Seinen-Kai, Oouchi Primary School	Narahara-Cho, Minami-Aizu-Gun

Total viewers for *Sports Revue*

Number of viewers	Title	Other titles in the package
1,000	Sports Revue	• Panama Canal • Beware of Fire
1,000	,,	,,
800	,,	,,
2,000	,,	,,
1,000	,,	,,
250	,,	,,
500	,,	,,
800	,,	,,
800	,,	,,
1,500	,,	,,
1,000	,,	,,
500	,,	,,
1,600	,,	,,
1,000	,,	,,
1,000	,,	,,
1,000	,,	,,
1,500	,,	,,
300	,,	,,
1,000	,,	,,
800	,,	,,
1,000	,,	,,
1,500	,,	,,
21,850		

(Table continues)

Date	Venue	Town
8/18/50	A square	Aza Noito, Tateiwa-Mura, Minami-Aizu-Gun
8/19/50	Tateiwa-Mura Primary School	Tateiwa-Mura, Minami-Aizu-Gun
8/20/50	Ina-Mura Primary School	Ina-Mura, Minami-Aizu-Gun
8/21/50	Ookawa Mura Primary School	Ookawa Mura, Minami-Aizu-Gun
8/22/50	Shinden Village Square	Aza Shinden, Oomiya-Mura, Minami-Aizu-Gun
8/23/50	Amusement square in Oomiya Kouzan	Aza Oomiya Kouzan (Mine), Minami-Aizu-Gun
8/24/50	Oomiya Primary School	Oomiya-Mura, Minami-Aizu-Gun
8/25/50	Izumida Primary School	Aza Izumida, Tomita-Mura, Minami-Aizu-Gun
8/26/50	Katagai Primary School	Aza Katagai, Tomita-Mura, Minami-Aizu-Gun
8/27/50	Asahi-Mura Primary School	Asahi-Mura, Minami-Aizu-Gun
8/28/50	Meiwa-Mura Primary School	Meiwa-Mura, Minami-Aizu-Gun
9/1/50	Asahi-Mura Primary School	Asahi-Mura, Oonuma-Gun
9/2/50	Arai-Mura Primary School	Arai-Mura, Oonuma-Gun
9/3/50	Miyashita Primary School	Miyashita-Cho, Oonuma-Gun
9/4/50	Wakamiya Shrine precinct	Wakamiya-Mura, Oonuma-Gun
9/8/50	Inside Manpiku-Ji (temple)	Baba-Nagoya-Cho, Wakamatsu-Shi
9/10/50	Office of Fukushima Branch of the Nippon Culture Association	Amida-Cho, Wakamatsu-Shi
9/12/50	Town square	Nishi-Sakae-Cho, Wakamatsu-Shi
Total viewers for *Sports' Golden Age*		

Number of viewers	Title	Other titles in the package
Villagers: 600	*Sports' Golden Age*	*Northern Ireland*
Students & parents: 1,200	,,	,,
Villagers: 1,000	,,	,,
Students & PTA: 1,500	,,	,,
Villagers: 300	,,	,,
Miners: 300	,,	,,
Students: 800	,,	,,
Students & general public: 1,000	,,	,,
Students & general public: 700	,,	,,
Villagers: 1,000	,,	,,
Villagers: 1,000	,,	,,
Students & villagers: 1,500	,,	,,
Students & villagers: 1,200	,,	,,
Students & general public: 1,500	,,	,,
Villagers: 600	,,	,,
General public: 200	,,	,,
General public: 100	,,	,,
General public: 300	,,	,,
14,800		

(Table continues)

Date	Venue	Town
9/20/50	Office of Fukushima Branch of the Nippon Culture Association	Amida-Cho, Wakamatsu-Shi
9/22/50	Kitakata Educational Association	Kitakata-Cho, Yama-Gun
9/24/50	Wakamatsu National Hospital	Tsurugaoka-Cho, Wakamatsu-Shi
9/25/50	Takeda Hospital	Sakae-Cho, Wakamatsu-Shi
9/27/50	Higashiyama-Mura Primary & Middle School	Higashiyama-Mura, Kita-Aizu-Gun
9/28/50	Matsuyama-Mura Primary School	Matsuyama-Mura, Yama-Gun
9/30/50	Kamisannomiya-Mura Primary & Middle School	Kamisannomiya-Mura, Yama-Gun
10/2/50	Bandai-Mura Primary & Middle School	Bandai-Mura, Yama-Gun
10/3/50	Oodera Seinen-Kai Square	Aza Oodera, Bandai-Mura, Yama-Gun
10/4/50	Kamisairen Square	Aza Kamisairen, Bandai-Mura, Yama-Gun
10/6/50	Sakashita Civic Hall	Sakashita-Cho, Kawanuma-Gun
10/7/50	Yanaizu Community Center	Yanaizu-Cho, Oonuma-Gun
10/9/50	Miyashita Primary & Middle School	Miyashita-Cho, Oonuma-Gun
10/11/50	Kouzashi-Mura Primary & Middle School	Kouzashi-Mura, Kita-Aizu-Gun
10/14/50	Nishisakae-Cho 1 Chome Seinen-Kai	Nishisakae-Cho, Wakamatsu-Shi
10/17/50	A square in front of the town hall	Sakae-Cho, Wakamatsu-Shi

Total viewers for *Vacation Sports*

Number of viewers	Title	Other titles in the package
200	*Vacation Sports*	• *New Traffic* • *The Care Story* • *Lobster Town*
Students, teachers & general public: 2,000	,,	,,
Managerial staff, patients & general public: 250	,,	,,
Managerial staff, patients & general public: 3,000	,,	,,
Students & general public: 1,500	,,	,,
Students & general public: 800	,,	,,
Students & general public: 800	,,	,,
Students & general public: 1,500	,,	,,
600	,,	,,
500	,,	,,
2,000	,,	,,
2,000	,,	,,
Students & general public: 700	,,	,,
Students & parents: 1,000	,,	,,
500	,,	,,
General public: 3,000	,,	,,
20,350		

(Table continues)

Date	Venue	Town
10/29/50	Kamimiyori Workshop Square	Aza Kamimiyori, Ooto-Mura, Kita-Aizu-Gun
10/30/50	Schoolhouse of Kuragawa Primary School	Aza Kuragawa, Ooto-Mura, Kita-Aizu-Gun
11/3/50	Niou Theater	Aza Niou, Omata-Mura, Oonuma-Gun
11/4/50	Katakado Primary School auditorium	Katakado-Mura, Kawanuma-Gun
11/5/50	Yawata-Mura Primary School	Yawata-Mura, Kawanuma-Gun
11/6/50	Yaizu-Cho Primary School	Yanaizu-Cho, Kawanuma-Gun
11/7/50	Sakashita-Cho Primary School	Sakashita-Cho, Kawanuma-Gun
11/8/50	Niitsuru-Mura Primary School	Niitsuru-Mura, Oonuma-Gun
11/9/50	Doojima-Mura Primary School	Doujima-Mura, Kawanuma-Gun
11/10/50	Takada-Cho Primary School	Takada-Cho, Oonuma-Gun
11/11/50	Nagaino-Mura Primary School	Nagaino-Mura, Oonuma-Gun
11/13/50	Egawa-Mura Community Center	Egawa-Mura, Minami-Aizu-Gun
11/14/50	Narahara-Mura Primary School	Narahara-Mura, Minami-Aizu-Gun
11/15/50	Arajai-Mura Primary School	Arakai-Mura, Minami-Aizu-Gun
11/16/50	Schoolhouse of Itosawa Branch School	Aza Itosawa, Arakai-Mura, Minami-Aizu-Gun
11/17/50	Hizawa-Mura Primary School	Hizawa-Mura, Minami-Aizu-Gun
11/18/50	Tateiwa-Mura Primary School auditorium	Tateiwa-Mura, Minami-Aizu-Gun
11/19/50	Ina-Mura Primary School	Ina-Mura, Minami-Aizu-Gun
11/20/50	Ookawa-Mura Primary School auditorium	Ookawa-Mura, Minami-Aizu-Gun
11/22/50	Eiwa Primary & Middle School auditorium	Aza Eiwa, Machikita-Mura, Kita-Aizu-Gun
11/25/50	Aizu Seika (fruit & vegetable) Company warehouse	Nishi-Sakae-Cho 2 Cho-Me, Wakamatsu-Shi
Total viewers for *Boys' Baseball League*		
Total viewers for *Let's Square Dance*		
Total viewers for all five films		

Number of viewers	Title	Other titles in the package
Villagers: 1,000	• *Boys' Baseball League* • *Let's Square Dance*	• *Burroughs Newsboys' Foundation* • *Floating Theater*
Students & villagers: 700	,,	,,
Villagers: 500	*Boys' Baseball League*	,,
Young Men & Women's Association, PTA: 800	• *Boys' Baseball League* • *Let's Square Dance*	,,
Villagers: 700	,,	,,
Yanaizu Cultural Association, PTA & students: 1,000	,,	,,
Students & PTA: 1,000	,,	,,
PTA & students: 850	,,	,,
Students & PTA: 800	,,	,,
PTA & students: 1,000	,,	,,
Young Men & Women's Association, PTA & villagers: 800	,,	,,
Villagers: 350	,,	,,
Students & PTA: 700	,,	,,
Students & villagers: 1,000	,,	,,
Students & parents: 300	,,	,,
Young Men's Association, villagers: 700	,,	,,
Villagers & Young Men's Association: 800	,,	,,
Villagers: 700	,,	,,
Students & PTA: 700	,,	,,
Students & villagers: 850	,,	,,
General public: 750	,,	,,
16,000		
15,500		
88,500		

Bibliography

Archival Materials

National Archives and Records Administration, College Park, Maryland

CI&E documents, Records of the Supreme Commander for the Allied Powers (RG 331)

Records of the United States Information Agency (RG 306)

State Department Central File 1950–54 (RG 59)

State Department Decimal File (RG 59)

State Department Lot File (Public) (RG 59)

Records of the Office of War Information (RG 208)

'Five Years After Baseball', Tokyo, Japan, 09/11/1950 ARC Identifier 22422／Local Identifier 111-ADC-8657, Motion Picture, Sound, and Video Records Section, Special Media Archives Services Division

National Archives and Records Administration, New York City, New York

Records of the Department of State (RG 306)

Records of the United States Information Agency (RG 306)

Periodicals from the Gordon W. Prange Collection, University of Maryland Libraries, College Park, Maryland

All Sports (オール・スポーツ)

'Boxing Champion Shirai Yoshio wo Kakonde' (Round table talk with Yoshio Shirai, a champion of boxing), No. 15, June 1949, All-Sports-Sha, pp. 18–19 (「BOXING・チャンピオン白井義男を囲んで座談会」、『オールスポーツ』第15号、1949年6月、オールスポーツ社、18〜19頁).

'Undou-Kyougi no Minshushugi ni Oyobosu Eikyo' (Effects of democracy's adaptation to sports), October 15, 1946, All-Sports-Sha, p.　5 (「運動競技の民主々義に及ぼす影響」、『オールスポーツ』創刊号、1946年10月、オールスポーツ社、5頁).

Ayumi (あゆみ)

'Gyouji-Nisshi: Kenka Keisatsu-Shokuin Kendo-Taikai' (Event diary: Kendo match for prefectural police officers), October 1949, Kobe-City Police Department, p. 79 (「行事日誌：縣下警察職員剣道大会」、『あゆみ』1949年10月号、神戸市警察局発行、79頁).

Baseball Magazine (ベースボールマガジン)

'Ma-Gensui Sou-Kei-Sen ni Shukuji' (Gen. MacArthur sent a congratulatory message to the Sou-Kei-Sen), Vol. 4, No. 10, August 1949, Koubun-Sha, p. 48 (「マ元帥早慶戦に祝辞」、『ベースボールマガジン』第4巻第10号、1949年8月、恒文社、48頁).

Miyake, Daisuke. 'Yakyu wo Kagaku seyo!' (Think about *yakyu* scientifically), Vol. 2, No. 4, May 1947, Koubun-Sha, pp. 9–12 (三宅大輔「野球を科学せよ!」、『ベースボールマガジン』第2巻第4号、1947年5月、恒文社、9～12頁).

Ohashi, Masamichi. 'Jackie Robinson', Vol. 2, No. 5, June 1947, Koubun-Sha, pp. 20–21 (大橋正路「ジャッキー・ロビンソン」、『ベースボールマガジン』第2巻第5号、6月号、20～21頁).

Sakaguchi, Ango. 'Nihon-Yakyu-wa-Puro-ni-Arazu' (Japan's professional baseball won't be professional), Vol. 3, No. 8, August 1948, Koubun-Sha, pp. 16–17 (坂口安吾「日本野球はプロに非ず」、『ベースボールマガジン』第3巻第8号、1948年8月、恒文社、16～17頁).

Sato, Hachiro. 'Seals Gun wo Mukaeru Waga besuto nain wo utau' (Lyricize our best nine who will meet the Seals), Vol. 4, No. 14, November 1949, Koubun-Sha, pp. 50–51 (サトウ・ハチロー「シールス軍を迎えるわがベスト・ナインを歌う」、『ベースボールマガジン』第4巻第14号、11月号、50～51頁).

Baseball News (ベースボール・ニュース)

Okamoto, Hiroshi. 'Kyoui no Mato Kokujin-Senshu: Dodgers no Jackie Robinson: Hatsu no Saiyuushuu-Senshu to Naruka: Saikin no America Kyuukai Tanshin' (Amazing black player: Jackie Robinson from the Dodgers: Will he be chosen as the first Negro MVP?: A brief note on the recent American baseball world), No. 637, Nihon-Taiiku-Shuuhou-Sha, pp. 40–41 (岡本寛「驚異の的黒人選手：ドジャーズのジャッキー・ロビンソン：初の最優秀選手となるか：最近のアメリカ球界短信」、『ベースボールニュース』、第637号、日本体育週報社、40～41頁).

Boucho-Keiyu (防長警友)

Tahara, 'Shuuki-Ju-Kendo-Taikai Ki' (Note on the autumn judo-kendo match), 1949 New Year Issue, Yamaguchi Prefecture Police Department, p. 26 (田原生「秋季柔剣道大会記」、『防長警友』1949年新年号、山口県警察部発行、26頁).

Boxing (*gekkan kento*) (ボクシング　月刊拳闘)

'Nihon no Bokushingu ha Moukarunoka?' (Does Japan's boxing make a profit?), Vol. 10, No. 2, February 1948, Kento-Sha, p. 8 (「日本のボクシングは儲かるか!?」、『ボクシング　月刊拳闘』10巻2号、1948年2月、拳闘社、8頁).

Boxing Digest (ボクシングダイヂェスト)

Asama, Chiyohiko. 'Bokushingu Zuiso' (Essay on boxing), inaugural issue, December 1947, Boxing Digest-Sha, p. 6 (浅間千代彦「ボクシング随想」、『ボクシングダイヂェスト』創刊号、1947年12月、ボクシングダイヂェスト社、6頁).

Eiga Star (Movie Star) (映画スタア)

'Coca Cola Sweet Girl', Vol. 1, No. 7, September 1949, Romance-Sha, pp. 26–27 (「コカ・コーラ・スイート・ガール」、『映画スタア』1949年9月号、ロマンス社、26〜27頁).

Home Run (ホームラン)

Mizuhara, Shuuoushi. 'Korakuen Kyujou Nite' (At Korakuen Stadium), Vol. 3, No. 10, October 1948, Homurun-Sha, p. 13 (水原秋櫻子「後楽園球場にて」、『ホームラン』第3巻第10号、1948年10月、ホームラン社、13頁).

Izumi (いづみ)

Ooki, Akira. 'Judo-Kendo Kyougi-Taikai Ki' (Note on a judo-kendo match), No. 2, February 1947, Hiroshima Police Association Branch, p. 39 (大木明「柔道剣道競技大会記」、『いづみ』、第2号、警察協会広島支部発行、1947年2月号、39頁).

Judo (柔道)

Kanou, Risei. 'Kaitaku subeki Judo no Nimensei' (Two aspects of judo to be developed), Vol. 19, No. 12, December 1948, Kodokan, p. 1 (嘉納履正「開拓すべき柔道の二方面」、『柔道』第19巻第12号、1948年12月、講道館、1頁).

Moriwaki, Ichiro. 'Supoutsu toshiteno Judo' (Judo as a sport), Vol. 20, No. 1, December 1948, Kodokan, pp. 17–19 (森脇一郎「スポーツとしての柔道」、『柔道』第20巻第1号、1948年12月、講道館、17〜19頁).

Okabe, Heita. 'Judo no Shourai' (The future of Judo), Vol. 20, No. 5, April 1949, Kodokan, pp. 17–19 (岡部平太「柔道の将来」、『柔道』第20巻第5号、1949年4月、講道館、8〜9頁).

Kagaribi (かゞりび)

> Adachi, Fumio. 'Akarui Heiwa-Nihon no Saisei to Keisatsu-Budo' (Rebuilding glorious, peaceful Japan and police *budo*), No. 5, May 1948, Ehime Prefecture Police Department, pp. 68–70 (阿達文男「明るい平和日本の再建と警察武道」、『かゞりび』第5号、1948年5月、愛媛県庁警察課、68〜70頁).

Kagoshima-ken Kyoiku-Iinkai Geppou (Kagoshima Prefecture Education Committee Monthly Report) (鹿児島縣教育委員会月報)

> 'Kagoshima-ken Shinsei-Kendo-Dokokai ni Nozomu' (Anticipating the Kagoshima Prefecture Newborn Kendo Club), inaugural issue, 1949, Kagoshima-ken kyouiku-Iinkai, p. 20 (「鹿児島県新生剣道同好会に望む」、『鹿児島縣教育委員会月報』創刊号（1949年）、鹿児島縣教育委員会発行、20頁).

Keiko (警鼓)

> Matsuda, 'Tai-sho Budo Taikai' (*Budo* tournament among departments), Vol. 24, No. 21 (The first issue after the war), December 1946, Nagasaki-ken Kei-Min Kyokai, pp. 23–24 (松田生「対署武道大会」、『警鼓』第24巻第21号（再刊第1号）、1946年12月、長崎県警民協会、23〜24頁).

Kento Fan (拳闘ファン)

> Matsuoka, 'Bosu no Issou' (Removal of bosses; in the 'Voices from the fans' section), Vol. 2, No. 2, December 1946, Kento-Fan-Sha, p. 14 (松岡生「ボスの一掃」（「ファンの声」欄）、『拳闘ファン』巻2号、1946年12月、拳闘ファン社、14頁).

Kento Gazette (拳闘ガゼット)

> Haggins, Frank B. 'Nihon-Kento-kai ni Ata'u (Giving to the Japanese boxing world), Vol. 22, No. 5, October 1946, Kento-Gazette-Sha, p. 3 (フランク・ビー・ハギンス「日本拳闘界に与ふ」、『拳闘ガゼット』22巻5号、1946年10月、拳闘ガゼット社、3頁).

Kindai Yakyu (近代野球)

> 'Rokudaigaku Seals to Tatakauka' (Will Six-University fight the Seals?)', September 1949, Kindai Yakyu-Sha, p. 27 (「六大学シールズと戦うか」、『近代野球』、近代野球社、1949年9月号、27頁).

Seinen-Fukushima (青年ふくしま)

> 'Yomigaetta Kendo: Fencing-Kisoku wo Kami' (Revived kendo: Adding fencing regulations), Fukushima-Minpo-Sha, December 1948, p. 12 (「"よみがえった剣道"フェンシング規則を加味」、『青年ふくしま』1948年12月号、福島県連合青年会編集・福島民報社発行、12頁).

Shufu no Tomo (主婦の友)

> Kuwabara, Kimi. 'Kendo-gu no Hodoki de Gesshuu Sanbyaku-en Zengo' (Earning three hundred yen per month by unfastening kendo equipment), Shufu-no-Tomo-Sha, January 1947, p. 97 (桑原きみ「剣道具のほどきで月収三百圓前後」、『主婦の友』1947年新年号、主婦の友社、1947年1月1日発行、97頁).

Shukan Asahi (週刊朝日)

> 'Kendo', in the column 'Rotary', May 29, 1949, Asahi-Shimbun Tokyo Honsha, p. 19 (「剣道」、『週刊朝日』1949年5月29日号、朝日新聞大阪本社、19頁「ロータリー」).

Sports (スポーツ)

> Itaru, Nii. 'Supōtsu to Minshushugi' (Sports and democracy), June 1946 (inaugural issue), Taiiku Nihon-Sha, pp. 6–7 (新居格「スポーツと民主主義」、『スポーツ』創刊号、1946年6月、體育日本社、6～7頁).

> Norviel, Maj. John W. 'Nihon Supōtsu no Tameni' (For the progress of Japan's sports), June 1946, Taiiku Nihon-Sha, p. 9 (連合軍総司令部民間教育情報部ジョン・ノーヴィル少佐「日本スポーツ發展の爲に」、『スポーツ』創刊号、1946年6月、體育日本社、9頁).

Sumo (相撲)

> Fatabayama, Sadaji. 'Shin-Hossoku ni Atatte' (Facing the new start), Vol. 11, Nos. 4–7, July 1946, Dai-Nippon Sumo Kyokai, pp. 8–9 (双葉山定次「新発足にあたって」、『相撲』第11巻第4・5・6・7号(新年号／創刊十周年記念　本場所待望号、1946年7月、大日本相撲協会) 8～9頁).

> Uemura, Mutsuo, Motoi Soma, Saburo Hara, Koichi Yamaguchi, Tsuyoshi Kasugano, Hidemitsu Fujishima, Koichiro Sadogatake and Kozo Hikoyama, 'Sumo-kai Kikyoku Kokufuku Shin-Doukou Sakuan Zadankai' (Round table talk about overcoming difficulties and planning the new approach of the sumo world), Vol. 11, Nos. 2–3, March 1946, Dai-Nippon Sumo Kyokai, pp. 26–47 (植村陸郎、相馬基、原三郎、山口幸一、春日野剛史、藤島秀光、佐渡嶽高一郎、彦山光三「相撲界危局克服新動向策案座談会」、『相撲』第11巻第2・3号、1946年3月、大日本相撲協会、26～47頁).

Yakyu-Fan (野球ファン)

> Nakamura, Seikichi. 'Bei Dai-Rīgu Wadai: Bob Feller to Jackie Robinson' (Topics of the Major League: Bob Feller and Jackie Robinson), Vol. 3, No. 7, August 1949, Yakyu Fan-Sha, pp. 46–49 (中村清吉「米大リーグ話題　ボッブ・フェラーとジヤツキー・ロビンソン」、『野球ファン』第3巻第7号、8月号、野球ファン社、46～49頁).

Yakyu-kai (野球界)

> Hirose, Kenzo. 'Saiken Nihon Yakyu: Tosai-Taikou-Yakyu Kansenki' (Rebuilding Japanese baseball: Watching the East-West game), Vol. 36, No. 1, January 1946, Hakubunkan, pp. 4–5 (広瀬謙三「再建日本野球　東西対抗野球戦記」、『野球界』、1946年1月=36巻1号、博文館、4～5頁).

> Kawakami, Tetsuharu. 'Seals to Tatakatte' (After fighting the Seals), December 1949, Hakuyu-Sha, p. 42 (川上哲治「シールズと対戦して」、『野球界』、博友社、1949年12月号、42頁).

Yakyu Shonen (野球少年)

> Fukuyu, Yutaka. 'Supōtsu wo Aisareru Tennōheika to Mikasanomiya' (Sports lovers: The Emperor Hirohito and Sir Mikasanomiya) October 1947, Shoubunkan, pp. 2–3 (福湯豊「スポーツを愛される天皇陛下と三笠宮」、『野球少年』1947年10月特大号、尚文館、2～3頁).

Yomiuri Sports (読売スポーツ)

> Cahn, Alvin R. (Kaneo Nakamura). 'New Champion Shirai Yoshio wo Kataru: Kaan-Hakase no Shuki' (Talk about the new champion, Yoshio Shirai: Dr. Cahn's essay), Vol. 2, No. 4, April 1949, Yomiuri Shimbun-Sha, pp. 42–46 (アール・カーン（中村金雄）「ニューチャンピオン白井義男を語る：カーン博士の手記」、『読売スポーツ』2巻4号、1949年4月、読売新聞社、42～46頁).

Yowa Kai Shi (養和会誌)

> 'Shinchu-Gun ga Budo Keiko' (Occupation troops officer practicing *budo*), No. 174, Mitsubishi Yowa Kai, p. 32 (「進駐軍が武道稽古」、『養和会誌』第174号、三菱養和会発行、32頁).

Books and monographs
(written in English)

American Film Institute Catalog of Motion Pictures Produced in the United States: Feature Films, 1941–1950, Film Entries A–L (AFI Volume F4). University of California Press, 1999.

Ashby, LeRoy. *With Amusement for All: A History of American Popular Culture Since 1830.* University Press of Kentucky, 2006.

Belmonte, Laura A. *Selling the American Way: U.S. Propaganda and the Cold War.* University of Pennsylvania Press, 2008.

Bogle, Donald. *Toms, Coons, Mulattoes, Mammies, and Bucks: An Interpretive History of Blacks in American Films*, 4ᵗʰ edition. Continuum International Publishing Group Ltd., 2001.

Crawford, Russ. *The Use of Sports to Promote the American Way of Life during the Cold War: Cultural Propaganda, 1945–1963*. The Edwin Mellen Press, 2008.

Cull, Nicholas J. *The Cold War and the United States Information Agency: American Propaganda and Public Diplomacy, 1945–1989*. Cambridge University Press, 2008.

Dower, John W. *Embracing the Defeat: Japan in the Wake of World War II*. W. W. Norton and Co., 2000.

Drinson, Joseph and Warmud, Joram. *Jackie Robinson: Race, Sports, and the American Dream*. M.E. Sharpe, 1998.

Duberman, Martin Bauml. *Paul Robeson*. Knopf, 1989.

Durso, Joseph. *Casey & Mr. McGraw*. The Sporting News, 1989.

Eig, Jonathan. *Opening Day: The Story of Jackie Robinson's First Season*. Simon & Schuster, 2007.

Elder, Robert E. *The Information Machine: The United States Information Agency and American Foreign Policy*. Syracuse University Press, 1968.

Engel, Jeffrey A., ed. *Local Consequences of the Global Cold War*. Woodrow Wilson Center Press & Stanford University Press, 2007.

Falkner, David. *Great Time Coming: The Life of Jackie Robinson from Baseball to Birmingham*. Simon & Schuster, 1995.

Gevinson, Alan, ed. *Within Our Gates: Ethnicity in American Films, 1911–1960*. AFI, 1977.

Guthrie-Shimizu, Sayuri. *Transpacific Field of Dreams: How Baseball Linked the United States and Japan in Peace and War*. University of North Carolina Press, 2012.

Hirano, Kyoko. *Mr. Smith Goes to Tokyo: Japanese Cinema Under the American Occupation, 1945–1952*. Smithsonian Institution Press, 1992.

Hixson, Walter L. *Parting the Curtain: Propaganda, Culture, and the Cold War, 1945–1951*. St. Martin's Griffin, New York, 1998.

Klein, Christina. *Cold War Orientalism: Asia in the Middlebrow Imagination, 1945–1961*. University of California Press, 2003.

Leutzinger, Richard. *Lefty O'Doul: The Legend that Baseball Nearly Forgot*. Carmel Bay Publishing, 1997.

Maltby, Richard. 'The Production Code and the Hays Office'. In Tino Balio, ed., *Grand Design: Hollywood as a Modern Business Enterprise, 1930–1939*. University of California Press, 1995.

Matsuda, Takeshi. *Soft Power and Its Perils: U.S. Cultural Policy in Early Postwar Japan and Permanent Dependency*. Woodrow Wilson Center Press & Stanford University Press, 2007.

Nash, Jay Robert, and Ross, Stanley Ralph. *The Motion Picture Guide H–K 1927–1983*. Cinebooks, 1986.

Oldenziel, Ruth, and Zachmann, Karen, eds. *Cold War Kitchen: Americanization, Technology, and European Users*. The MIT Press, 2009.

Osgood, Kenneth. *Total Cold War: Eisenhower's Secret Propaganda Battle at Home and Abroad*. University Press of Kansas, 2006.

Prince, Carl. *Brooklyn's Dodgers: The Bums, the Borough and the Best of Baseball, 1947–1957*. Oxford University Press, 1996.

Rampersad, Arnold. *Jackie Robinson: A Biography*. Alfred A. Knopf, 1997.

Robinson, Jackie (As Told to Wendell Smith). *Jackie Robinson: My Own Story*. Greenberg, 1948.

Robinson, Jackie (As Told to Alfred Duckett). *I Never Had It Made*. G. P. Putnam's Sons, 1972.

Rubin, Ronald I. *The Objectives of the U.S. Information Agency: Controversies and Answers*. Praeger Special Studies in International Politics and Public Affairs, Frederick A. Praeger Publishers, 1966.

Rutkoff, Peter M., ed. *The Cooperstown Symposium on Baseball and American Culture, 1997 (Jackie Robinson)*. McFarland, 2000.

Saeki, Chizuru. *U.S. Cultural Propaganda in Cold War Japan: Promoting Democracy 1948–1960*. The Edwin Mellen Press, 2007.

Shaw, Tony, and Youngblood, Denise J. *Cinematic Cold War: The American and Soviet Struggle for Hearts and Minds*. University Press of Kansas, 2010.

Shulman, Holly Cowan. *The Voice of America: Propaganda and Democracy, 1941–1945*. University of Wisconsin Press, 1990.

Simon, Scott. *Jackie Robinson and the Integration of Baseball*. John Wiley & Sons, 2002.

Tygiel, Jules, ed. *The Jackie Robinson Reader: Perspectives on an American Hero*. Dutton, 1997.

Von Eschen, Penny M. *Satchmo Blows Up the World: Jazz Ambassadors Play the Cold War*. Harvard University Press, 2004.

Books and monographs
(written in Japanese)

1934-2004 Pro-Yakyu 70 Nen-Shi (1934-2004　プロ野球70年史／1934–2004: 70 years of professional baseball). Baseball Magazine-Sha, 2004.

Abe, Akira. *Sengo Chihou-Kyouiku-Seido Seiritsu Katei no Kenkyu* (戦後地方教育制度成立過程の研究／A study on the developmental process of the post-war regional education system). Kazama-Shobou, 1983.

Aku, Yu. *Setouchi Shonen Yakyu Dan* (『瀬戸内少年野球団』／MacArthur's children). Bungeishunju, 1979.

Aisarete 30 Nen (愛されて30年／30 years of being loved). Coca-Cola (Japan) Company, Limited, 1987.

Cohen, Theodore. *Nihon-Senryou-Kakumei: GHQ karano Shougen* (日本占領革命　GHQからの証言／The third turn: MacArthur, the Americans and the rebirth of Japan), Vol. 1. Translated by Omae Masaomi. TBS Britannica, 1983.

Domoto, Akihiko. *Kendo Shugyou: Shudou Gakuin no Seishun* (剣道修行: 修道学院の青春／Kendo training: Young days at Shudou Gakuin). Ski Journal Publisher Inc., 1985.

Ginga Kyokai, ed. *Chaplin no Sekai* (チャップリンの世界／The world of Chaplin). Eichi Shuppan, 1978.

Hata, Akio, ed. *Nijusseiki America Eiga Jiten* (20世紀アメリカ映画事典／The encyclopedia of 20th century American movies). Cataloghouse, 2002.

Hatano, Masaru. *Nichibei Yakyu Shi: Major wo Oikaketa 70 Nen* (日米野球史メジャーを追いかけた70年／The history of U.S.-Japan baseball: 70 years chasing the Major League). PHP, 2001.

Hatano, Masaru. *Nichibei Yakyu no Kakehashi: Suzuki Sotaro no Jinsei to Shoriki Matsutaro* (日米野球の架け橋　鈴木惣太郎の人生と正力松太郎／Bridge over Japan-U.S. baseball: The life of Suzuki Sotaro and Shoriki Matsutaro). Fuyo Shobo Shuppan, 2013.

Hazumi, Arihiro, et al., ed. *Sengo Kokai America-Eiga Daihyakka* (戦後公開アメリカ映画大百科／Encyclopedia of American films), Shiryou-Hen PART2 45-78 Nihon-Koukai-Zensakuhin-Jiten (Vol. 11: Data PARTII 45-78 Dictionary of All Films distributed in Post-War Japan). Nihon Book Library, 1979.

Ichioka, Hiroshige, and Fukunaga, Ami. *Pro Yakyu wo Sukutta Otoko Cappy Harada* (プロ野球を救った男　キャピー原田／Cappy Harada: The man who saved professional baseball). Soft Bank Creative, 2009.

Imada, Juzen. *Dokankai: Harite Ichidai Maedayama Eigoro: Kokusaika wo Kakenuketa Otoko* (どかんかい　張り手一代　前田山英五郎／Get out of my sight: Eigoro Maedayama, 'Harite' sumo wrestler). BAB Japan, 1995.

Iwasaki, Akira. *Gendai Nihon no Eiga: Sono Shisou to Fuzoku* (現代日本の映画　その思想と風俗／Modern Japanese films: Their ideology and customs). Chuo-Koron-Sha, 1958.

Kawamura, Kazuhiko. *Sengoshi GHQ no Kensho* (戦後史GHQの検証／Post-World War II history: Verifying the GHQ). Hon-no Fuukei-sha, 2014.

Keishicho Budo 90 Nen-Shi (警視庁武道九十年史／90 years of *budo* at the police department). Education Section of the Police Department, 1965.

Kimura, Ki. *Nihon Supōtsu Bunka-Shi* (日本スポーツ文化史／History of Japanese sports culture). Baseball Magazine-Sha, 1978.

Kishi, Toshihiko, and Tsuchiya, Yuka, eds. *Bunka-Reisen no Jidai: America to Asia* (文化冷戦の時代　アメリカとアジア／De-centering the Cultural Cold War: The U.S. and Asia). Kokusai-Shoin, 2009.

Korakuen no 25 Nen (後楽園の25年／25 years of Korakuen). Korakuen Stadium, 1963.

Leutzinger, Richard. *Densetsu no Lefty O'Doul* (伝説のレフティ・オドール／Lefty O'Doul: The legend that baseball nearly forgot). Translated by Sayama Kazuo. Baseball Magazine-Sha, 1998.

Miyata, Noboru. *Honyakuken no Sengoshi* (翻訳権の戦後史／Post-war history of translation rights). Misuzu-Shobou, 1999.

Murakami, Yumiko. *Yellow Face: Hollywood Eiga ni miru Asia-jin no Shouzo* (イエロー・フェイス　ハリウッド映画にみるアジア人の肖像／Yellow face: Portraits of Asians through Hollywood films). Asahi Sensho, 1993.

Nagata, Yoichi. *Baseball no Shakaishi: Jimmie Horio to Nichibei-Yakyu* (ベースボールの社会史　ジミー堀尾と日米野球／A social history of baseball). Tohou-Shuppan, 1994.

Nagata, Yoichi. *Tokyo Giants Hokubei-Tairiku Ensei-Ki* (東京ジャイアンツ北米大陸遠征記／The Tokyo Giants North American tour of 1935). Tohou-Shuppan, 2007.

Nakamura, Tamio. *Kendo-Jiten: Gijutsu to Bunka no Rekishi* (剣道事典技術と文化の歴史／Kendo dictionary: History of its skills and culture). Tokyo: Shimazu-Shobou, 1994.

Nakano, Haruyuki. *Kyudan Shometsu: Maboroshi no Yushou-Chīmu Robins to Tamura Komajiro* (球団消滅　幻の優勝チーム・ロビンスと田村駒次郎／The team has vanished: Robins, a visionary pennant winning team and Komajiro Tamura). Chikuma-Shobou, 2000.

Nihon no Yakyu Hattatsushi (日本野球発達史／A pictorial history of baseball in Japan). Tosei Godo Tsushin-Sha, 1959.

Nippon Shirīzu no Kiseki (日本シリーズの軌跡／Nippon series history since 1950). Baseball-Magazine-Sha, 2001.

Sakai, Yasuyuki. *Haran Koubou no Kyufu: Ushinawareta Lions-Shi wo Motomete* (波瀾興亡の球譜　失われたライオンズ史を求めて／A record of baseball in storms and rise and fall: Seeking the lost history of the Lions). Baseball Magazine-Sha, 1995.

Sakaue, Yasuhiro. *Nippon Yakyu-no-Keifugaku* (にっぽん野球の系譜学／A genealogical study of Japanese baseball). Seikyusha Library 15, 2001.

Sasaki, Takuya. *Eisenhower Seiken no Fuujikome-Seisaku* (アイゼンハワー政権の封じ込め政策／A containment policy of the Eisenhower administration). Yuhikaku, 2008.

Sato, Hideo, ed. *Sengo Kyouiku Kaikaku Shiryou 2: Rengoukaku Saiko-Shireikan Soushireibu Minkan Jouhou Kyouiku Kyoku no Jinji to Kikou* (戦後教育改革資料2: 連合国最高司令官総司令部民間情報教育局の人事と機構／Post-war education reform documents 2: The staff rosters and organizational charts of CI&E, GHQ/SCAP: Compiled from 'GHQ/SCAP telephone directories'). Kokuritsu Kyouikugaku-Kenkyujo, 1984.

Sato, Tadao. *Chushingura: Iji no Keifu* (忠臣蔵　意地の系譜／Chushingura: A genealogy of stubbornness). Asahi Sensho, 1976.

Sekine, Junzo. *Sekine Junzo Yakyu Houdan: Yakyu ga dekite Arigatou* (関根潤三野球放談　野球ができてありがとう／Sekine Junzo's essay on baseball: Thanks for letting me play baseball). Shougakukan, 1998.

Shimoda, Tatsuo. *Bokushingu Kenbunki* (ボクシング見聞記／A record of personal experiences in boxing). Baseball Magazine-Sha, 1982.

Shirai, Yoshio. *The Champion* (ザ・チャンピオン). Tokyo Shinbun Shuppan-kyoku, 1987.

Showa no Ozumo Kankou Iinkai, ed. *Showa no Ozumo* (昭和の大相撲／Ozumo in the Showa Era). TBS Britannica, 1989.

Suzuki, Ryuji. *Suzuki Ryuji Kaikoroku* (鈴木龍二回顧録／Memoir of Ryuji Suzuki). Baseball Magazine-Sha, 1980.

Suzuki, Sotaro. *Nihon Pro-Yakyu Gaishi* (日本プロ野球外史／Another history of Japanese professional baseball). Baseball Magazine-Sha, 1976.

Takanaga, Taketoshi. *Sumo Showa-Shi: Gekidou no Kiseki* (相撲昭和史激動の軌跡／History of sumo in the Showa Era: The track in convulsions). Kobun-Sha, 1982.

Tanikawa, Takeshi. *America-Eiga to Senryou Seisaku* (アメリカ映画と占領政策／American films and occupation policy). Kyoto University Press, 2002.

Tanikawa, Takeshi. *Sengo Chushingura-Eiga no Zenbou* (戦後「忠臣蔵」映画の全貌／All about post-World War II Chushingura films). Shueisha Creative, 2013.

Tanikawa, Takeshi, ed. *Senryouki no Key Word 100: 1945-1952* (占領期のキーワード100: 1945-1952／100 key words in the occupation era: 1945–1952). Seikyuu-Sha, 2011.

Tsuchiya, Yuka. *Shinbei-Nihon no Kouchiku: America no Tainichi Jouhou-Kyouiku Seisaku to Nihon-Senryou* (親米日本の構築——アメリカの対日情報・教育政策と日本占領／Constructing a pro-U.S. Japan: U.S. information and education policy and the occupation of Japan). Akashi-Shoten, 2009.

Tsuchiya, Yuka and Yoshimi, Shunya. *Occupying Eyes, Occupying Voices: CIE/USIS Films and VOA Radio in Asia during the Cold War* (占領する眼・占領する声——CIE／USIS映画とVOAラジオ). University of Tokyo Press, 2012.

Tsunashima, Ritomo. *Pro Yakyu Unifōmu Monogatari* (プロ野球ユニフォーム物語／The history of the uniform). Baseball Magazine-Sha, 2005.

Visual Ban DENTSU Koukoku-Keiki-Nenhyou 1945-2003 (ビジュアル版DENTSU広告景気年表 1945-2003／Visual version of DENTSU chronological table of advertisement and the economy 1945–2003). DENTSU, 2004.

Watanabe, Yuko. *Sebangou 42: Mejā Rīgu no Isan---Jackie Robinson to America-Shakai niokeru 'Jinshu'* (背番号42　メジャー・リーグの遺産——ジャッキー・ロビンソンとアメリカ社会における「人種」／Uniform number 42: Inheritance of the Major League——Jackie Robinson and 'race' in American society). Bungeisha, 2009.

Yamamoto, Reiko. *Beikoku-Tainichi-Senryo-Seisaku to Budo-Kyouiku: Dainihon-Butokukai no Koubou* (米国対日占領政策と武道教育／大日本武徳会の興亡／U.S. occupation policy and *budo* education: The rise and fall of the Dainihon-Butokukai). Nihon-Tosho-Center, 2003.

Yamamoto, Shigeru. *Cahn Hakase no Shouzou* (カーン博士の肖像／A portrait of Dr. Cahn). Baseball Magazine-Sha, 1986.

Yamamoto, Taketoshi, ed. *Senryouki Bunka wo Hiraku: Zasshi no Shosou* (占領期文化をひらく　雑誌の諸相／Open the culture in occupied Japan: Various images of magazines). Waseda University Press, 2006.

Yamamuro, Hiroyuki. *Pro Yakyu Fukko-Shi: MacArthur kara Nagashima 4 Sanshin made* (プロ野球復興史　マッカーサーから長嶋4三振まで／History of the revival of professional baseball: From MacArthur to Nagashima four struck out). Chuko Shinsho, 2012.

Yamato, Kyushi. *Shinsetsu Nihon Yakyuu-shi: Showa hen sonogo* (真説・日本野球史: 昭和篇その五／True history of Japanese baseball: Showa Era Vol. 5). Baseball Magazine-Sha, 1979.

Yamazaki, Mitsuo. *Rashhu no Ouja: Kensei Piston Horiguchi Den* (ラッシュの王者　拳聖・ピストン堀口伝／King of rush: Biography of Piston Horiguchi, a holy boxer). Bungei Shunju, 1994.

Yasuoka, Masahiro. *Unmei wo Tsukuru: Ningen-Gaku Kouwa* (運命を創る人間学講話／Creating destiny: Anthropology lecture). President-Sha, 1985.

Zen-Ken-Ren 30 Nen Kinenshi Editing Committee, ed. *30 Nen-Shi* (三十年史／30 years). Zaidan-Hojin Zen-Nihon Kendo Renmei, 1982.

Articles, chapters and pamphlets
(written in English)

'Army-Navy Baseball Game' pamphlet, Annapolis, Maryland, May 29, 1920.

'HQ&SV.GP. Special Services Presents 4th of July Sports Program Tokyo Japan, 1949' pamphlet, GHQ/SCAP, 1949.

Jackie Robinson: Baseball Hero. Fawcett Publications, May 1950.

'San Francisco Seals Goodwill Baseball Tour of Japan, October 1949', souvenir program, Seals Sinzen-Yakyu Fukyu-Kai (Seals Goodwill Baseball Association), *Shinzen Nichibei-Yakyu: San Francisco Seals—Zen Nihon Gun, Zen Kaisai Gun, Zen Kanto Gun, Kyojin Gun, showa 24 Nen 10 Gatsu*, 1949.

Serafino, Nina, Tarnoff, Curt and Nanto, Dick K. *U.S. Occupation Assistance: Iraq, Germany and Japan Compared, CRS Report for Congress* (Received through the CRS Web／Order Code RL33331), March 23, 2006, Accession Number: ADA458270.

'The 47 Ronin: The Most Popular Play in Japan Reveals the Bloodthirsty Character of Our Enemy', *Life*, November 1, 1943

Articles, chapters and pamphlets

(written in Japanese)

Abe, Tetsushi. 'Kendo ni okeru Kokusaika no Shomondai' (剣道における国際化の諸問題／Various problems of the internationalization of kendo), *Budo Ronshu, No.III,: 'Global Jidai no Budo'* (武道論集III: グローバル時代の武道／*Budo* in the global age), Budo & Sports Science Research Institute, International Budo University, 2012.

Bowers, Faubion. Interview: 'Senryou ha Nihon no Bunka wo Hakai shita (kikite: Takeshi Tanikawa)' (インタビュー　占領は日本の文化を破壊したフォービアン・パワーズ(聞き手:谷川建司)／ The occupation destroyed Japanese culture), *Senryouki-Zasshi-Shiryou-Taikei: Taishui-Bunka-Hen* (占領期雑誌資料大系』大衆文化編／The occupation period periodical materials compendium: Popular culture series), Geppou 1 (月報1／Monthly Newsletter 1), Iwanami-Shoten, 2008.

Ikawa, Mitsuo. 'Sengo VOA Nihongo-Housou no Saikai' (戦後VOA日本語放送の再開／Resumption of VOA Japanese language broadcasts after World War II), *Media History*, Vol. 12, 2002.

Ikawa, Mitsuo. 'Reisen-ki niokeru VOA risunā Chousa: Nihongohousou wo Rei ni' (冷戦期におけるVOAリスナー調査:　日本語放送を例に／VOA listener survey during the Cold War era: A case study of VOA Japanese language broadcasts), *The Journal of Applied Sociology*, Rikkyo University, No. 51, 2009.

Jackie Robinson, a supplement of *Chugakusei no Tomo* (中学生の友／Junior high school students' companion), Vol. 27, No. 3, Shogakukan, June 1950.

Jijitsushin Nikkan Eiga-Geinou-Ban (時事通信日刊映画芸能版／Jijitsushin Daily Movie & Entertainment Issue), May 18, 1948.

Kangei San Francisco Seals 1949 (歓迎　San Francisco Seals 1949／Welcome San Francisco Seals 1949), Nihon Yakyu Renmei (Japanese Baseball Association), 1949.

Misaki, Tomeko. 'GHQ/CIE Kyouiku-Eiga to sono Eikyou: Sengo Minshushugi to Dining Kitchen' (GHQ/CIE教育映画とその影響―戦後民主主義とダイニング・キッチン／GHQ/CIE films and their influence), *Image and Gender*, Vol. 7, March 2007.

Morooka, Tatsuichi. 'San Francisco Seals to Fumin-sho: Showa 24 nen niokeru Yakyu Ninshiki no Shougeki—Mutodoke-teki Score sheet kara Zen 6 Shiai wo Shousai ni Kenshou' (サンフランシスコ・シールズと不眠症 昭和二四年（1949）における野球認識の衝撃—無届的スコアシート から 全6試合を詳細に検証／San Francisco Seals and insomnia: Impact of baseball recognition in 1949—Verifying all 6 games from the unofficial score sheet), *Baseballogy*, No. 2, 2001.

Sakaue, Yasuhiro. 'Kendo-Yougu to Sono Rekishi: Hitotsu no Kenkyuu Josetsu toshite' (「剣道用具とその歴史—ひとつの研究序説として—」／Kendo equipment and its history: An introduction), *Supoutsu-Yougu-shi-Kenkyu no Genjou to Kadai to* (The situation and the subjects in studies of sports equipment), Mizno Sports Shinkoukai, Research Report of 1999 Research Grant, 2000.

'San Francisco Seals Japan Tour' pamphlet (歓迎 San Francisco SEALS 1949), All Japan Baseball Association, 1949.

Shimizu, Akira. '20・9・22 Kara 23・8・19 made—Senryou-ka no Eiga-Kai no Kiroku' (20・9・22から23・8・19まで—占領下の映画界の記録／From September 22, 1945 to August 19, 1948: A record of the motion picture industry under the occupation), *Film Center*, No. 7, 1973.

Tanikawa, Takeshi. 'Chushingura wo tsuujite miru Senryo Shitamono to Saretamono no Mentality' (『忠臣蔵』を通じてみる、占領した者とされた 者のメンタリティ／The mentality of occupier and occupied people through observing Chushingura), *Bungaku*, September-October 2003.

Tanikawa, Takeshi. 'Senryouki no Tainichi Supōtsu Seisaku—Baseball to Coca-Cola wo megutte' (占領期の対日スポーツ政策—ベース ボールとコカ・コーラを巡って／U.S. sports policy toward occupied Japan — Regarding baseball and Coca-Cola), *Intelligence*, No. 3, 2003, pp. 30–41.

Tanikawa, Takeshi. 'Senryouki no Tainichi Budo Seisaku—Chanbara kinshi to Kendo e no taiou wo megutte' (占領期の対日武道政策—チャンバラ 禁止と剣道への対応を巡って／U.S. *budo* policy toward occupied Japan—Regarding the ban of *chanbara* and response to kendo), *Studies of Korean & Chinese Humanities*, No. 18, 2006, pp. 403–427.

Tanikawa, Takeshi. 'Senryouki no Tezuka Osamu' (占領期の手塚治虫／Osamu Tezuka in occupied Japan). In Taketoshi Yamamoto, ed., *Senryouki Bunka wo Hiraku: Zasshi no Shosou* (占領期文化をひらく 雑誌 の諸相／Open the culture in occupied Japan: Various images of magazines). Waseda University Press, 2006.

Tanikawa, Takeshi. 'Kaisetsu' (Chapter 1) (解説(第一章)、7-15 頁). In Taketoshi Yamamoto, ed.-in-chief, Kenichi Harada, Hitoshi Ishii and Takeshi Tanikawa, eds, *Senryouki-Zasshi-Shiryou-Taikei: Taishu-Bunka-Hen*, *Vol. I* (占領期雑誌資料大系大衆文化編第一巻：虚脱からの目覚め／Magazine materials in the occupation period, popular culture version, volume I: Democracy fever), pp. 7–15. Iwanami Shoten, 2008.

Tanikawa, Takeshi. 'Kaisetsu' (Chapter 6) (解説(第六章)、213-219頁). In Taketoshi Yamamoto, ed.-in-chief, Kenichi Harada, Hitoshi Ishii and Takeshi Tanikawa, eds, *Senryouki-Zasshi-Shiryou-Taikei: Taishu-Bunka-Hen*, *Vol. II* (占領期雑誌資料大系大衆文化編　第二巻：デモクラシー旋風／Magazine materials in the occupation period, popular culture version, volume II: Democracy fever), pp. 213–219. Iwanami Shoten, 2008.

Tanikawa, Takeshi. 'Kaisetsu' (Chapter 5) (解説(第五章)、211-217頁). In Taketoshi Yamamoto, ed.-in-chief, Kenichi Harada, Hitoshi Ishii and Takeshi Tanikawa, eds, *Senryouki-Zasshi-Shiryou-Taikei: Taishu-Bunka-Hen*, *Vol. IV* (占領期雑誌資料大系大衆文化編第四巻：躍動する肉体／Magazine materials in the occupation period, popular culture version, volume IV: Democracy fever), pp. 211–217. Iwanami Shoten, 2009.

Tanikawa, Takeshi. 'Beikoku Seifu Soshiki to Hollywood Eiga-Sangyoukai tono Sougo-Izonkankei' (米国政府とハリウッド映画産業界との相互依存関係／Interdependence of the U.S. Government and the Hollywood motion picture industry). In Toshihilo Kishi and Yuka Tsuchiya, *Bunka-Reisen no Jidai; America to Asia* (文化冷戦の時代　アメリカとアジア／De-centering the Cultural Cold War: The U.S. and Asia). Kokusai-Shoin, 2009.

Tanikawa, Takeshi. 'Senryoki no amerika kouhou gaikou to supōtsu—CIE eiga to VOA rajio housou niokeru supōtsu kanren contentsu no sekkyokuteki riyou' (占領期のアメリカ広報外交とスポーツ—CIE映画とVOAラジオ放送におけるスポーツ関連コンテンツの積極的利用／U.S. public diplomacy and sports in occupied Japan—Active use of sports-related contents on CIE films and VOA radio programs). In Yuka Tsuchiya and Shunya Yoshimi, eds, *Occupying Eyes, Occupying Voices: CIE/USIS Films and VOA Radio in Asia during the Cold War* (占領する眼・占領する声 — CIE／USIS映画とVOAラジオ). University of Tokyo Press, 2012, pp. 185–212.

Tsuchimoto, Takeshi. 'Mis-Jajji ni taisuru Nihon-Gata Taio: Olympic Danshi Judo 100 kg Cho-Kyu Kesshousen' (誤審(ミスジャッジ)に対する日本型対応: オリンピック男子柔道100キロ超級決勝戦／Japanese way of corresponding over misjudgment: Final match of the male judo over 100 kg class at the Olympics), *Sousa Kenkyu*, No. 590, 2000.

Tsuchiya, Yuka. 'The USIA and the privatization of overseas information activities' (米国広報文化交流庁(USIA)による広報宣伝の「民営化」). In Toshihiko Kishi and Yuka Tsuchiya, eds, *Bunka-Reisen no Jidai: America to Asia* (文化冷戦の時代　アメリカとアジア／De-centering the Cultural Cold War: The U.S. and Asia), Kokusai-Shoin, 2009.

USIS Film Catalog for Japan 1953 (USIS映画目録1953), prepared by Distribution Section, Motion Picture Branch, American Embassy, Tokyo.

USIS Film Catalog for Japan 1959 (USIS映画目録1959年版), prepared by Distribution Section, Motion Picture Branch, American Embassy, Tokyo.

Magazine articles

Asahigraph (アサヒグラフ),
Shinzen' (Goodwill), Vol. 52, No. 20, November 11, 1949, Asahi Shimbun Tokyo Honsha (「親善」、『アサヒグラフ』、朝日新聞東京本社、第52巻20号).

Baseball Magazine (ベースボールマガジン)
'USIS Teikyou: Robinson Monogatari' (USIS Presents: Robinson story), Vol. 5, No. 110, October 1950, Koubun-Sha, pp. 86–87 (USIS提供「ロビンソン物語」、『ベースボールマガジン』第5巻・第110号、10月号、恒文社86～87頁).

Baseball News (ベースボール・ニュース)
'Kyujou no Ninkimono' (Popular shop in the ballpark), No. 640, November 1949, Nihon-Taiiku-Shuuhou-Sha, p. 53 (「球場の人気者」、『ベースボールニュース』、日本体育週報社、第640号、53頁).

Home Run (ホームラン)
'Seals Shikin Hyakuman-en Shinpan-bu e' (A million yen of Seals' fund goes to Umpire Division), February 1950, Homurun-Sha, p. 45 (「シールズ資金　百万円審判部へ(ボールペン)」(『ホームラン』、ホームラン社、1950年2月号、45頁).

Yakyu News (野球ニュース)

Arima, Tadashi. 'Seals Sen wo Mite: Roku-Daigaku no Shourai' (Watching the game with the Seals: The future of the Six-University League), No. 40, Yakyu News-Sha, December 1949, pp. 40–41 (有馬直「シールズ戦を見て　六大学の将来」、『野球ニュース』、野球ニュース社、1949年12月号、40～41頁).

Newspaper articles

New York Times, April 21, 1949.
New York Times, July 19, 1949.
Nikkan Sports (日刊スポーツ), No. 1343, November 18, 1949

'Seals-gun Tokuhou' (Seals special report), supplement for the December 1949 issue of *Shounen Shoujo Tankai* (少年少女譚海)
Stars and Stripes, November 17, 1945.
Tokyo Nichi-Nichi Shimbun (東京日日新聞), May 22, 1949.

Interview

Tatsuichi Morooka, December 22, 2015, Tokyo.

Websites

20thdb.jp/

20th Century Media Information Database (20世紀メディア情報データベース).

http://2689web.com/nb.html

Nippon Professional Baseball Records homepage.

http://comicbookrealm.com/series/23181/218194/Jackie%20Robinson

Comic Book Realm.com.

http://comics.lib.msu.edu/rri/frri/fawc_p.htm

Michigan State University Libraries, Special Collections Division, Reading Room Index to the Comic Art Collection 'Fawcett Publications' (A–Z titles).

http://kirokueiga-hozon.jp/cie/
>Search Data System for CIE/USIS Movies (CIE・USIS映画　検索
>データベース).

http://www.archives.gov/publications/prologue/1997/summer/jackie-robinson.html
>Vernon, John. 'An Archival Odyssey: The Search for Jackie Robinson,
>Federal Records and African American History' (*Prologue Magazine*,
>Vol. 29, No. 2, Summer 1997).

http://www.cmn.hs.h.kyoto-u.ac.jp/CMN6/nakamura.htm
>Nakamura, Hideyuki. 'Senryouka Beikoku-Kyouiku-Eiga nitsuite no
>Oboegaki: 'Eiga-Kyoushitsu'Shi nimiru Natco (Eishaki) to CIE Eiga
>no Juyou nitsuite' (占領下米国記録映画についての覚書—「映画教室」
>誌におけるナトコ(映写機)とCIE映画の受容について／Memorandum
>of American educational films under the occupation: Demands
>for NATCO projectors and CIE films through observing 'Eiga-
>Kyoushitsu'), *CineMagaziNet*, No. 6, 2002.

http://www.comicvine.com/fawcetts-baseball-heroes/4050-26321/
>Fawcett's Baseball Heroes (COMIC VINE).

http://www.criticalpast.com/video/65675024538_international-programs_King-
Paul_Queen-Frederika_William-Portner
>USIS program including the musical *Porgy and Bess* and orchestra,
>sprinter Jesse Owens, writer William Faulkner and a trade show
>(CRITICALPAST.).

http://www.insidevoa.com/content/a-13-34-beginning-of-an-american-voice-
111602684/177526.html
>Inside VOA: Our People, Programs & Events.

http://www.insidevoa.com/content/a-13-34-2007-reorganizing-us-international-
broadcasting-in-the-1990s-111602649/177524.html
>Inside VOA: Our People, Programs & Events.

http://www.jackierobinson.com/about/stats/html
>The Official Site of Jackie Robinson, stats page.

http://www.joedimaggio.com/the-ballplayer/pre-yankees/
        Joe DiMaggio.com (Joe DiMaggio Children's
        Hospital Foundation).

http://www.kidsneedbaseball.com/index.php?option=com_content&view=article&i
d=212:college-feature-1&catid=50:foundation&Itemid=477
        Lefty O'Doul's Foundation for Kids.

http://www.pepsi.co.jp/history/
        PEPSI homepage.

http://www.profootballhof.com/hof/member.aspx?PLAYER_ID=242
        Pro Football Hall of Fame.

http://www.sonypictures.jp/corp/history/28386
        Sony Pictures Japan homepage.

https://archive.org/stream/JackieRobinson/robsn3_djvu.txt
        Full text of 'Jackie Robinson FBI Files' (a new internet archive).

https://www.cocacola.co.jp/ history_
        Coca-Cola homepage.

https://www.meridian.org/pacificpitch/
        Pacific Pitch: U.S.-Japan Baseball Diplomacy homepage.

▌DVD

        The Jackie Robinson Story, MMIII Miracle Pictures a Division of
        PMC Corp. De., 2004.

Index

Subject Index

Personal Name